God's
Own Untouchables

God's
Own Untouchables

Ulahannan Thoppil

Published by Renu Kaul Verma for
Vitasta Publishing Pvt. Ltd.
2/15, Ansari Road, Daryaganj,
New Delhi - 110 002
info@vitastapublishing.com

ISBN 978-93-80828-72-5

All the names and the characters in this book are fictitious. Resemblance to anyone, living or dead, is purely coincidental.

Cover Design and Layout by Vitasta Publishing Pvt. Ltd.
Printed by Vits Press, New Delhi

Marketed and Distributed exclusively in India & Sub-Continent by:

Times Group Books
(A division of Bennett, Coleman and Company Limited)
Times Annexe, Express Building
9-10 Bahadur Shah Zafar Marg, New Delhi-110 002

To

The sacred memory of my parents
Augustine and Rosma Thoppil

In the autumn of the Year 2000 Anno Domini,
in the fiftieth year of
The sovereign, democratic, socialist, secular
Republic of India,
And in the fourth year of the Presidency of
Kocherryl Raman Narayanan,
there stood in humility, veneration and
anticipation before the Altar of
The Roman Catholic Cathedral of
THE SACRED HEART,
In Lutyens city of New Delhi, capital of the Republic of India
REVEREND AARON PATHROSE MICAH,
a Dalit Catholic Priest, whose parents lived as Untouchables,
awaiting the announcement of his being elevated to
the titular Bishopric of
THE SEE OF ARBA.

One

The blue sky over Lutyens New Delhi looked serene and awesome. The monsoon crossing over the Vindhya Range had become tame, leaving the earth rejuvenated. A rush of autumnal colours hung all over the ambience in brilliant drapes; wiping the blues of the summer with the sun straying southward.

Under the azure dome of the September sky, snow-white patches of cloud stood mutely cornicing the steeples of the Cathedral. Outside, the arrival of droves of nuns ruffled the quietude of the few men lingering about in anticipation

Inside, Most Reverent Allen D'Lastic, the Archbishop of Delhi, led a silent procession of the Faithful towards the altar. Priest RevAaron Micah walked close behind him. In his early 40s, dusky, black haired, the Priest had his head bent down, eyes half closed with both his palms held close to his chest. He walked with measured steps as an unwilling martyr to the gallows. He looked solemn; an early rush of perspiration moistening his face even though the welcome chill of autumn had soothed the earth.

The procession entered the sanctuary at the east end of the nave as some of Priests occupied the pews. The Master of Ceremony, Monsignor Ben D'Silva standing behind the Archbishop, directed the Priest, Rev Aaron Micah to occupy a chair on the right side of the sanctuary. He sat down unobtrusively, still holding his head bent and palms joined at his chest.

Monsignor D'Silva, whispered a few words to the Archbishop. The Archbishop promptly got up but waited for a second to commence the rituals as the Master of Ceremony placed the mitre on his head. The Archbishop bowed before the tabernacle and slowly moved forward. The MC handed him a folded white sheet of paper. He didn't open it, perhaps aware of its contents.

"Dear Brethren in Jesus Christ." A rare glow on his face, the jubilant Archbishop raised his chin and stood gazing at the assembled congregation. The Priest sitting next to him neither lifted his face up nor pined for what his Apostolic shepherd was about to say.

The Faithful, unmindful of the martyred face of their Priest, sat looking intently at the inviting face of their Archbishop for a cheerful message for the congregation.

"Today I am immensely pleased to make a very important and joyous announcement."

"Our Most Holy Father, Pope John Paul the Second, has appointed our brother Priest Reverend Aaron Pathrose Micah the titular Bishop of the See of Arba and Auxiliary to the Archdiocese of God's Own Country."

"Our Vicar General will now read the Papal Bull."
The Archbishop resumed his seat as Rev Ben D'Silva moved to the microphone. The Cathedral bells started chiming as he read the Papal Bull, announcing the joyous news to the world outside. At the same hour Bells also chimed in St Peter's Square in Rome, emphasising the universality of the event. The congregation joined the Cathedral choir to sing Tadeum.

The Archbishop shook the Bishop designate's hands as Rev Aaron Micah humbly kissed the pastoral ring of his superior.

"Congratulations Monsignor Aaron Micah, I invoke God's blessings on you in your mission to serve His folk." As the Archbishop again took Rev Aaron Micah's palms in his own, the newly titled Monsignor kissed the Archbishop's ring once again.

The crowd waiting in the nave, impatiently started entering the sanctuary to congratulate the Bishop designate. Msgr Micah walked down the steps of the isle shaking hands with everybody and speaking a word or two. The broad smile on his face revealing a row of white teeth now replaced the solemn look.

Soon the crowd swelled. Msgr. Micah stood reciprocating and appreciating, yet embarrassed by the boisterous crowd at the consecrated ground. The arrival of a fellow Priest saved the situation for him.

The Archbishop wanted to speak to him and his fellow Priests wanted to congratulate him before they returned to their stations around the city. It was quite late by the time he could free himself of his well-wishers and admirers who chased him indiscreetly. He looked exhausted. The night turned out to be shorter with visitors arriving unannounced and long distance callers. Late night news gatherers lingered to ferret out every strand of his personal life to cook up an exotic story that a *Pulaya* Priest was appointed the Archbishop of God's Own Country.

"Are you a *Pulaya*?" The Special Correspondent of a leading Malayalam daily asked. Sensing the veiled insinuation in the question he replied firmly, "Yes, I am one as the colour of my skin perhaps testifies but not certainly by my blood that has little to distinguish between." The journalist silenced by his reply left him alone.

Never ashamed of his past, Msgr. Micah admitted his parents lived untouchables, converted neo Christians but he was a born Christian.

"Caste is not in the blood," another journalist made a comment.

"Then, where is it, in the skin?" The question remained unanswered.

"Sir, I have a question," another journalist ventured.

"Yes, shoot."

"In God's Own Country, as their shepherd do you anticipate any trouble from your sheep?" the man seemed to have a good feel of the pulse of the folks back home.

"I will have no trouble with them; for that matter with any body." He saw another hand waving to catch his attention.

"Sir, I understand that in God's Own Country where the Missionaries had ushered in a social revolution, based on the Christian teaching that God is the Father and men are His children. In simple terms it meant universal brotherhood and human equality and it attracted a good number of untouchables to the church. But sadly, they are now deserting the church in large numbers, rather disillusioned. My question is one, what is the reason for their turning renegades? and two, how do you propose to reverse the trend?"

The laboured question bewildered many, confusing the bishop-designate himself; after a moment he answered with a smile.

"Friend, your question is an essay one, but only a treatise can answer all the points you have rightly raised. The question is well thought out and relevant. I thank you."

"In the beginning, the land was the sole means of production in the hands of those who worked it. Powerful hordes which rode into the land later, usurped the land to become the masters. The dispossessed became outcastes and lived untouchables on their own home turf. As the Millennia passed silently before their eyes, the disinherited remained docile, unaware of their rights on this earth, living a life, shackled and barren."

"It is in this context that one has to examine the role of the church. Over a period of time, its teachings, particularly its social contours, expanded. The church taught men to empower themselves."

"In God's Own Country the Faith was brought by the West Asian traders not as evangelists but as well respected wealth creators, who had trading posts down the shore, at a time, when caste division was unheard of. Eventually, when the region went into the caste mode these traders found themselves recognized as *Vaishya;* the ruling class little bothered by the fact *that they were* practising Christians. The relationship between the traders and the rulers remained cordial, and mutually beneficial."

"Until the arrival of the Missionaries, the inhuman living conditions of the untouchables never pricked the Christian conscience. They concentrated on their business, accumulating wealth and worshipping of their God in their churches. The Missionaries championed social justice, extended health mission to take care of the poor and opened schools where untouchable children were admitted. Their activities attracted the downtrodden who joined the church in large numbers, finding naturally and ally in them. As long as their endeavour didn't affect their economic interest, the high castes remained indifferent to all this. What bothered them were the inconvenient questions the educated untouchables began to ask in due course."

"The Christian teachings of social justice and equality were eventually accepted universally. When India became independent, the church's preachings of equality and social justice found expression in the country's Constitution as core principles of the State Policy. The framers of the Constitution abolished untouchability declaring it a crime against humanity and provided for constitutionally guaranteed rights with sufficient financial support. It was a moment of great triumph for the church.

"But this social justice, proclaimed by the Constitution for the former untouchables, was exclusively for those within the Hindu fold, claiming that Christianity didn't practice untouchability and the untouchables who had joined the church earlier had no such disability. The reverse exodus that my friend referred to, is not because those men are disillusioned with Christianity as such; for they are still fired by what the church has taught them; the flight is merely to gain economic advantage." Taking a brief break, Msgr Micah looked at the face of the man who had raised the question,

"Do you agree or disagree?" he asked

"Yes, what you say does seem to be a valid argument."

"Thank you. Now I would like to add a few more points." The men listened quietly.

"The constitutional provision for the former untouchables is an act of restitution for the social oppression they were subjected to, from time immemorial. Those who took a brief shelter for a few decades under the humanitarian umbrella of Christianity, could never justly be treated ineligible for recompense; for they too had been equally victimized under the old regime for thousands of years. Again, if a convert alleged to have shed his religious label on becoming a Christian, returned to the Hindu fold, he was reclaimed as a prodigal son and admitted to his original caste and declared eligible for the privileges available to former untouchables' no questions asked. This is sheer discrimination."

"The Indian society is caste-based and caste is static. If a *Pulaya* accepts Christianity he becomes a Christian *Pulaya*, the caste follows him."

"Is Christianity the villain, the spoilsport therefore?"

"Reverend, you have presented your case cogently. Will you fight for the cause?"

"Of course; not physically, but by convincing the authorities of the injustice."

Monsignor I have a question. You talk so much about the former untouchables, could you please tell us something about your own ancestry? I understand you are one among them." It was apparent that the man was from God's Own Country.

"Of course I am. I am glad that you raised this question. My origin is not lost in the obscurity of an untouchable caste. It's because my father was literate and I was raised in socially unmolested environs; my parents ensured that I received a reasonably good education."

"I am the son of former untouchables turned Christian parents; our story is unique and eventful. For the *Pulaya*s, life was never a bowl of cherries. In the hands of their masters, they were slaves risking life and limbs."

"Yours is a unique story, part of our social history. Why don't you write a memoir for posterity?"

ꕤ 7 ꕤ

"That's an idea. Perhaps I will."

Yet the questions didn't stop.

"The church is well entrenched in God's Own Country. But why has the State gone Red?" The Priest responded with a a tentative smile as he paused but stood his ground.

"There too you might find the unseen influence of the Gospel that proclaimed universal love and justice; the Missionaries sowed the seeds of a bloodless revolution. They educated the touchables and untouchables and they dared to ask questions."

"Knowledge is power and that's what the Missionaries had sown in the fertile soil of God's Own Country." He concluded.

"Good night. Wish you all the best."

He wondered why the Holy See had suddenly decided to elevate him for an ecclesiastical position. He was well aware of the Christian community's strength and weakness in comparison to the community he was born into.

Derisively called a lunatic asylum of castes, the static society had been impacted by the Christian community, led by forces unleashed by the church, bringing about perceptual changes, transforming human life. The force with which the gospel moved the conscience of men to demolish the iniquity of caste was historic. But ironically now the fence was devouring the crop; the church that took up cudgels against injustice had become more castist than the former tormentors.

The church is divided vertically and horizontally, Christian Rites replaced the Hindu castes, becoming more dominant than the gospel. Endowed with aristocratic pretensions, these rites claimed descent from Brahmins and untouchables; treating adherents of certain Rites as a kind of ritual untouchables. Aptly, Christianity in God's Own Country has become a lunatic asylum of Rites, both competitive and combative.

Education, once the basic idiom of Christian concern, slowly ceased to be a service and became a source of power, influence and lucre. The proliferation of private education shored up by the charisma of the church and the brand attraction of the 'Missionary School' elevated the church to a commanding height in the field of education.

He wondered how a gospel that proclaimed equality of all men on earth based on universal love and brotherhood could abandon its true spirit.

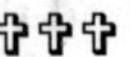

Two

Msgr Micah was holding the fort while the Archbishop was away in Rome and the Cathedral Vicar and the Chancellor were in Calcutta attending an eccleastical plenum. The task was rather arduous as he could be called upon at any time from anywhere in the city.

He shut himself in his room and went to sleep. A sudden phone call woke him up. It was from a nearby Convent; the caller sounded rather vexed,

"Yes, I am Father Micah; please tell me what's the matter?"

"May I speak to His Grace the Archbishop?"

"He is away and I am the only Priest available." The phone suddenly got disconnected, but rang again after a while. Another caller had the same request.

"The Archbishop is away and I am the only Priest available."

"Oh! Father, our Sister Maria Thomasina is sinking; she craves for extreme unction, immediately."

He felt the nuns were crazy; they wanted the Archbishop even for administering the last Sacrament in the dead of night. He paused for a minute and told the caller: "I shall come soon."

Msgr Micah changed his dress and collected the clerical clothing. He guessed the Holy oil and Holy Eucharist would be available in the convent chapel; he rode off on his Lambretta Scooter. Two nuns were waiting at the gate to escort him; he followed them quietly.

"How old is Sister Thomasina, Sister?"

"She is seventy five-plus, Father"

"She is really holy with a strong faith and her love goes out to everybody. She is always willing to sacrifice her comforts to make life pleasant for others. When she said that she was sinking we called you immediately." The nuns briefed him.

He stopped by the chapel and asked the nuns.

"Does she want to make her confession too?" Msgr Micah was sure a dying person would certainly go for a last confession.

"I think so. I will ask her to get ready." The nuns disappeared behind the curtain as the Priest waited in the chapel for their return.

The two nuns walked Sister Thomasina to the Confessional in the side room. The frail and weak Sister was provided with a chair. The two nuns discreetly drew back, leaving the confessor and the penitent.

The nun made the sign of the Cross, remorsefully declaring, mea culpa, mea culpa, and then she abruptly lapsed into silence. She resumed slowly,

"A week since my last confession."

"Yes. Have you fulfilled the expiation awarded?"

"Yes Father," the nun meekly submitted. Msgr. Micah wondered whether the nun was really sinking; her speech was clear and memory was sound; though she looked fragile and weak.

She sat quiet for a while groping for words to convey her extra ordinary state of mind and a bizarre sin. It was an old misdemeanour that she had failed to confess all these years that tormented her; she feared the Priest might frown upon her for hiding a sin. She was desperate to make a clean confession, particularly about the old sin.

One night she was in the chapel for many hours, keeping company with the Lord, who was alone in the tabernacle like a prisoner. She thought she saw him beckoning her. It thrilled her to realise how much Jesus loved her, though a sinner. Then she heard a voice which she believed was His.

"I will call you to my Father's mansion soon; be prepared."

She wanted to discuss the matter with some one but found no one worthy of sharing this rare revelation. She was uncertain but excited that Jesus had spoken to her. A few weeks later in a second vision, Jesus repeated his words. She was convinced that the vision was real. Now she wanted to be ready to go with him when he willed. The third time he came, she sat weeping in the chapel when she realised how much Jesus had cared for her even though she was a sinner.

"To be his spouse I shall have to remain clean and I have to make a full confession and obtain remission of all my sins past and present." She vowed. She searched her conscience and thought her present record warranted little re-examination but when she traversed back she stumbled upon the event that had been churning her wakeful hours.

"I have been hiding a wrong man in my thoughts; I have to get rid of him."

"Father, almost fifty years ago I committed an error, unintentionally though. I fell in love with a soldier of low caste, who visited my home and stayed with my parents over night. We lived in poverty; my parents failed to get me married as they could not raise the dowry. My grandfather proposed me to the visitor who accepted and I too agreed. But my brother opposed the match; he assaulted him and I was forced to forget him. Though hurt I abided by his decision." The nun paused unable to proceed further.

"You haven't committed any sin in this matter." The confessor enlightened her, but doubts still lingered in her mind and she continued to sit quiet with tears rushing down her cheeks. An eerie silence reigned between the confessor and the confessant, prompting the Priest to ray.

"Do you have anything more to say?"

"Yes father...I, I kissed him." She abruptly stopped with words choking her parched throat .

"You kissed him?" Taken aback by these words coming from a nun's mouth the Priest asked her: "How and where did this happen?"

Sister Thomasina felt the confessor had suddenly become stern. The nun, rather frightened, whispered:

"On his lips father." Her answer troubled the Priest further; he wanted to probe to determine the enormity of the sin.

"Were you alone with the man?"

"No Father, there were several people around."

"Was it after you had entered the convent or before?"

"Before, Father."

"But you failed to confess it even at the time of your vestition?" The Priest thought it was a venial sin; still he wanted to know the circumstances.

"I was sad that he was assaulted by my brother. The next day when I went to the church to pray for him, I saw a small crowd in the cemetery to bury a dead man. I too joined them. When I looked at the face of the dead man I discovered it was the same young man who had offered to marry me without any dowry. The sight shattered me and silently I wept for him. As they lifted the coffin I rushed forward. I unveiled his serene face and kissed him. Yes father, I kissed him on his lips. Some one pushed me aside. I fell down, hurting my head. I sprang up crying aloud. I don't remember anything more. My grandfather rebuked me for disturbing the peace."

"Did you have a dream, my daughter?" Her grandfather had asked her.

"Yes, grandpa… I had a dream."

"He made a sign of the cross on my forehead and asked me to sleep."

"Nobody commits a sin in a dream, forget it." Msgr. Micah consoled her.

"But, Father ever since this man has stayed in my mind; when I went for a bath in the stream I found him with me, when I slept alone in our kitchen, I saw him sharing the mat with me but he never attempted to violate me. I wanted to chase him away and I wanted to call my brother but I didn't, fearing he would kill the poor man. I didn't want the man to suffer for my sake, again. When I joined the convent he followed me. His shadow casts a spell on me. He comes alive before my eyes. I am afraid I might lose my soul."

For the Priest it was an odd disclosure; he could not comprehend the pain of a septuagenarian woman, a votary of chastity and obedience, still carrying in the depth of her heart the baggage of a conscientious prick, of half a century old juvenile foible. He concluded that the man might have highly impressed her, under the state of privation that her family had been condemned to live in. The Priest asked her: "Did you ever meet him after the breakdown of the proposal?"

"No. I never met him." She affirmed.

"Did you ever feel a desire to meet him, casually as a friend?"

"No, never." Her reply was firm and definite.

"Would you meet him, in case he came to meet you?"

Sister Maria Thomasina hesitated for a minute but affirmed: "I don't think I would seek a meeting with him but if he comes I may not refuse to meet him."

"Have you ever regretted that you lost his hand?"

Again she stayed lost in thoughts but faced the question truthfully.

"Initially yes, because my parents worried a lot about their inability to get me married. Our neighbours constantly harried them on this matter. I was disappointed that I continued to be a burden on them."

"Is he still alive?"

"I don't know Father."

"Do you keep any memento of him?"

The nun again lapsed into silence. She remembered she had picked up his blood stained scapular from the site where her brother had attacked him. She came to know of the incident two days later when their neighbour narrated the events to her grandfather. The next day, on her way to church she stopped at the spot, casually looking around. She found the scapular hanging from a broken bush by the side of the water course. She guessed that that was the spot where he had been felled.

"Nothing, except a scapular that I had picked up from the spot. I considered it as a holy relic."

"A juvenile foible!" Msgr Micah concluded.

"Sister Thomasina, you have not committed any sin. I gather from all that you have narrated, that the unexpected arrival of this striking young man at a time when your parents were desperately scouting for a groom, and one that you too had been anticipating, after several failures, created a commotion in your family, and more so in your psyche. Your parents were excited and obviously you too had entertained great expectations. But the violence your brother let loose on this person wounded your conscience. You naturally sympathized with him, perhaps your heart bled for him and finally you identified with his suffering. His fate troubled you and you imagined him knocking at your door, even though he might be unaware of the existence of a Maria Thomasina grieving for him. You are troubled by a guilty conscience."

"Whenever he appears before your mind, you enthrone Jesus in his place. He will save you." Msgr Micah concluded his post confessional counselling. He continued to sit in the confessional for a while praying for her.

As the Priest came out of the chapel Sister Maria appeared before him with a pleasant face and a bright smile. She looked composed.

"Father, I have found real consolation. I thank you."

She looked at his face, her gaze slowly turning into a stare and the smile vanished from her lips. To her, his face appeared strikingly familiar, the replica of an original that she had seen and long cherished. She had seen the Priest earlier too but the similarity of his face to another old face had gone unnoticed.

'Almost fifty years ago; still the face hasn't aged.' She thought; even the voice echoed another voice heard long ago.

"Lord, are you still testing me? She thought she was going to burst out. The two nuns who had escorted her were still in the chapel, believing the confession, being the last one, would take a little extra time.

"Father, may I know your name please?" She asked him; she sounded troubled.

"I am Father Aaron Micah." The Priest casually answered her; she appeared mystified.

☙ 15 ❧

"Aaron Micah...Pathrose Micah." She mumbled as she stood supporting herself on the arms of a sofa.

"Pathrose Micah is my father, sister. Do you know him?" He too looked surprised

"Pathrose Micah's son... Aaron Micah… yes… the son I bore him not..."

Rev Aaron Micah heard the mystifying incoherent words; he stood intrigued as he watched her suddenly dragging her feet, almost tottering. He waited until she walked into her room and shut the doors behind her.

That night he had a disturbed sleep, overwhelmed by the face of the nun, the young and impressive face of the one who had been tormenting herself for half a century, and finally, his own face, throwing her thoughts into chaos. He felt compelled to unravel the mystery; he guessed only Sister Maria Thomasina could throw more light on the matter. Particularly, her words 'the son who I bore him not' aroused his curiosity; he wanted to explore and decided to visit her.

Despite the disturbed night he was up with the lark in the morning. As he was readying himself for the morning Mass, the telephone rang up. His first impulse was to ignore the call but on second thought he realized that a Priest should be available to his flock anytime. He picked up the receiver.

"Father, I am sorry to inform you that our Sister Maria Thomasina expired early this morning. We will call you later to give the details." The nun assured him. The news badly shook Msgr Micah; he felt it was a personal loss so soon after his acquaintance with her. His need to get to the mystery behind her intriguing soliloquy remained compulsive.

Msgr Micah visited the convent in the evening; the dead body looked almost abandoned with a solitary nun keeping vigil.

A couple arrived a little before the commencement of the funeral procession. They stood solemnly by the coffin with their heads bowed. The man had two candles with him, which he lighted and fixed on either side of the coffin. He kissed the nun's forehead The man drew back with the woman following him.

✠✠✠

Three

"…the son I bore him not…."

Her exclamation, distressed Msgr Aaron Micah. Keen to unravel the mystery; he found her words buried deep within her with her sudden demise; no one on earth could perhaps discover the truth. The spectre of those words troubled him. Her reference to a soldier of low caste and, therefore, unacceptable, and her brother assaulting him admitted one question and one answer.

"Was that soldier my father? For, he was a soldier of low caste." Besides, available evidence finds him fitting the bill.

Sister Thomasina's last statement continued to vex him; his efforts to untangle the mystery bore no fruit; he had almost closed the chapter.

But one evening as he said requiem Mass in the Cathedral for the soul of the departed nun, he saw man in his 60s approaching the communion table. He could not recognize him but he guessed the face was the one he was looking for. As he concluded the Mass, he rushed out to meet him.

"I am Father Aaron Micah. I believe I saw you at Sister Thomasina's funeral."

"Yes Father, I am George Thomas, her nephew." Msgr Micah remained silent groping for words; he was glad he had met the nun's nephew who, he hoped, could answer some of his questions.

"I believe you are the son of Mr Pathrose Micah."

"Yes. I am; my father is still alive. Do you know him?"

"Yes, I remember having met him, about fifty years ago." What he said was in line with what Father Micah had assumed.

George remembered the face clearly and he believed the Priest resembled his father minutely; but he hesitated to speak about him. For, the man's visit to their home and the events that followed had unflattering memories.

It was the years of the Great War. With his fourth standard education, Pathrose Micah joined the Indian Army and fought five years on the Burmese front. On cessation of hostilities he was granted home leave. On his way home he stopped at Ottapalam to visit his late senior colleague Govindan's father in a nearby village. Govindan had died in action.

"Thomakutty, the man with the shoulder bag is looking for you." A man standing at a shop counter alerted Thomakutty. Seeing Micah walk towards the shop, Thomakutty the land broker and stead-bull owner stepped into the street, watching the visitor to assess his worth.

"Are you on your way?" Thomakutty asked his first question feigning a contrived familiarity. Micah ignored him as he stepped into the teashop.

Thomakutty concluded the visitor was a Travancore Christian; scapular around his neck helping to fix his Christian identity.

Thomakutty was a smart guy, proud of his innate talents. He had meagre land holdings but was blessed with the gift of the gab. He excelled as a land broker, his clients being the land hungry Travancore Christians and, the cash strapped local caste aristocracy who owned the land but utterly lacked the skill to raise the crops. The Christian green thumbs filled the gap. Thomakutty was acceptable to both as a friend in high quarters.

Assuming the visitor had come to buy land, he welcomed him, claiming they were kins. Micah knew the man was wrong; a *Pulaya* could never be a kinsman of a Syrian Christian; he parried the probing observation as Thomakutty stood racking his brain to divert their conversation to business matters.

The broker slowly tried to open up the subject though the visitor's coldness dampened his enthusiasm; he wondered how a Travancore Christian could be indifferent to the offer of a fertile tract of land. Micah brushed him aside and stepped onto the road, without even looking back. This overbearing attitude incited the broker and he quipped,

"He isn't a Christian, a damn *Pulaya*." Micah's extra ordinarily dark skin further provoked Thomakutty to malign him. He left quietly, unleashing a stud bull he had tethered by the sacred grove where the grass was fresh and green.

Micah walked almost a mile and stopped in front of a nondescript hut. Its low roof thatched with Palmyra leaves and a bunch of ripening bananas hanging over the front entrance confirmed that it was food vendor. A young girl in her late teens was sitting at the entrance, apparently guarding the business. Seeing a stranger approaching, she instinctively sprang to her feet.

"Do you have some eatables?" Micah asked the girl as he stopped in front of the hut. A stranger in olive green uniform overawed the girl who stood alarmed to face him. Micah saw two big eyes peering at him. As he repeated his question he heard a male voice yelling from behind the hut, "Kaali, who is there?"

Kaali had no idea who the man was but she knew he was a big man, unlike her father or their customers. She rushed to her father to describe him. Only her father could understand her strange language and he easily grasped what she conveyed to him.

"He's a big man with a bag and wearing a *kuppayam*; he wants some thing to eat." She told him. Her father went to meet the visitor, and he too felt the man was really big. But he found it strange that the big man was as black as himself, he wondered how a black man would be so big. Pokkan stopped at the corner of the yard. Micah looked at him casually, sure that he was also a *Pulaya*; his mien and speech confirmed it beyond doubt.

"I am hungry. Do you have something that I can eat?" The question surprised Pokkan, who asked the visitor timidly.

"I am a *Pulaya*; how can you eat from my humble shop?"

"I don't care what you are. I am hungry and need something to eat. I am also a *Pulaya*. Can't you see I am black too?"

"Whatever I cooked in the morning is sold out; nothing is left. Pokkan explained his helplessness.

"But you have eggs, I suppose?" Micah saw a pair of hens passing by.

"Ah! I'll get you two eggs." Micah's enquiry brightened Pokkan's face; he asked his visitor to wait for a while until he boiled two eggs. Pokkan rushed to the rear of the hut taking Kaali with him. Micah entered the hut but he found no bench to seat the customers; he guessed that invariably Pokkan's clients were untouchables who sat on the floor; keeping an elevated seat would have invited the wrath of the caste men. Micah sat by a corner leaning against a post that supported the roof. Hunger and lack of sleep the previous night drove him into a slumber, making him forget about the hen and the eggs.

Busy with the birds outside, Kaali came to the rear opening of the hut to steal a glimpse of the man; finding him asleep she drew back silently. Micah slept soundly. He finally woke up to the rays of the sun falling vertically on the floor.

"Kaali…." He yelled for the girl; she appeared promptly with her big eyes peering at him with awe and veneration.

"Haven't you boiled the eggs? Where is your *Achha*? I have to leave soon."

She had no answers for him; for Pokkan did not tell her where he was going, or anything about the eggs. She withdrew her innocent gaze to avert the teardrops, brimming up in her eyes.

"Why? What happened?" Micah sprang to his feet and hurried towards her, "Why do you cry?"

Kaali walked past him wiping her eyes with the back of her palm. She quietly squatted by a reed basket turned upside down on the ground. She slouched forward and carefully lifted the basket a little by its edge peering into it as she groped inside with her hand, provoking a cackle of protest from the two hens trapped inside.

"No luck; they haven't laid any egg." Kaali concluded. She looked straight into his face with tears welling up again in her eyes.

"Never mind, don't cry. I don't need any eggs. I am leaving; tell your father when he returns." Micah ferreted a small packet of biscuits from his bag; (saved from his military ration). He extended it to the girl; who stood bewildered, her enormous eyes staring at him.

"Come on, take it; they are nice." He persuaded the hesitant girl. Finally, he thrust the packet into her hands. She looked at it, unable to figure out what it was and what to do with it. She wanted to ask him but only her eyes could pose the question that Micah failed to grasp.

"Kaali, have you had any egg?" Pokkan asked his daughter as he returned with a few cassava tubers. She shook her head sadly, as Micah added:

"The fowls refused to oblige me."

"But I have some thing for you that you, being a Travancorean, will enjoy; please give me a little more time."

The sight of the tapioca tubers thrilled Micah; he decided to stay back until Pokkan steamed them. Tapioca had always been a *manna* for the Travancoreans since the Portuguese introduced the stumps of the plant in the State. Over the years tapioca, together with fish had become the piece de resistance of the poor man's diet.

"I bought it from Avirah *Chettan's* farm; he is your fellow country man. If you have time I will take you to them; really good people." Pokkan recommended but Micah appeared less than enthusiastic. Pokkan thought the Travancore Christian, though dark, was a suitable groom for Avirachettan's daughter, Mariachi; dowry rocking the boat, she had remained single far too long because of dowry.

"Maybe when I come next."Micah excused himself as he stepped out.

"Kaali I am leaving." She nodded without lifting up her eyes, denying him the pleasure of a last gaze of those big eyes.

"Would you like to come with me?" He asked. She shook her head with her eyes silently piercing the earth.

"She doesn't speak?" Micah finally discovered the painful truth. Kaali again shook her head, as her father said: "She is dumb."

Micah heard the truth, cruel and painful. He stepped into the mud road and walked on gloomily leaving behind the father and the daughter, the innocent face of the girl looming large in his mind.

The sight of a tamarind tree that stood by the side of a gatehouse caught his attention; he found that he stood right in front of the house he was searching for. The cut-stone oil lamp that protruded from the wall met with the description Govindan had given, except the sump was dry with no wicks in place. He thought it was a lamp that had ceased to light the nights. He stood in front of the wooden door that barred entry into the compound; a casual knock at the door sent the shutters up prompting a yell from the house.

"*Aaraa*…who is there?" Raghavan Nambiar skewed his eyes to catch a glimpse of the unannounced visitor at this odd hour; he couldn't recognize the man he saw walking towards the house. "Rama, go and see who he is."

"*Aaraa*, where do you come from?" Raman Nair repeated the question.

"I have come to visit Govindan Nambiar's father. I am from the army."

Raghavan Nambiar jumped up from his seat and rushed towards the man are Raman Nair following.

"What does it mean? Is Govindan alive?"He asked Raman, who clarified,

"The man didn't say anything of the sort."

Nambiar thought the man from the army had come to tell that his son was not dead.

"What did you say your name is?" Nambiar asked.

"Micah." The name sounded a puzzler, revealing neither his caste nor his religion.

"Not Hindu, either Muslim or Christian." He concluded.

"Are you a Christian? You are, I suppose."

"Yes, I am a Christian."

Nambiar thought the nonchalant tone of his reply sounded assertive; he looked unaffected. Nambiar guessed the man might be a Travancore Christian.

The day had become very hot with the merciless summer sky scorching the earth; wind had ceased to blow, except for the occasional light breeze that rustled the crown of the Palmyra. Micah felt exhausted and thirsty. He had left behind his water bottle believing that water was aplenty in the land.

"Could you please get me some water to drink?" He asked.

The request for drinking water startled Raghavan Nambiar; he pretended that he hadn't heard the request as he turned to Raman for a tête-à-tête. Customarily, the family never served food or water to those from outside the fourfold. Those who were familiar with the system never sought any. Raman Nair too looked embarrassed.

"This man has worked with our Govindan; he has come visiting you as a friend of your dead son. It's cruel to refuse him water." Raman Nair counselled him.

"Rama, bring that *kindy* and pour some water into his palms. After all he had worked with my son." He needed an excuse to justify his deviation from the custom. The servant brought the *kindi* which always remained filled with water for the old man to wash his feet when he returned from his outings.

Micah stood with his head lowered and palms scooped together close to his lips, and drank the water that Raman siphoned into the scooped up palms. Micah felt neither surprised nor offended at the indignity, which he believed was part of their social system.

"Govindan and I have been together in the army. We have drunk from the same mug, eaten from the same plate, and sat huddled together in one trench."

"Why to conceal the truth, Life in the army has taught us great lessons of human dignity; the army is a powerful social leveller."

Micah understood that the man still refused to take him into the house, intending to dismiss him unceremoniously. He walked towards the gatehouse, Raman following him. Micah walked behind them.

Micah knew it was time for him to return but he dared not breach the silence that Raghavan Nambiar sat engrossed in. The sun had descended to the western slope of the sky; though Micah stood before him for quite a while the senior Nambiar didn't speak to him. It was only Raman who had been speaking or asking questions.

"I wish to take leave of you, Sir." The old man stirred, hailing his servant.

"Rama…this man had no food. Why don't you get him a measure of rice and some vegetables, and all that he needs to cook a meal for himself? Give him some old utensils." Turning to Micah he continued.

"We don't serve food to outsiders. Raman will show you a place where you can cook your own food as you like."

"I am not good at cooking; you need not bother about me. I will eat something available on the way."

"You won't get anything to eat on the way until you reach Ottapalam, and you don't get a bus to Ottapalam until tomorrow morning."

"There is a shop by the mud road where I can buy something." Micah thought he could sleep overnight in the hut to catch the morning bus.

"Where, Pokkan's shop? *Shiva…Shiva…* Do you intend to eat from his shop? He is an untouchable, *Pulaya.*" Micah didn't miss the scowl on his face.

"A soldier eats any food served by any person." Micah told him. Raghavan Nambiar slowly lapsed into silence again; he wanted to feed the man who was his son's companion. He believed it unfair to send him away empty handed. He beckoned Raman Nair again.

"Rama, you ask Thomakutty to see me immediately." He seemed to have hit upon an idea.

"Return with him soon." He called the servant from behind and urged him.

Micah noticed that the man had not asked him to take a seat even though he had been standing in the courtyard for quite a while . Being a soldier standing for hours never tired him, nor did the insult hurt him for he knew that was how the system treated the lowly.

"Thomakutty?" Raghavan Nambiar introduced Micah, explaining who he was, his association with Nambiar's son and how grateful he was for his visit.

"He is a Christian like you, and from Kottayam too as you are…"

"Maybe some relation…." Raman Nair interrupted to throw in a cynical remark apparently to belittle both but Raghavan Nambiar's face conveyed that he was displeased. Raman Nair drew back sheepishly.

"I want you to take him with you for the night; he plans to leave by the morning bus." Nambiar was sure Thomakutty would oblige him; the request was a mere formality.

"Yes Sir. I will do as you command." Thomakutty assured him.

Micah took leave of Raghavan Nambiar and he walked behind Thomakutty, clutching his bag close to his chest. He stopped at the outhouse gate for a last look and saw Nambiar still sitting immobile with Raman Nair close behind, both lost in thoughts. Beyond, the soulless big, old house appeared ghostly.

✞✞✞

Four

Micah stayed overnight with Thomakutty. His grandfather Thomman Master was highly impressed by the young man in Olive Green from Kottayam. He had arrived at a time when they were looking for a groom for his granddaughter, Mariachi. Their inability to raise dowry had failed all the proposals. Theirs was once a prosperous family in Kottayam but they now lived in poverty eking out a miserable life. Yet they boasted of an aristocratic origin, claiming descent from a Brahmin family converted by the Apostle, St Thomas, almost two millennia ago. Thomman Master was happy that Micah was also in the service of the Emperor like him.

But they found his unusually dark skin damning. Thomakutty's wife Chinnamma concluded he was a *Pulaya* but the grandpa overruled her. In the night they hosted him a grand dinner with drinks and lots of eats. Thomman Master tacitly extracted from him a promise that he would accept Mariachi's hand with no dowry demanded.

In the morning Micah left for his home, seen off by Mariachi who alone rose up early to attend on the departing guest. When asked whether he would visit them again, he promised he would if her grandfather invited him. Micah left for home entertaining the fond hope that Mariachi would be his soon, though he being a *Pulaya* the odds were formidable.

Thomman Master was unhappy with his son and grandson; their

failure to see off Micah properly irked him. He believed that he had talked around Micah and his response was favourable. He thought he had found a suitable boy for the girl.

One morning Mariachi dressed herself up in her white attire with the *Kavani* pulled over her head. Chinnamma looked mystified at the sudden pious pretensions of her sister-in-law. She protested a bit but the grandpa overruled her and Mariachi found nothing to fear.

"Why do you think that man will marry Mariachi?" Thomakutty asked, ending a long harangue of his grandfather. "Thomakutty, a young man marries a young woman whom he finds lovable. My daughter is really adorable, and I am sure he will marry her if we offer her in marriage."

They debated for days, speculating about his job, family and their social connections. Though poor, they insisted the groom be from a respectable family with a good background.

"Don't rush into decisions without proper enquiry." Thomakutty warned.

"Who said not to enquire? But first you have to talk to him."

"Let us ask Mariachi first." Chinnamma wanted to hear from the horse's mouth. Mariachi was promptly called in, though young girls were seldom consulted by the elders on decisions of their marriage. She stepped in and stood hiding behind the thatched screen.

"Mariachi, have you seen Micahchan?"

Mariachi stood quiet, biting her lips silently. She felt abashed at the unexpected question. An unmarried woman was not expected to look at a stranger. She had in fact not merely seen him but stared at him while he had his bath by the well curb and when she served him coffee as he was departing. How could she deny the truth?

"Yes… I saw him in your midst." Mariachi hedged but preferred to speak the truth.

"Do you like him?" Chinnamma shot a question deliberately to embarrass her. Mariachi didn't answer though she was sure she loved him. She stood blushing. Her silence didn't deter Thomman Master from asking further: "If we propose him will you agree to marry him?"

Mariachi was sure that she would but pretended she was unconcerned. Her silence irritated Thomakutty, who said:

"You don't need her consent; we decide whom she should marry." That was the inviolable rule of the old world. But Thomman Master insisted that he hear from Mariachi. He concluded the man was a good Catholic Christian, the scapular around his neck mutely testified. He repeated his question, turning his face towards her. Mariachi remained ossified into her shell.

"Mariachi, you have to answer some thing." Thomman Master raised his voice; his only concern was Micah's unusually dark complexion.

"I will go by your decision." She whispered though she had the desire to announce 'yea' from the top of the roof for the entire world to know:

"I will marry none but him."

She scuttled across, into the sick room of her mother. A brief lull followed; the men sat lost in their thoughts wondering how to retrieve the lost opportunity; finally Thomman Master came out with a suggestion.

"Thomakutty, you write him an urgent letter asking him to visit us formally to finalise the proposal."

Thomakutty wrote the letter, read it to them, put it into an old envelope, and personally dropped it into the post box. Mariachi daily watched for the postman whose routine she was now familiar with. She guessed her conspicuous presence would serve a reminder to the postman if he needed one; but no letter came. However, Mariachi kept her vigil; she was certain he would come; she stayed hopeful.

One night Mariachi overheard Thomakutty talking to his wife in a hushed tone

"I don't expect this marriage to take place."

"Why? Now what's the problem?"

"I have news that he is a *Pulaya*. Poor Mariachi! She has big dreams; and poor *Valliappachan* thought he had found a husband for his granddaughter. He was happy the man demanded no dowry, a stumbling block upon which many proposals have petered out."

"When I told you what I had thought about him you came hissing at me; now what? Where did you get the news?" Thomakutty declined to reveal his source but he insisted what he had heard was true.

"These *Pulayas* might have been converted by some foreign missionaries." Between them they decided not to disclose to anybody what they had heard, and Thomakutty added with vehemence:

"It's good for him if he doesn't come; if he comes I will teach him a lesson."

This midnight conversation did little to daunt Mariachi; she continued with her devotion at the Mass, and her vigil after church in the churchyard that overlooked the village bus stop.

Finally he arrived. As she stood scrutinizing every face that alighted from the bus, she saw a dark face emerging wearing the same old olive green. She stood overwhelmed, watching him slowly walking onto the mud road that led to her home.

Suddenly, she remembered the midnight conversation and the vow her brother had made. Knowing that Thomakutty was satanic when in a vengeful mood her sole hope was her grandfather, but age had rendered him helpless. His only weapon was his sharp tongue, which was no match for Thomakutty's brawn. She wanted to warn Micah and also find out whether all that she had heard was true.

Yet she stayed put, wavering, unable to muster enough courage to face him; the rigid concept of modesty disapproved of a young woman socializing with a person of opposite sex. Micah was a mere acquaintance of her brother; still she knew for certain why he was visiting them and what peril awaited him at the hands of her brother. She wanted to caution him but how.

Fear numbed her legs, which refused to sprint off despite a firm urge. Doubts plagued her mind, and the timorous young woman she had been raised to become, she failed to act. When she came out of the thoughts cocooning her mind she found the bus stop deserted; all the men had disappeared.

Mariachi panicked; she conjured up the ghastly vision of Micah meekly facing a brutal Thomakutty with Thomman Master watching helplessly. She wanted to reach home ahead of Micah. Taking a short cut, she ran across the paddy fields that skirted several hillocks. She reached home to find Thomakutty's children quietly basking in the morning sun. Chinnamma was busy in the kitchen. She felt relieved that Micah hadn't arrived yet.

"Mariachi, the Virgin Mother hasn't answered your prayers." Thommam Master said aimlessly as he saw Mariachi rushing back from church. Tired and gloomy; she paid little attention to the old man's words as she walked into the kitchen with a sullen face.

"I am sure the Holy Mother will answer my prayers if not Mariachi's."

Thomakutty's words had a ring of doubt. The old man quickly reacted.

"Why? Don't we all pray for her marriage with Micahchan?" Thomman Master appeared annoyed.

"I don't know, and I don't care whether it's Micah or some one else. I wish we find her a good match."

"Achacha…that man is coming." George who had rushed in from the paddy fields announced jubilantly.

"Who…. who?" Thomman Master sprang up on his feet anxiously, gazing into the distance and alternately staring into the eyes of the young boy; Micah had stepped into the courtyard.

"It's Micahchan; he is coming. Thomakutty you go and meet him. Where is Avirachan? Mariachi you ask him to come soon." An excited Thomman master jumped into the courtyard on his staff and walked towards the mud path with George following close behind. He stopped under the jackfruit tree beyond which the descent was rather steep. He looked back to see whether his son and grandson were following him to receive the guests. He discovered Thomakutty lurking behind the cattle shed busying himself with the bull and Avirachan away in the vegetable garden; he found their absence unmannerly.

"Micahcha, I am glad that you have arrived finally. Did you get our letter?" The old man took Micah's hand in his as he escorted him.

"Who is this young man with you?" Looking into Anthony's face he asked Micah.

"He is my cousin.... and, where are Thomakutty and Avirachayan?" He enquired casually though their absence was of little concern immediately. They quietly climbed the veranda and Thomman Master seated them on the old bench. He sat on his ancient cot.

"Thomakutty, come and see who is here." The old man summoned his grandson to meet the guests. Thomakutty was slow to appear, his face surly and hostile; he stayed put in the courtyard, giving instructions to his son; he saw George tarrying around watching the guests whom he thought had come to marry his aunt. His tardiness incensed. Thomakutty who dashed towards the veranda where the boy was standing close by Micah. He caught him by his arm and pulled him out, thrashing him. The boy stood whimpering. The boy's cries brought his mother out.

"Why do you take out your anger on the boy?" Chinnamma was in a fighting mood. Micah felt uneasy at the odd behaviour of Thomakutty. He too intervened on behalf of the boy.

"He is a small boy; how can you be so harsh with him?"

Thomakutty resented Micah's interferenve and anger clouded his face; he stood, sternly looking intoMicah's eyes; he thought it was the right time to show him his place.

"He's our concern; I don't allow any one to interfere."

"Thomakutty." Thomman Master reacted to his grandson's madness, adding:

"Have you gone out of your mind? Don't you know what Micahchan is to us? He is to marry your sister and he is here at your invitation; I don't stomach such behaviour in my house."

Micah sat petrified at this display of anger. Anthony looked scared and humiliated. Mariachi was busy in the kitchen scraping coconut to bake pancakes for the guests; she didnot expect such an outburst though she had feared her brother's anger. She believed her grandfather would support Micah. Leaving behind the scraper and the coconut she moved into the room by the veranda, that allowed her, without being seen, a full view of the crowd in the veranda. Thomakutty still remained in the courtyard, his eyes roving over every face. He finally resolved to break the imbroglio; he was determined to expose the man who had come to marry his sister. He moved closer to the veranda and positioned himself between Micah and his grandfather.

"Micah, what kind of a Christian are you?" Thomakutty fired his first question that surprised both Micah and Antony as much as it riled Thomman Master.

"What nonsense? Don't you know he is a Christian like any one of us?" Thomman Master raised his voice.

"*Valliappacha*, you please wait; let him answer."

Micah answered boldly,

"Yes I am a born Christian, born of Christian parents."

"So, what more do you want? He bears a Christian name, wears a scapular like every devout Catholic. Do you want him to recite a few prayers for a proof?" Thomman Master was sure that simple test would satisfy everybody.

"But what is your caste?" Thomakutty fired the next shot.

"I believe that being a Christian I am above castes."

"You may believe anything you like but the truth is, that in this country everyone has a caste, whether one likes it or not; if you have any doubt you ask Raman Nair." Raman Nair's timely arrival gave him a chance to build up his case. He exultantly invited Raman to give his judgment, and to impart validity to his verdict. He added: "He is a former teacher and a scholar."

"But Thomakutty, I am not interested in what he says. You please tell me what your caste is." Micah's unexpected question startled Thomakutty; he had never expected Micah to fluster him by throwing a counterquestion. He stood wavering.

"My caste? Our caste? But we have no caste for, we are Christians." Thomakutty had become defensive.

"So am I. I told you I am a Christian, and I have no caste," Micah asserted, but Thomakutty persisted as if the rule was not applicable to Micah.

"Aren't you a *Pulaya*? I know you are one."

"Yes I was a *Pulaya*." His reply rattled everybody in the household, except perhaps Mariachi. A stunned Thomman Master sat brooding over the matter; he was totally defenceless against the damaging revelation. What Micah admitted dashed his last hope of getting the girl decently married away; he looked sad.

"How could I give my granddaughter in marriage to a *Pulaya*?" Thomman Master cursed his folly in making a thoughtless proposal; he knew that the wrath of his forefathers would be upon him and the scorn of the community would be unbearable. He felt Thomakutty's righteous anger was justified.

"You have tried to cheat us; you have come with your companion to kidnap our girl. I shall not let you go. I am going to call the Police." His threat had little impact on Micah who sat unmoved, unmindful of the tirade Thomakutty had let loose against him; his nonchalant attitude irked Thomakutty further. He vowed:

"Whoever tries to cheat me has to face the consequences. This intimidation provoked Micah; he said firmly but without losing his calm.

"Thomakutty, better you mind your words. I am a soldier, I have seen death and killed enemies; your threats donot frighten a warhorse. I have my own weapon to kill in self defence." Micah's words, firm and clear resounded across, sending a clear message.

"Mariachi, you come here." Chinnamma summoned Mariachi, and she came meekly, head down, silently wiping off the tears in her eyes. The sight of Mariachi peeved Chinnamma, who asked rather tauntingly:

"What saddens you to shed tears ? Do you want to go with that *Pulaya* and bring disgrace to the family?" Chinnamma's insinuation broke her heart. She darted out of the kitchen to escape her. Chinnamma pursued her into the courtyard, picking up the scraped coconut and rice dough that Mariachi had mixed for pancakes. She dumped the stuff into the waste heap. Mariachi stood still miserably watching the chickens jostling for the food.

"I am here to decide whom to give what to; no more shall I serve him with food nor shall I wash his plates." Chinnamma rushed back into the kitchen to throw out the boiling water to brew coffee for the guests. The earthen pot crash-landed in a corner of the yard splashing the hot water. Mariachi strode into the inner room to escape her wrath. She silently grieved over her fate.

The situation in the front yard was no less stormy with Thomakutty yelling and shouting. This attracted the attention of many a passerby. A few stopped by silently watching Thomakutty; the presence of the two strangers made them suspects in the eyes of the crowd. Thomakutty guessed the mood of the crowd was hostile and wanted to take advantage of this hostility.

"Do you know these *Pulayas* have come to kidnap our Mariachi? you tell me what should I do with them."

"Hand them over to the Police." One man suggested, raising his voice.

"Why Police? We know how to handle them; break their legs and throw them into the ditch. Let jackals feast on their flesh."

"Atrocious! *Pulayas* daring to kidnap a Christian girl?"

"He seems to be a Christian." Some one who had spotted a scapular around Micah's neck whispered into the ears of the next man.

"May be; these days there are many *Pulaya* Christians, just converts."

"But aren't all Christians converts?"

"True, but *Pulayas* are neo-converts; they are still treated as untouchables."

"Perhaps, your sister connived with him; otherwise why should a man travel all the way to this village to kidnap an unknown girl?"

"It's a very relevant question; you better call out Mariachi. Let us hear her."

Mariachi thought it her duty not to conceal the truth; the truth that would free her of any complicity and absolve Micah of the alleged malevolence; yet she hesitated to speak out against her own brother; she felt herself thrown between the devil and the deep sea.

"Hiding the truth would put an innocent man in peril. I must speak the truth." And she spoke the truth, hiding herself behind the thatch curtain only showing her face.

"No… he hasn't come to kidnap me; he has come at the invitation of my brother." She repeated and what she said silenced the men. Mariachi's intervention emboldened Micah to speak for himself.

"*Chettans* I am a Christian as my name would confirm, and perhaps this scapular would suggest." Micah paused for a moment looking into the eyes of the men around him, holding the scapular raised between his thumb and index finger, adding: "But I am of *Pulaya* parentage."

His assertion, unusually daring, sounded like a bolt from the blue leaving the crowd shocked and disoriented. For them too, offering an original Christian girl in marriage to a *Pulaya,* though Christianized was unacceptable; the enigmatic look that quickly clouded their face dampened his zeal. Micah thought it was time for him to play his trump-card. He picked out a white crumpled sheet of paper from his pocket and unfolding it he told them.

"Look, this is the letter that I had from Thomakutty, Mariachi's brother inviting me to visit them to finalise my marriage with his sister. Does he deny his letter?"

"Do you deny the letter?" The crowd that had turned skeptical confronted Thomakutty, demanding an answer. He stayed dithering, searching for an answer to save his face; his silence exposed his dubious intentions. Some thought he might have invited the man to extract money under the pretext of giving his sister in marriage.

"The man being a soldier might be flush with cash." One man concluded. Thomakutty found himself deflated with his sister spilling the beans, and Micah taking advantage of the disclosure; he stood balking.

The crowd insisted that Thomakutty give an answer; he felt compelled and he racked his brains for a plausible story, though unsuccessfully. Finally he admitted, averting his eyes from the crowd.

"It's true that I wrote the letter but it was as dictated by my grandfather."

Thomman Master who had been sitting on his cot silently watching the goings on lifted up his face with determination to announce:

"Yes. It's true I had asked him to write this letter, inviting Micahchan to visit us to finalise his marriage with my granddaughter Mariachi. I want my community to know that Micahchan is a soldier, in the service of the king emperor. I know only brave men can be soldiers and brave men are of high castes. And Micahchan being a soldier is of high caste though you might prefer to call him a *Pulaya*." Thomman Master stopped briefly, cleared his throat and clutched his staff firmly, as if he was getting ready for an act; he said looking into the eyes of the assembled, more particularly staring into the face of Thomakutty:

"Yes, I certainly stand by my decision."

Micah found himself frustrated at Thomakutty's sudden volte-face. His contention that he had come at their invitation carried little impact. The crowd too found it unacceptable for a *Pulaya*, though Christian, to seek a bride from a Christian family, though poor. Even Thomman Master had become sullen. Mariachi, the voiceless sat inside by a corner of her mother's sick bed.

Deeply humiliated, Micah and Anthony walked down the hills silently, Micah cursing his temerity to equate himself with the aristocratic Christians. Anthony thought that Micah was rather naive.

"We have been Pulayas; now we have become Christian Pulayas." He said.

"Aren't you hungry?" Micah wished to change the topic. They had skipped their breakfast hoping a feast at the gir's home. Micah guessed they might get something at his old friend Pokkan's shop. In fact, Pokkan was expecting them; for his daughter had seen them walking to Thomman Master's house. Romour was afloat that a soldier was to marry the Master's granddaughter Mariachi. Pokkan felt hurt they had avoided his hut. Yet he came out running to receive them. Kaali too rushed out but drew back seeing a stranger with Micah.

"Pokkacha, do you have something for us to eat?" Micah asked him as he held the old man's hands into his.

Pokkan offered them boiled tapioca, soaked over night in water with chilly chutney.

Micah's story saddened Pokkan but he was helpless.

"They are good but bad too," Pokkan observed.

"How?" Anthony asked.

"They don't practice untouchability but they think they alone are God's own.

" Kaali would you like to come with us?" Micah asked her. She shook her head and looked at her father for guidance.

Anthony suddenly had an idea; he had a word with Micah who stood listening attentively. After the humble tapioca meal they left for home.

A week later they reached Pokkan's hut along with Sarah, Micah's mother and a fortnight later, Kaali, who was christened Miriam travelled to Delhi along with Pathrose Micah as his wife. They lived happily, unmolested in the capital city.

Msgr. Aaron Micah was happy that his father stood acquitted of the moral turpitude the nun had alleged. He was at peace with himself.

✞✞✞

Five

The train slowly crossed the river at Neelimangalam; it was late night and he was uncertain of what awaited him at the station. He expected a tumultuous and a jubilant reception.

Msgr Micah stepped down onto an almost deserted platform. He looked around for a familiar face but found none; even his father was absent; nor was there the Vicar or any one else from the parish whom his father had talked about rather eloquently. His own kin, the scions of the *Thonnurans* who had walked into the church long ago, along with his father and grandmother, were conspicuous by their absence. A public reception at the railhead and a procession to escort him to the parish centre with speeches concluded with fire works, were what the old man had dreamt for his son, the bishop designate. With the shattered dreams he wondered whether his father was hiding somewhere. Msgr. Micah was not upset though he wondered whether it was a total boycott… But the absence of his own father began to trouble him; then he understood that a *bandh* in this part of the country was a formidable block which even gods failed to overcome.

Leisurely he looked for the tribe in frightful red that bullied the unwary passengers, claiming their right to carry the luggage. Instead, he spotted the new incarnates in blue who appeared less intimidating. Lush with cash the wiser passengers too had become liberal and bought peace on arrival in the home land. The portico was, however, crowded with cab and autorikshaw drivers chasing the fatigued passengers. Unhurriedly, Msgr. Micah climbed up the steps and waited undecided where to go. He found the yard had become deserted.

An autorikshaw, driven into the station yard came to a screeching halt two yards ahead of the lone passenger, who by a deft jerk of his torso saved himself from a direct hit; the driver, rather emboldened looked back expecting the passenger to run towards him to hire the vehicle. Msgr. Micah feigned that he hadn't noticed him. The driver guessed, the man being a Priest would be a soft prey. Besides, a couple of oversized boxes in his possession was an attractive lure for the driver. He reversed the auto and stopped by him, enquiring: "Where do you want to go, Father?"

"Well, I am not sure, I am waiting for some one to pick me up." Msgr. Micah ignored him, turning away his face, showing no interest.

"I can wait for you.' The driver sounded tame.

"Not necessary."

"Father, I am a Christian, and I expect you to travel by my auto."

"Oh! I never knew that one's faith is a factor in hiring a vehicle; but then if you are a Christian why do you exhibit a picture of *Ayyappan* on your vehicle?" The question embarrassed him but he made an effort to wriggle out by inventing an alibi; he said that the auto belonged to a friend, a devotee of *Shree Ayyappan*. His stratagem amused Msgr. Micah, who enjoyed talking to the auto driver.

"What is your name?"

"My name is…Mathai….Varkey." He sounded not quite sure.

"Is it Mathai or Varkey?"

"Does it make much difference? Mathai or Varkey, both are Christian names; they are my friends too."

"I don't want your friends' names. I wish to know what your name is."

"I am Varkey."

"All right Mr. Varkey. How far is Kudamaloor?"

"It's fifteen kilometres" The driver looked at the Priest hopefully; guessing the Priest was not familiar with the town. Assured that he could take the Priest for a ride the driver was also unsure whether more passengers would arrive at night after a *bandh.*

"No. the last time when I visited, the fare meter showed the distance six kilometres only; now Kudamaloor seems to have drifted away from the station. How?" Msgr. Micah looked into the eyes of the driver. Haggling was not his practice yet he wanted to know how honest the man was. Finally, he agreed to hire his vehicle on condition the fare would be what the meter recorded, twenty five per cent extra for the night service.

Msgr. Micah was visiting his father's house after a gap of seven years. He had forgotten the exact location of the house. He remembered it was down Pulimchode, towards north as one walked to the river. The driver seemed to have grasped the direction. Msgr. Micah boarded the auto and the man drove off; he crossed the level crossing at Kumaranalloor and drove westward, passing the bo tree junction, off the temple. The road at the junction was partially blocked with heaps of rubble strewn on the road. The driver slowed down the auto, cautiously looking around lest his vehicle ram into the rubble heap.

" The road seems to have been blocked, Why?" Msgr. Micah asked, noticing the chaotic road condition.

"Don't you know that we had a *bandh* for three days? This road was blocked like a fortress; in the darkness, an unwary motor cyclist rammed into the road block sustaining serious injuries. I think he died in the hospital and a man who took him to the hospital was arrested for man slaughter." The driver narrated the events of the previous night.

"Very bad." Msgr. Micah felt sorry for the dead man and the Good Samaritan who was booked by the police.

"Father, we are at Pulimchode." The driver looked at the passenger for further direction. The driver turned around as Msgr. Micah was slow to respond.

"Well, I think you can take me to the church; that's easy for you."

At the junction the driver took the road on the right and drove fast; he stopped in front of the Priests' residence.

It was past midnight. The church and other buildings in the compound appeared in nocturnal slumber. A lone light shining above the cross on the façade, failed to brighten the yard. Msgr. Micah knew the location of the Vicar's bedroom on the first floor; he asked the driver to wait for a moment as he confidently climbed up the steps. He found the door bolted from inside; he stood debating whether to knock or not. He was not sure how the Vicar would react to be woken up in the dead of night. He knocked finally, waiting anxiously as there was no response. The thought of a second knock was repugnant to his sense of propriety. However, he had no choice, and he knocked again loud enough to reach the message indoors.

"Who is there?" the response sounded jarringly loud.

"Father, I am Father Aaron Micah from Delhi," he said rather meekly. The Vicar slowly opened the door but kept it ajar, apparently to prevent the visitor from rushing inside.

"Yes?" He sounded rather gruff.

"Father I am a Priest from the Archdiocese of Delhi, on official assignment to meet with the Archbishop. I am late to come to you because of the *bandh*. I need accommodation for a few days."

They stood quiet for a while with their eyes locked; the Vicar was well aware of the purpose of the visit of soldier Pathrose Micah's son and his credentials as bishop designate; yet he feigned ignorance. Msgr. Micah didn't miss the bland expression on his face. The Vicar was slow to respond and he appeared unhappy.

I don't know you, and you didnot not inform me earlier. Sorry, it's past midnight . I can't help you." He stood at the door expecting the visitor to withdraw.

"All right Father; its past midnight but that is my problem . Good night, may the Lord Bless you." Msgr. Micah walked down as the Vicar stood watching the unsolicited visitor stepping down.

"Now, we will take the road to the *Laksham* colony."

"Father, do you live in the *Laksham* colony?" The driver couldn't believe a respectable Priest living in a ghetto; the name itself was stigmatic, poverty being its hallmark and gang wars its daily routine.

"Yes, my father lives there and I plan to stay with him."

It was a narrow lane, the surface broken with pot holes and the sides cluttered with domestic waste. The auto rattled down the lanes braving packs of stray dogs which roamed about defying intruders, as if they were the local vigilantes.

It was a borderless settlement, all the tenements looking alike. Flag masts with fluttering party flags stood sentinel at the entrance to the colony from the main lane, proclaiming the political affiliation of the residents

"Here, please turn left."

A tricolour that fluttered atop the mast was familiar to Msgr. Micah. Behind the mast was the first house of the colony that belonged to one Shourie, the local chieftain of the party that had hoisted the tricolour. Msgr. Micah knew that his father's house was the last one on the bylane with an open ground on its left. He asked the driver to stop in front of the house.

"My father lives here, but the door is locked." Msgr. Micah climbed up the steps of the veranda, looking around for his father. It was quiet with no sign of life inside. He stood wondering what to do; he stacked the three boxes on the veranda with the driver helping him.

"How much do I owe you?" He demanded of the driver, who waited unusually meek and self effacing. The Priest noted that the distance covered was seven kilometres, but with no return passengers in the night, he thought it reasonable to pay him an extra fare besides, something to compensate for the night driving.

"How much do you expect? You tell me whatever the reasonable fare is." Msgr. Micah looked into his eyes, reciprocating his humility.

"A hundred rupees, Father?"

"All right, here it is." He handed over to him one hundred and fifty rupees, asking him: "Are you happy?"

"Yes, Father, certainly." As he proceeded to start his vehicle, Msgr. Micah asked:

"You didn't tell me what your real name is."

"Yes Father, sorry, my name is Shivkumar."

"Well Shivkumar, we will meet again."

Shivkumar silently drove away wondering how a Priest could live in a slum house. He doubted whether he was a real Priest; he wanted to go back to verify whether he was fake or real.

✞✞✞

Six

Msgr Micah stood confounded, unable to unravel the mystery of his father's sudden disappearance. He couldn't find a place to sit, with the furniture locked inside. His father's absence at the station was understandable, uncertainty of traffic during the bandh being its cause. But to find him missing from his own home was intriguing. The failure of his father's grandiose scheme to accord a royal welcome to his son, a bishop designate, might have hurt his self esteem. That was not a reason for absenting himself from his own home. He wondered where to look for him and whom to ask.

Msgr. Micah was tired and travel weary. He was hungry and was expecting a hot meal. The neighbourhood was in deep slumber.

He decided to wait until day break, which was not very far. He needed rest but was unsure where to lie down. Finding a pragmatic solution, he placed his three boxes on the floor next to each other in a row with a sheet spread over it; his small bag came handy as a headrest. He removed his cassock, folded and kept it under the sheet. He lay on the improvised bed with his eyes closed. But pangs of hunger and painful thoughts of his missing father kept him awake for a long time. Finally, worried and exhausted he slept on for hours.

The bylane had come alive; menfolk came out in the veranda, smoking and exchanging greetings. The morning sun rose in the east;

Msgr. Micah slept on, unmindful of the advancing rays that embraced him. A passerby noticed a stranger sleeping in the veranda of Pathrose's house which was locked; he alerted the neighbours who collected in front of the house, but seemed reluctant to dare him.

"I don't think he is a burglar; a robber never comes with heavy luggage." One person reasoned. Another climbed on the veranda to verify whether the person was dead or alive. For, the way he slept totally still, caused some concern. He placed his palm over his nose and declared: "He is alive, for sure."

Sourie, who was a late riser, rushed to Pathrose's house alerted by the crowd. His son Reji had told him about a stranger on Pathrose's veranda.

"That must be his son, the bishop."

"His son, a bishop? Can a *Pulaya* be a bishop?" They could not believe that a bishop would come from their slum; that too the son of a *Pulaya*.

"Yes, his son is a bishop; Pathrose had told me that he would be arriving soon. In fact he wanted me to go to the railway station to receive him."

"Now, where has this Pathrose Micah gone, locking the house?"

The commotion in front of the house finally woke up the bishop designate; he sat on the box looking into the faces of the neighbours watching him with awe and admiration. Sourie jumped on to the veranda, extending his palm to grab the bishop's hand to give the conventional kiss on the ring. Micah, took his hand, shaking it heartily, thwarting his attempt to kiss the still vacant ring finger. Following Sourie a few more stepped onto the veranda seeking the bishop's blessings.

Suddenly Msgr. Micah realized that he was in lay dress. He turned towards the wall, pulled out his cassock and donned as he turned towards them. The crowd clapped their hands in appreciation.

"It is for the first time that a bishop visits us."

In no time the whole colony assembled in front of Micah's house as if a miracle had happened. The people watched him, tried to touch him and admired him.

"Pathrose *chettan* is a blessed man; his son is a bishop." Sourie's mother Kathreena opined.

"Yes, yes he is a blessed man". It was a consensus.

"But where is Pathrose *chettan* ?" Nobody had an answer to the puzzling question, though everybody remembered having seen him just the other day, morning or evening.

"My Lord." Sourie addressed him, wanting to make an enquiry.

"Please, don't address me as My Lord or Your Excellency; just 'Father' is enough," Msgr. Micah corrected them.

Sourie still hesitated but asked him. "When did you arrive? Yesterday night? I was out in my veranda until midnight past; a little later I heard the rattling of an auto. I thought it was Pathrose *chettan* returning."

"No, perhaps it was the one that I came by."

Fish hawker Mark's wife brought him a glass of hot coffee and also plain water for him to wash his mouth. Msgr. Micah couldn't ignore her generous offer. He promptly washed his mouth with the water from the glass and drank the coffee, though the glass smelt of fish.

"Thank you." He returned the glass. As she walked home she told her daughter, "I never thought a bishop would drink anything from our hands."

"He seems to be a humble person. May God bless him?"

"Will he become our bishop?"

"I don't think. Don't you know that he is a *Pulaya* and we are Syrian Christians?" Every Syrian Christian, rich or poor was mindful of his identity.

Sourie lingered around; he thought it ill-mannered to leave the bishop alone in the strange circumstances. Besides, he saw a delicate situation with no facility for the exalted person to answer the call of nature. The colony notoriously lacked any such provision with lot of open space around under the sky. In anticipation of his son's arrival Pathrose had added a privy to his house with an external entrance; but he kept it locked and the key was with him. Shourie casually examined the frail padlock; with a slight pull it came away, opening up the tin-sheet shutter. Sourie brought a bucket of water and an earthen bowl to serve the guest's morning business.

"*Pithave*, there is some facility for you to wash your face and …" Shourie stopped short of what he wanted to convey and Msgr. Micah didn't miss the suggestion. Still the nagging question of his father's absence troubled him. Quietly he walked into the privy. Sourie felt reassured. He felt reluctant to try his hand on the lock on the front door which appeared stronger.

"*Pithave*, I feel miserable to see you sitting atop your box like a stranded passenger on a railway platform. I don't know when Pathrose *Chettan* will return.

I will open the room for you if you allow me." He waited for Msgr. Micah's response. "You are his son and I open the room in your presence; and I am sure he will appreciate my action."he added:

"You can do that." Msgr. Micah agreed.

Shourie knew the old man never carried the key with him. He also knew where he kept the key when he went out. The key was found in the axils of a plantain in his backyard. Sourie opened the house and Msgr. Micah formally entered his father's house with his luggage.

Msgr. Micah felt relieved. He was however distracted, slowly turning restive. The room was unusually small with a tiny window sparsely letting in any breeze. His father's absence left him shaken. Away from Delhi's bustle he felt like a fish out of water.

He looked out of the window; the lane was almost deserted except for groups of children walking to the school in their bright uniforms, carrying a load too heavy for their age; the girls nosily blabbering and the boys rowdily retorting. Smoke billowed from the roof of a few houses.

By noon Sourie's mother came along with her daughter-in-law, carrying covered plates and a tiffin carrier. They found Micah's door closed. Unsure about how to call him, they hesitated Reji came to their help.

He knocked at the door which slowly opened from inside. Msgr. Micah came out:

"What makes you visit me at this time?"

"My Lord..."

"No, not My Lord; call me Father."

"Yes Father. We have some food for you." The women waited for his response, and the bishop designate to was really hungry. Sourie returned in the meanwhile. The women left the food with him. For Msgr. Micah this was his breakfast and lunch put together, consisting of a heap of boiled rice, curried sardine in deep, red gravy, and a full length mackerel, deep fried in coconut oil.

"*Ediyey*, the food is for a bishop; it shouldn't lack in salt, spice and must be tangy too." The old woman had warned her daughter-in-law.

"I know mamma." The daughter-in-law assured. And she was liberal with the condiments.

Sourie spread the plates on a small desk. He dumped the whole rice in a heap onto the plate and emptied the entire red gravy over the rice with half a dozen sardines topping the heap The fried mackerel too found a precarious place by the side of the plate, The room was thick with the smell of fish. And, finally there was a lump of chutney, mashed coconut with green cinnamon in tamarind and chilly paste.

The spread on the table surprised the Priest. Sourie was apologetic.

"My Lord, I am sorry, I had no time to buy a chicken; you will have chicken for dinner." Sourie assured him. Msgr. Micah smiled at him.

"Sourie, I eat very simple food, I need only one-third of what you have placed before me. Sardine is good and so is mackerel; both are good for heart but not coconut oil and too much of spice."

Sourie brought another spoon from the kitchen Msgr. Micah took a portion of the food onto another plate.

"You ate very little." Souri said as he cleared up the table.

"Yes, Sourie, I eat little so that I live to eat more." The riddle was beyond Sourie.

After lunch he sat out on the veranda looking at the vacant sky. Sourie guessed he was disturbed, his eyes and face grim.

"Sourie, tell me where do I look for my father? I don't have much contact with any one. The Parish Priest doesn't seem to be helpful. Do you have any suggestion?" Msgr. Micah knew that Sourie was not very resourceful but he seemed to have contacts, at least to make some enquires.

Sourie was also concerned though he knew the old veteran habitually vanished from home unannounced. But his disappearance today was intriguing.

"*Pithave*, you please take rest. I am just going out; shall try to return soon."

Sourie had no idea where to look for him. As he walked down he casually stopped at the Bo tree junction where, by the side of a partially demolished road block, a relic of the bandh, he saw a few men engaged in discussion; they talked about the events of the previous night. Not very far from the site was the damaged cab of Devasia parked by the road.

"It's cruel that the police implicated an innocent Ex-Serviceman in a murder; his crime was he took the victim of an accident to the hospital. The poor chap is in the police lock up now."

"Do you know who the man is? Sourie asked though he could make a guess. He rushed to the police Station where he spotted Pathrose sitting on the floor behind the bars. Sourie's request to meet the man was turned down. He felt awful at the thought of returning to Msgr. Micah without his father, just to inform his father was in police custody.

Sourie remembered a member of the Local *Panchayat* who had the knack to negotiate with the police. Sourie was determined that he would return home with Pathrose only. He hired an auto-rikshaw to search for the Member; he found him and explained the matter to him.

"He is the father of a bishop who is waiting for him now; it's totally embarrassing for him to be in jail when his son the bishop waits at home. Please help." He pleaded.

"What will the bishop do for me?" The Member demanded.

"Any thing you ask. I will get it done."

"Okay!" Both agreed.

✠✠✠

Seven

Communities prided themselves on a past that eulogized their grand deeds and immortalised their great path finders; the *Pulayas* too had a share in what man's great story is today. But the sweat, blood and life they had shed always remained unsung. Their story remained obscure as they lived untouchables, inauspicious to sight and despicable to the gods.

Msgr. Aaron Micah earnestly wanted to delve into their past, at least the immediate past when they had begun to receive social attention; for the recent past had broken many taboos unleashing great potentialities and unlocking new vistas. The Missionaries provided them with the impetus to change.

Shivanandan had agreed to cooperate in the venture. Apart from Pathrose Micah, Suresh Kuttan an old friend of Msgr. Micah was the resource person; He was familiar with their story for four generations that commenced with Poomachee who was like a great-grandmother to Msgr. Aaron Micah. The grand lady had raised Pathrose Micah's father Meenan whose grandson now was the bishop designate.

Pathrose Micah had never seen Poomachee or his father ; but what he had heard by word of mouth was quite poignant. Pathrose Micah had a vivid vision of her from those who had known her. She was a simple woman, who lived unobtrusively, never crossing the path of men who abhorred the sight of the untouchables.

Pathrose Micah recollected how in her death she had became a threat, almost hundred years ago.

Meenan and Athai, the *Pulaya* youths, were good friends; one night they had gone fishing in the river. The catch was good; each had a string of fish dangling, some dead and some still struggling to die.

Poomachee, the old woman, hadn't been keeping well for quite some time but she would never complain of her ill-health; keeping away such matters from her son Meenan. A few days ago she was sitting out in the hot sun warming herself.

"Are you going to roast yourself in the hot sun?" Meenan chided her.

"I feel chilled to the bone." She muttered without lifting her face. She tried to expose her bare bosom to the warm rays of the sun. Meenan sat beside her, placing his palm over her forehead pushing aside a few flocks of tangled white hair from her face.

"You have fever *ammachee*." He discovered, lending her a hand to lift her, he persuaded her to go inside the hut.

"Leave me alone for a while". She resisted; she felt comfortable in the warm sun.

"I shall make some hot *Kapi* for you that will warm your chest" Meenan rushed into the hut to make coffee for her; he found some coffee husk at the bottom of an earthen pot by the side of the hearth. He brought in a pot of fresh water from the river.

"*Ayyo ammachee.*"

As he walked in, he saw her falling down, with her eyeballs rolling. Meenan panicked and his fingers lost them grip on the pot in his hand; the pot dropped crashing on the ground. Lifting her up in his arms he laid her on a mat. Weak and dizzy, she had fainted.

She is light as a chaff." He mumbled as he stood confused, not knowing what to do; there was no one in the neighbourhood to consult with. Her strenuous breathing really frightened him. He poured some cold water on her face. She responded and slowly opened her eyes, grasping his arm.

"Nothing to worry.... I am alright." She assured him. He felt relieved but the drag in her speech caused him anxiety.. Meenan brewed black *kapi* for her; the steaming brew seemed to energize her as she sipped it silently.

"Are you well *ammachee*?"

"I am very well, my son." She tried to calm him down, and he believed her. But he had a lurking fear that everything was not well with her. She preferred to lie on the mat never stirring out.

In the evening she had a little rice gruel; she took a lot of time to eat it. Sleep seemed to have deserted her in the night except for a brief spell in the early hours of the daybreak. Throughout the night she remained restless, suddenly waking up in the midst of sleep, attempting to get up or sit down. Her troubled state worried him. He too couldn't sleep except in the wee hours when, in fact, he over slept. The morning sun slowly rolled over their roof. Meenan jumped off of his mat to find her sleeping with uneven breathing that he thought was not a good sign.

He stepped into the open yard looking around for any one moving along the river. It was a borderless watery expanse before him with dwellings few and far between. Chathans's hut was the nearest.

The placid water remained still with no sign of any canoe moving. Gradually he spotted a sleek canoe emerging from the east with Chathan rowing, down stream. Meenan rushed towards the river bank clapping his palms to catch his attention. He slowed down the canoe, and looked at him enquiringly.

"*Ammachee* is sick; will you please come and see her? I don't know what to do". Meenan expressed his helplessness. Chathan's presence lightened his heart. He looked at him earnestly for his response.

Chathan moored the canoe and walked towards the hut; Meenan followed him.

"*Poomachee.*" Chathan called out her to wake her up. Slowly she opened her eyes, staring at him intently; she had difficulty in recognizing him.

She appears to be in a daze, he observed. He didn't have much of to answer for Meenan's doubts.

"She is quite old," he observed looking at her. He was not sure whether she could be cured, he felt it was a problem of old age.

"I don't think she needs any medicine; you brew some *kapi* with pepper and ginger, he added; "our traditional medicine will see her fit," he prescribed.

"Don't you think it's better to take her to a *Vaidyan*?" Meenan suggested.

"Do you have money to take her to *Olassa Thirumeni*? They won't even allow the untouchables to enter their compound" Chathan's screwed up face cowed Mennan. He too knew that *Olassa* was unapproachable for an untouchable. He kept quiet.

In the evening as the news reached them, Ettanu came along with his wife, Pakkothi and, Athai his eldest son. Pakkothi grasped Poomachee's hand and stood looking at her intently. She turned her face away and wiped her eyes that had welled up with tears. She feared that Poomachee was beyond cure.

"Athai, tonight you better stay with Meenachan; your Amma will also stay back" Ettanu instructed his son. He felt that Meenan needed support in case something happened during the night. He looked apprehensive.

Inside the hut Poomachee still lay on the mat with her eyes half closed. "*Ammachee*...it's me, your Meenan. He sat besides her, and held her face in his cupped palms. She slowly opened her eyes and looked at him eagerly.

"Where did you go, my son?" She sounded feeble and her speech remained inaudible.

Ammachee, why don't you eat a little conji?" He looked into her eyes little realizing that those eyes had lost the shine that had lighted her face.

"Poomachee, here is kanji for you." Pakkothi offered to feed her.

"No. I don't want." She closed her eyes again.

"*Ammachee*, please, a little; you will be alright soon".Meenan implored.

"Only a little." She agreed, perhaps to please her son. Pakkothi warmed the left over gruel and brought it to Poomachee in an earthen bowl. Athai had collected a few jack tree leaves, the lamina of which he shaped into a cone, pinned to position as a ladle. Meenan helped her to sup with the leaf spoon. After a few helpings she refused to open her mouth.

"No. I don't need more."

"Don't force-feed her; she doesn't need more." Pakkothi advised Meenan; he kept the bowl on the floor.

"At least she had some thing." he consoled himself.

Dusk fell under the canopy of the summer sky; darkness gradually crept into the hut as the tiny earthen lamp tried valiantly to ward off the advancing night. Soon the lamp went out with no kerosene in its tank. Pakkothi tried to light a fire in the hearth thrusting tinders on the embers. Poomachee was quiet, as she had slipped into sleep. Meenan thought everything was under control as he moved out along with Athai to sit on the grassy bank of the river, silently watching the water flowing down. Pakkothi remained inside the hut observing the old woman.

As Poomachee lay on the mat, Pakkothi sat by the side of the hearth eating the gruel; more water with a spatter of cooked grain. Darkness did not impede her eating, accustomed as she was to eating and sleeping in darkness.

Meenan had a good heap of tinders stocked which he brought inside. Pakothi kindled a fresh fire in the hearth; slowly the flame leaped up. The sudden rush of bright light dazzled Pakkothi who tried to shade her eyes with her palm. Poomachee cared not to open her eyes to greet the bright golden yellow light.

Poomachee showed no sign of revival. The only sure sign of life was the slow, feeble breath that lingered. They sat around watching her. Pakkothi called out to her once again to see whether she would respond, and she made a weak attempt; moving her lips and opening her heavy eyelids. She made another bold attempt, and called out:

"M…E…E…N…A…"

He was sitting next to her with a blank look on his face. As she called him out he grasped her right hand and held it tightly in his palms. Her tongue was heavy and sound buried deep in her throat. Poomachee strenuously lifted her hands to hold Meenan's; she slowly opened her eyes. She pulled him towards her bosom and held him tightly in her arms. He held her head in his left arm pressing her against his breast. Her eyes had become dim and dull; the eyelids involuntarily closed over the eyeballs. She forced open her eyes, perhaps, for a last glimpse of her son. No words came out of her mouth nor did any light pass into her eyes. She collapsed into his arms.

"This chapter truthfully portrays the pathetic end of a *Pulaya* woman a hundred years ago." Msgr. Micah affirmed.

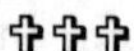

Eight

Death is always unbearable but burial presented a traumatic experience for the *Pulayas*. For they had no right to claim six feet from this earth as their bodies polluted the land on which rested the feet of the gods. The sight of their dead was equally disgusting. The *Pulayas* were condescended to dump their dead at the far end of the river, strictly carried in the night. Poomachee's death repeated the same question.

By midnight the *Pulayas* in the neighbourhood reached Poomachee's hut; the women sat huddled together lamenting the departed, who was really a heroine for them. The men squatted together in the open yard in front of the hut discussing how to dispose of the body. Meenan stood behind them mutely watching and listening. They never thought it necessary to hear him nor did he make any suggestion except one.

"Meenan desires that his mother be buried in the backyard of their hut." Athai told the elders. Meenan anxiously looked at them for their reaction. Athai explained why it should be, and he added:

"He wants to light a lamp at the spot to keep her memory alive."

Kandan, who had a daub of wet lime at the tip of his index finger to coat the split betel leaf with, stopped abruptly, and looked at the boys; his puckered brow surprised the boys who appeared sheepish among the elders.

"How could that be? This earth is not ours; we have no right to bury our dead in this soil." Kandan patiently tried to make them understand the difference.

"Yes sons, we have no right to what comes out of this soil and no right to go under it, only destined to stride on it unseen and unheard of". Ettanu sounded melancholic and dejected at their fate. Someone had declared long, ago that fire was sacred not to be defiled by consigning to it a dead *Pulaya* and, mother earth dear, not to be polluted by burying the dead of the *Pulayas*.

They were allowed only to sink their dead in the bosom of the river. Meenachil had been carrying in her bosom their ancestors and Poomachee was to follow them soon, faithfully. The dead body could only be consigned beyond the dwellings of the high castes where the river entered the Kuttanadan expanse. It couldn't be carried along the course of the river at daytime, as it would pollute ceremonial bathers.

Their Priest the *Achon* arrived, escorted by Athai. The few women standing at the door of the hut hurriedly made way for him;.Chirtutha and the other women who sat wailing abruptly ended the mournful ode when they saw the *Achon*, with his mace, peering at them. The frightened women squeezed out of his presence, taking shelter behind the hut.

He began to swirl his mace vigorously, making three rounds of the corpse, and stopped at its head; he sat cross-legged placing the mace over the deceased. He pulled out a red scarf from the folder and wore it from his shoulder across his breast imitating the Brahmin Priest. Both his palms were placed on his knees opening upward. A long litany of jarring invocations followed. On concluding the rituals he bundled up the dead body and signalled to the men that they could proceed. He rose up holding his mace high over his head. As he went around the body the bells jingled announcing the final journey to the watery grave. At the end of the third round, as the Priest emerged at the door, those crowded at the door made way for him. The dead body was solemnly carried to the waiting barge.

The day was breaking in the east and the men who sat huddled together in the *savathoni* loathed light; for, darkness gave them security, making them invisible. Ettanu feared the day would soon break, exposing them. The *Savathoni* slowly emerged winding still west where the reach was broad and deep. The punters noticed the barge swerving leftward, and instinctively manoeuvred to correct the course. Down stream, on their left gradually emerged a sprawling compound with stone masonry embankment to protect it against the ravages of floodwaters. The sight of the compound stunned the occupants of the barge who looked at each other apprehensively. They appeared afraid to look directly at the compound to avoid looking into someone's face.

For it was almost the hour of the day when the inhabitants of the household would come out in the open to take their morning bath in the river. If they happened to see a dead body being carried in front of the house at daybreak it would certainly invite their wrath upon them.

Sensing the threat posed by the situation Ettanu peered surreptitiously for any sign of movement in the compound. As the cortege moved down he warned the punters against crossing the mid line of the river to avoid violation of *Theendal* distance. He was uncertain whether the customary distance of sixty cubits was good enough for a dead woman. Sixty cubits was the distance a living person was decreed to keep off but a dead woman's potency to pollute was perhaps greater. The punters laboured hard to keep their course to the right; they treaded a risky line. The boat was left to drift down as the river flowed. The punters remained perplexed leaving the poles flitting across the surface of the water.

At the bathing ghat Ettanu saw a man who stood fully stripped, immersed in water with his long hair dishevelled and half closed eyes focussed on the young morning sun in the east. Slowly and deliberately he took three deep dips ceremoniously in quick succession reciting a hymn venerating the sun god. He posted himself erect at the virgin moment witnessing the emergence of the coppery sun beginning a new day. He had his hands held above his head. In a moment, as he felt relaxed, he wiped his forehead with his hands and brushed back his water dripping long hair in position.

The cortege continued to glide over the water, uninterrupted. The only sound that broke the silence of the morning was the rapid pounding of the mourners' hearts. The tiny waves that had rushed to kiss the sides of the boat seemed to have restrained themselves. The faceless bundle that was Poomachee, rested on the mid thwart of the barge, unaware of the brewing commotion caused by the accident of her death.

"*Thampran*!" Ettanu lipped under his suppressed breath.

"Kottamana Namboodiripad." They thought the breeze had whispered into their ears. The panicked boat men looked at each other seeking an answer to a question that they dared not ask. Slowly it dawned on them, that to the world they were committing the most obnoxious violation of the rules laid by the mighty. They felt as if they were stepping into the jaws of a tiger. None could expect to come out alive. Ettanu thought he heard the rumbling of thunder and the flash of lightening from the summer sky, though the sky was clear and the morning calm. Beleaguered by anxiety and fear, the men crowded together in numb bewilderment with their parched throats stilling even their stray thoughts.

"What to do now?" Ettanu asked in utter confusion.

"They will kill us. They will dump us along with Poomachee." They conjured up the vision of perishing along with the dead woman. A weird silence followed as a blank look descended on their faces.

"Come what may, let us move down quickly and get lost." Meenan boldly suggested, and looked at them for a response. The rattled men turned towards him with a look that wilted the young man. Meenan wanted to pacify them, so he said,

"It may not be easy for them to catch us; if it comes to that, we will dive deep into the water and get away, and I am sure they will never catch us" He sounded pragmatic but impulsive.

"What will you do with the dead body of this woman?"

"Let them take it; if it pollutes them, let them dispose it off."

They continued to ask questions. Chathan was the last one to ask a question.

"Where will you hide thereafter?"Every body knew, both the questions and its answers.

"They will catch us, one by one; no head shall remain upon any shoulders."

"No huts shall remain for us on this earth; every hut will be torched"

They knew that was how they settled scores with the untouchables. Those questions always remained unasked, as the poor were afraid to hear the painful answers.

"An untouchable, when dead, was a mere carcass to be dumped." Sivanandan commented as he read the story of Poomachee's last journey,

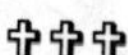

Nine

In the morning Ettanu, the head worker, noticed that the river was rising fast; the rapidity of the flow and the range of the flotsam served a warning. The high turbidity of the river alerted him of the brunt of the cloud burst on the hills; but the impact of the forebodings went largely unnoticed.

Floods had always been part of their life. Ettanu did not panic; he decided to stay back believing that the first lash of monsoon would be mild. Besides, he was responsible for maintaining the dykes that protected the paddy fields of his landlord against the rising water, a hectic job that wrecked one's head and heart.

"A *Pulaya* never runs away from his post when the flood threatens the paddy," he told his wife as he rushed to the farm when he found the river rising fast. Water had risen almost to a man's height above the ground where tillered paddy stood undulating in the squally wind. The floodwaters that rushed down the river knocked at the dykes tumbling down patches of earth. Round the clock vigil was needed to check every thing potential fault that threatened to breach the dyke. Teams of men worked by turns on the huge water wheels, draining the rain water that swelled the field. Ettanu knew the water in the river was rising at an alarming rate; he promptly reported this to Ravunni Achan, the landlord. With the flood threats the landlord had stopped visiting the farm, leaving the duty of saving the crop to the *Pulayas*.

"I leave the entire operations to you. You take care of it." A tired Ravunni Achan decided to call it a day, putting the load on his workmen. Ettanu worked hard along with his fellow men but the river turned out to be mightier.

In the afternoon, when every man was on the water wheels, Ettanu detected a minor opening at the upper end of the bund. He noticed it slowly widening into a gap; it continued to rain heavily..

"Kandacho....*pooyi.*" He screamed to his co-worker; nobody heard him, the roar of the rain drowning his scream. Ettanu was scared as the cavity had now become the size of an earthen pot denting the dyke. With little time to think and plan; his immediate concern was to stop the water from gushing into the field.

With a rare determination that only a man of strong conviction can summon, he lowered himself on the waterfront of the dyke and stood against the rushes that knocked at the dent. He pressed his chest against the cavity to seal it watertight. He seemed to have succeeded for a while with his torso snugly ceiling the opening. Water stopped flowing and Ettanu appeared happy as he stood protecting the property of his landlord, bravely, naively expecting his co-workers to respond to his shouts.

Hours passed but nobody came searching for him. Ettanu slowly realized that his feet were sinking deep into the slush at the bottom of the river forcing him to shift his legs frequently. The chilly wind that blew from the west weighed him down; the icy water he stood sunk in numbed him. He found himself losing his grip, as his flesh began to weaken. Each tap of rushing current tumbled a chip of the dyke that eventually widened the opening. Ettanu suddenly slumped onto the bund; a rush of water knocked at the cavity breaching the dyke. The bund collapsed letting the water cascade into the field. He was thrown in and washed away by the jet of water that rushed into the field.

The men on the water wheels felt the sudden surge of water on the wheels and guessed that the dyke had breached somewhere. Kandan came along with Koduvan looking for Ettanu. They discovered him lying half dead, his torso floating in water with the head resting on the wet earth. By evening the dyke had breached at several points and water stood level with that in the flooded river smothering the green saplings.

Ettanu was carried to the work shed and laid on the bare floor; he was insensate and cold. They lit a fire to warm up his body but couldn't find even a piece of dry rag to roll over his body. By turns they held their palms over the fire to warm and massage him,. It took much time to restore him; though alive he was weak and withered. Ettanu looked heart broken when he learnt that they had to abandon the crop overwhelmed by the deluge. Tears rushed down his cheeks.

In the evening they returned home, braving the rain and the turbulent river, carrying their empty baskets. For nobody had come to open the barn to measure out the day's wage. His co-workers escorted Ettanu home as they found him utterly wrecked and exhausted.

Floodwaters had risen up to knee level in his yard. He didn't think the flood posed him an immediate threat as it stood at least a cubit below his floor. The rain continued with no respite in the damp and chilly night.

Ettanu continued to live in his hut with his wife and children as did most of the other farm hands. They sat huddled in their huts staring at the bleak reality that threatened their lives, their limbs numbed by the wet floor. Through the night Ettanu didn't sleep, staying alert against the ravaging onslaught of monsoon. Boats and canoes had ceased to ply on the river.

Days passed uneventful but tense; the family hearth remained damp with no fire kindled; the Ettanus slept on empty stomachs.

One morning, the unceasing howling of his old dog suddenly woke up Ettanu Sharing the fate of the household the emaciated animal had been starving for almost a week. The dog seldom ventured out of the mound of ash he had sunk himself in; finding it warm enough to sustain him against the chilly weather that ate into the marrow of his bones. The humans it lived with, were worse than their canine companion; it could at least arrogate to itself the warmth that still lingered in the ash mound, heaped up soon after the last fire was kindled in the hearth.

The dog, with its eyes partially closed and mouth ajar exposing its canine teeth, occasionally growled when an intruding fly took the liberty to perch on him hoping to make a feast for itself. In a swift move the dog would close its jaws trapping the fly in its mouth.

With dark clouds in the sky, it was still raining outside. Ettanu struggled up on his feet and limped towards the front of the hut. He thought some one had come visiting him, perhaps, with a message; he was troubled and frightened.

"May be, the *Thampran* has sent some one with a few measures of paddy to help me fight hunger." the thought brightened his face as he stood at the entrance, hopefully.

"Or could it be some horrid news? Let it not be." He looked worried.

None appeared at the door. Ravunni didnot think of sending him two measures of paddy. Ettanu heaved a sigh of relief as there was no sad news either.

The river was in spate with the murky water knocking against any thing that blocked its onslaught. The grim picture portrayed by the monsoon clouds frightened Ettanu. The water had risen further and stood half a cubit below his floor, threatening to swamp the ground where his wife and children sat huddled together. Slowly they slipped into slumber on the bare mud floor on frayed mats with the youngest, two-year-old girl. Chakki, clinging to the bosom of her mother. His eldest son Athai slept with both his hands thrust between his thighs to keep himself warm.

Among his six surviving children, only Athai had some flesh covering his bones. Pakkothi, his wife, looked older than her age with a pale face and a wasted frame. The weariness of a life's suffering, and the anguish and strain associated with frequent child bearings; eight within a span of the first ten years they had lived together as man and wife, had seen her become gaunt with hollow eyes and prominent cheek bones. Her sparkling eyes and the unfailing stamina were the only remainders of her youth. Hunger and the bone freezing chillness of the rain-drenched wind crushed her will to endure.

She saw her children silently crying for a draught of gruel but she had nothing to offer. The pot that boiled the gruel remained as dry as their throats. They ate only when they had work, and with no work they starved without grumbling. The need to save was not their nature. The truth was that the meagre wage they earned was just enough for the day. The wage system discouraged them from saving as their masters ensured that they only received a survival wage.

Starving women and children went around begging, or scrambling to pick up plantain leaves thrown out with leftovers from the kitchens of rich households. Ettanu saw to it that his children never went begging, or fought with dogs for the leftovers. The flood marooned them denying the option of begging too.

Chakki, the youngest girl, clung to her mother's sagging breast, irritated as she found the breast dry, not yielding even a little watery serum to wet her mouth. She bit at the nipple, in bitterness. Tears were the only fluid that the mother could produce, copiously.

Pakkothi pulled her breasts away from the child's mouth with a spank on her cheek. In a huff the child wriggled out of her lap and began to blubber lying on the ground finally crying herself to sleep. Her cries woke up the other children who lay slumbering on the rain battered floor. One by one they rose up casting a sulky glance at their wretched mother. Athai didn't cry, he turned his sullen face away, quiet, with his eyes roving over the swift flowing water.

Ettanu knew his previous day in the nippy water had aggravated his chest congestion. Unable to find a way out, the children's starving faces pained him. Suddenly, the lone palm next to his hut, swaying its crown in the raging wind caught his attention. The nuts hanging invitingly from the tree were irresistible. His hope that a few nuts would drop down as the wind battered the crown remained a mere wish.

He had never in his life stolen anything. Today, in the face of starvation, he found himself tempted to do what he would never think of. Perhaps hunger and deprivation vitiated the human mind.

He slowly moved out of his hut almost knee deep in water, looking at the nut-laden tree that temptingly swayed its lush green head. Standing at the foot of the tree, he felt the trunk with his palms; it was slippery, the heavy coat of moss thriving on it making it dangerous to clamber up. He decided to ignore the hazards and climb up.

With his eyes closed, both palms placed on the trunk of the tree he offered a silent prayer to an unknown God as his witness and protector for a safe climb and return. He planted one foot on the bottom flank of the trunk and fixed his left palm on the tree front as a prop, and grasped the tree with the right arm in a catch. With the weight of his body on the prop arm he positioned himself in a squat, and leapt upward along the trunk, instantly lifting up each foot to a higher perch. He gained a few steps but suddenly began to slip losing his grip on the trunk. As he slipped down, he embraced the trunk with both his arms to avert a fall. That proved disastrous. As he slid along the crenulated trunk his chest rubbed against the trunk, exuding blood from the bruises. In no time he was back at the bottom of the tree, desperate and distraught. He wiped off the blood with the back of his palm, and stood nursing the injuries silently.

"The man is desperate; he will go to any extent to get some thing to eat." Athai thought to himself as he observed his father's discomfiture.

Looking at his father sympathetically, Athai stepped into the water. He waded through the flooded pathway towards the ferry point that lay submerged. Ettanu watched his son wading his feet getting dragged by the slushy earth. He waited patiently until his son had moved farther from their hut. His furtive manners confirmed more than what he wanted to conceal. Ettanu looked at the sleepy dog still in the ash mound enjoying a deep sleep with his eyes half closed as usual, and ears trained for stray sounds.

"Tippoo." Ettanu called and the dog trotted up to him faithfully wagging its tail; it shook its body vigorously to shed the ash it was covered with. It looked up to the master for his command, wagging his tail and sniffing at his feet. The poor animal was oblivious of the intentions of his master.

Ettanu knew that cat meat was good for health, especially for those who were consumptives. He concluded logically that dog meat too was equally good. Very reluctantly he decided to slaughter Tippoo for its meat as he could not bear any longer the suffering of his children. He knew that his children would never allow him to butcher their pet. Quietly, he drew the chopper from the fold of the thatch and stood watching.

The dog still waited at his feet, perhaps wondering why it was not given any command; its eyes rolled over the face of the master for a word but with no words coming from the master's mouth, Tipoo became impatient and began to howl. This woke up the slumbering household.

"You get lost." He chased the dog away as he saw the sleeping children popping up their heads, enquiringly; the dog timidly lingered for a while. He got annoyed at the dog's slothful insolence that invited a hard kick on its already shrunk belly. It meekly withdrew, whining at the irrational behaviour of the man. Ettanu did not up the idea of killing the dog but he understood that it couldn't be done with his children's knowledge. He broached the idea when Athai returned later.

"Do you want to kill the dog? You had better kill one of us."

"Don't we slaughter the cow, buffalo or goats that we rear at home?" Ettanu countered his son who cared not to answer him.

Ettanu had to hang his head in shame, and the dog saved its life by a mere chance. Yet it continued to bark unmindful of the kick it had from the master. It occasionally relapsed into loud growls with the hair on its neck standing erect and tail held straight, forcing Ettanu to look out. The dog appeared to be readying for a sudden jump as the man who was sluggish both in spirit and physique looked on, displeased; in fact, he hated the dog. Ettanu concluded that the dog was either hungry or afraid of the surging water. He had no reason to believe the dog was scared of the flood, as he had survived many a floods along with the family. The dog was a good swimmer too. The dog, however, continued to be agitated and restless, and moved in short circles sniffing at the corners and the folds of the thatch; it looked at him emotively, wondering, what had gone wrong with the man.

Finally, it stood at the entrance, apparently geared up for action, growling between his jaws, with his incisors unmasked, as was his wont when he was sure to jump on a victim. The fearsome, intent look on its face made Ettanu feel certain that the dog had gone mad. Again the thought of killing it rushed in to his mind; he wondered whether the flesh of a mad dog could be eaten; he casually looked out into the surging water to find what the dog was howling at.

Ettanu was taken aback when he saw a huge python lurking in the grass-covered mound of the palm tree that he had unsuccessfully attempted to climb up,.The python raised its head making a survey, with its eyes focussed on the dog apparently, anticipating its next move, which could be fatal to either.

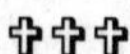

Ten

Monsoon continued to play havoc with the land and the hapless men. There was water everywhere; the sky had opened its spouts with vengeance and the rain gods acted ruthless. Rivers ran flooded, knocking down homesteads, man built dykes and submerging the tillers raised. The farmers had withdrawn, abandoning the farms and the workmen returned home with their wage basket empty. The white smoke that billowed over their roof ceased to appear with the hearth remaining damp.

They had a hand to mouth existence, earning a wage of two measures of raw grain at the end of each working day; no work meant no wage. They hardly had any surplus for a rainy day. When the great monsoon knocked at their doors, they sat huddled together under their thatch, hopeful for the rains to stop and sunny days to return.

The *Pulayas* enjoyed no rights on this earth which belonged to the high caste propertied class. They lived untouchables but worked the land to produce wealth. To ensure they served their masters the *Pulayas* were allowed to pitch their huts on properties of their lords; they lived bonded.

The rich never treated the *Pulayas* fairly; they exploited them with no succour to relieve their suffering. Laws were contrived to keep them suppressed illiterate and so that they posed no threats to their masters. Despite the flood and the misery it spread, the masters chose to keep their eyes closed.

Meenan believed that his Lord, Ravunni Achan, had a liking for him; it was true that the smart youth had been a favourite of the landlord. Meenan failed to realise that his lord's interest in him was purely personal. Ravunni found the youth handy to further certain covert interests.

Meenan's hut was on a higher plane with no immediate threat from the flood. But he too faced the stark reality of 'no grain'; he knew his fellow workmen fared no better. He racked his brains to discover a face that would answer his immediate need for two measures of paddy to sustain himself for a few days. Many faces paraded before his eyes but none fitted the bill; for they too were in no way better than him. And then a saviour appeared before his eyes.

"Ravunni Achan!", he exclaimed; he was sure he had found the answer. He wanted to present himself before his Lord, but he was unsure where to meet him and how to present his request. There was no precedent of a *Pulaya* visiting his Lord in his mansion and seeking a sort of loan of two measures of paddy. He thought he would perhaps have to wait a few hours for a chance vision of his lord.

Meenan had a boundless sea of water before him; crossing the flooded river to reach his Lord's mansion which was quite far off, was hazardous. Deciding to dare the river, he swam the swift flow diagonally, walking across the water logged palm lands to reach the mansion. He stopped at the *Pulathara* beyond which the untouchables were forbidden to tread. It was impolite to hail any person. He was expected to wait patiently until someone spotted him. He waited for a long while with no sign of any living being. Exhausted he decided to quit. He had no strength to slog the terrain and swim the torrent again.

As he walked down, he saw Ravunni Achan at the ghat by Emmanuel's house. He sat at the top flight of steps that led to the river. At the lower flight, by the inundated river was his wife, Nangeli. Meenan hesitated to appear before the Lord. Fearful of his wife who hated the *Pulayas* for no reason other than they were *Pulayas* and untouchables.

"Rosmaaa," Meenan heard the long intonation of Nangeli's hail seeking Rosma, Emmanuel's wife. Rosma felt uncomfortable at the morning visitor; her dangerous adventures in the river frightened Rosma. She was concerned as the weather was squally and the river in spate; the cloud burst in the hills had turned the river turbulent with a strong current devastating the bank. Fast swirling eddy that moved close to the bank posed a real threat to unwary swimmers. Nangeli was no less daring. Besides, Rosma was sure that her estranged partner, Ravunni would trail her seeking her out; he followed her like her shadow.

Rosma was the only person Nangeli enjoyed socialising with outside her own clan. The Emmanuels enjoyed substantial business connections with the *Tharawad* that stood them in good stead. Theirs was a time tested social bond though one was orthodox Hindu and the other a monotheistic Christian.

"Nangeli, the river is treacherously violent and the current is unusually rapid; it's not advisable to play in the swift flow. I suggest you return home." Rosma dissuaded the woman from entering the river.

"What makes you shoo me away like a cat on the prowl?"she protested excitedly and rushed towards the river with Rosma following her close behind.

"I have been bathing in the river…how long…for years when it was lean or in spate. I will bathe in the river today also." She ran down the cobbled steps but abruptly stopped when she saw Ravunni on the sidewalk.

"Oh! You are here to prevent me from entering the water; let me see who dares me" Nangeli challenged him but he preferred to look the other way. Rosma stood watching her helplessly, making a sign of the cross to give her wisdom not to venture too deep into the river.

"Rosma, why don't you join me for a swim? The water is cool and it has a sandal hue, but how come it has no fragrance?" She lifted up a scoopful of water and let it dribble down her fingers to find it smelling muddy.

"Who is making the water muddy?" She looked down stream and found Meenan, her bete noire around. Seeing the *thamprati* lazing in the water a frightened Meenan doubled up the steps so as not to expose himself. Detected, he stood exposed to the crime of polluting her.

"Who is that *Pulaya* who defiles me?" Her ire turned towards him.

Still Nangeli showed no sign of coming out of the river; she lowered herself in the water and stayed in, vigorously splashing water with both her hands.

"Nangeli, you please come out. *Kallappam* is ready for you." Rosma tried to lure her out reminding her of her favourite fare in the frying pan.

Rosma noticed that Nangeli was slowly moving into the deep where the current was tough. She lacked the skill to manipulate the deadly current, or strength to escape from the jaws of a killer whirl once sucked into. Rosma panicked and Ravunni looked confused, and both appeared helpless.

"You please come out; you are getting late for the temple." Rosma became more persuasive. Nangeli remained silent for a while and slowly climbed up a few steps. Rosma heaved a sigh of relief and Ravunni lifted himself up from his long squat, cautiously walking towards her.

She took another break, stopped for a while, then turned back, yelling: "Meenachi is my mother; she is inviting me. I want to join her in her bosom," she uttered as if possessed. Ravunni continued to climb as Rosma stood watching a tamed Nangeli moving up the steps. Before they could grasp what she had said she took a powerful leap, plunging herself into the depth of the river that she thought was her mother; moments dragged by but she failed to surface.

"Nangeli...*Ammay*...*Bhagavathee*..." Ravunni screamed in panic as he rushed down the steps. Rosma looked aghast with her tongue cleaving to the roof of her mouth. Meenan, who was waiting at the front yard of Rosma's house expecting her to return, heard the commotion; he rushed to the ghat, stopped away from Ravunni, lest he defile him. As Ravunni stood debating what to do, Rosma asked Meenan to act soon to search for Nangeli and rescue her. Meenan hesitated; unsure about what to do. He stood debating whether it was proper for him, an untouchable to touch an upper caste woman. "Where am I to find the *Thamprati*? After the plunge she hasn't surfaced even once. Even if I find her can I touch her? Will it offend you, Thampra?" Meenan's were genuine doubts that scared Ravunni. Meenan hesitated, watching the formidable spectacle the river was. Rosma got annoyed at his languid response.

"Meenan, don't wait to clear your doubts; take out the canoe, follow the course. She will surface soon and you catch her by her hair to be safe. Can't you do that much? The rest we will see."

He promptly boarded the sleek canoe shored by the ghat and pushed it down stream, looking around for a sign of the woman; the current swept his canoe rapidly downstream rendering his mission futile in case she surfaced up stream.

"Meenan, she's here…she's here… you come upstream soon." Both Rosma and Ravunni alerted him as they saw Nangeli surfacing for the first time. But Meenan sadly missed the chance as rowing upstream against the current posed a formidable feat. He rowed up vigorously, slouching at the stern with unwavering determination; the canoe inched up against the swift flow.

Bad luck awaited him; a rapid thrust of the current unexpectedly swept the canoe into a swirl. Rosma saw the canoe getting nearly swamped by the rising water. For a moment the muscle of the man seemed no match for the might of the water and, Meenan had to battle hard with the violent river for every moment he stayed. Finally he manoeuvred skirting a whirlpool on to an eddy. The eddy suddenly merged into a turbulent swirl and pulled the canoe towards its vortex. The small canoe moved in circles, at every turn its prow being pulled towards the central cavity. He too seemed to be fated for death.

Rosma panicked with no help available to save both Meenan and Nangeli; both seemed doomed but dear too. Ravunni stood by her side watching helplessly is Meenan fought an apparently losing battle. He was a good swimmer, familiar with every nook and corner of the River Meenachill, whose son he considered himself. Even its wild turbulence had always been tractable for him; but he shuddered at the thought of being sucked into the death well.

"Nangeli....Nangeli..." Rosma ran down the bank shouting as Nangeli surfaced for the second time for breath, further down from the first spot, but she sank back again. Meenan saw her face as she surfaced.

"Perhaps she will make one more attempt before she gives up the fight." He concluded it was the last chance for him to save her; he was determined to save her.

"*Ammay*..." He uttered a cry and in a quick move he caught hold of a palm trunk that lay submerged in the flood. Anchoring himself firmly with his legs entwining the trunk, he looked around for Nangeli to surface, hopefully for a last breath. He saw his abandoned canoe being sucked into the well of death.

He watched the movement of the current for any sign of Nangeli surfacing before sinking into the depth of the river. Down stream not very far from his perch, he noticed her head popping up briefly, and he took a leap; he missed her hair but caught her by her arm though he knew that catching a drowning person by the arm would endanger his own life. But he decided to risk his own life to save the woman. Frantically, Nangeli pulled him and held him tightly in her arms as one in the throes of death by drowning would attempt. Meenan found himself immobilized; he feared the danger of losing his own and her life as well. He struggled hard to disentangle himself from her tight grip. The more he tried to free himself the tighter her grip became. As they grappled under water she lost her hold on his torso but instantly her arm around his neck. Meenan gulped some muddy water, feeling he had little chance of surviving, when an idea flashed to him.

Nangeli's right biceps passed just across his mouth; he bit her resolutely, driving his teeth deep into the flesh; he tasted blood and she tasted pain; she instinctively loosened her grip. In no time Meenan extricated himself from the noose. He knew that the next moment was his own and he pushed her away from the tight embrace.

"Come what may, I shall save her" He quickly caught hold of her long hair and pulled her towards him, surfacing in no time, dragging her behind him. With little stamina to swim against the current he drifted down the stream along the flow slowly moving towards the riverbank. He touched firm ground under his feet to stand holding Nangeli in his arms.

A crowd had lined up the river bank, gesticulating and arguing as they watched Meenan grappling with Nangeli in the water. The high caste woman lying bare in the arms of Meenan, the *Pulaya*, was an outrageous sight for them. Many protested while a few accused him of mal-intention.

"He must have bared her."

"Where have her clothes gone?"

"Couldn't you find some one else to rescue her?" The wise among the crowd asked questions logical to them.. The spectators who had gathered along the river bank seemed more interested to watch the drama; they talked freely saving themselves from the surging water.

"*Thamprati* is still alive; you please lift her and take care of her." Meenan pleaded looking at the unconcerned crowd that stood watching the scene and passing comments.

Soon Ravunni arrived followed by his kin. Standing on the embankment they lowered a netting of a doubled cotton sheet into which Meenan placed Nangeli's bare body supine; he covered her breast with her own long hair which stopped short of the loin; seeing her haunch bare, reflexively he pulled off his own loin cloth to cover her.

✞✞✞

Elevan

"Don't blurt out that the *Pulaya*, Meenan has rescued Nangeli from drowning."

Konna Kaimal warned the onlookers. He considered it a disgrace. Nangeli was alive; her insensate body lay, still. The *Pulaya* youth's strip of cloth that had covered her loin had slipped nor was her long hair that covered her breast in place. Her body was placed on a make shift stretcher and carried away. Aghast at the callous handling of her exposed body, Rosma covered her torso with her *kawani.* The crowd slowly melted away. Meenan was still in the water with no loin cloth to cover his nakedness. He tarried in the river and climbed up the embankment after the crowd left. He covered his loin with a plantain leaf cut off with his teeth and, walked home.

It was an unflattering episode for a high caste house hold to watch helplessly an Untouchable, *Pulaya* youth grappling with a young woman of the *Tharawad;* though it was his brave feat that saved the woman from death. Still he drew censure instead of encomia. The unsung hero of the river was indignantly allowed to quit, saving his skin.

As Meenan faced a turbulent river and a drowning woman, his mentor Ettanu, hungry and emaciated, was struggling with a hungry python.

Ettanu stepped back cautiously, hoping the dog wouldn't act rashly before he returned equipped to deal with the intruder. He rushed towards the rear of the hut, where on the roof of the thatch he had a bow and a few arrows among his fishing tackle. He hurried back to the door with the bow and the arrow ready to be triggered.

He was late by a second; the dog sighted the head of the python again stealthily probing the trunk of the palm and, not to be outwitted, the dog jumped for its head but missed the target. The doggedness of the dog was no match for the wiliness of the reptile. The python seemed to be hungry, starving since it's descent from the hills washed by the flood waters.

In a swift move, it lowered itself below the surface of the water but kept ready its trunk and the tail to mount an assault on the dog. By a rapid move it knocked down the dog and caught it in the tight coils of its tail to choke it to death. The dog writhing in pain moaned hysterically struggling to escape from the tight coils, which the python had tightened to crush the bones of the victim. The dog's miserable gaze at him moved Ettanu; he stood immobilized, cursing his own helplessness in the face of the snakes strength, and he saw the dog gradually giving up. The feeble effort of the dog to free itself from the steeled coils of the python almost ended.

Ettanu saw the head of the python unhurriedly emerging from the water. It lifted up its head and readied itself with its jaw wide open to devour the prey. Ettanu had a glimpse of the python's head, crawling along the trunk of the palm. Emerging out of the inertia he had sunk in, Ettanu triggered the arrow hitting the snake on its head, pinning it down on the tree. He had the chopper ready and in one decisive stroke he cut off the head. It was the turn of the python; its head severed, the trunk quavered in the water turning it pale red. The trunk, life still lingering, squirmed in pain until the last breath. The python lay dead beside the dog that had the last gasp still trapped in its body. The head of the python remained sruck on the palm trunk, along with the arrow with blood oozing down

Ettanu uncoiled the dog and laid it on the floor; the dog lay immobilized, though not dead. Ettanu lifted up the heavy trunk of the python, and left it on the floor along with the dog, the former dead and the latter dying. He appeared wavering not knowing what to do with the carcass of the python and the dog; he knew both were good to eat. Python meat was very tasty, and its fat when melted had great potency in curing wounds, even leprosy. It fetched good money. He guessed it wouldn't be less than twenty-five *Panam*. For once he felt happy about the rain and flood that brought him misery and good luck as well.

He needed some one to help him prepare the meat and extract the oil from the fat. He had expected Meenan to visit him; he wondered why he hadn't come.

"Perhaps, he too might be caught in the flood." He concluded.

Flood waters that stood lapping at the bottom of the hut had dampened the floor. However, his wife and children had slumped into deep sleep fatigued by hunger and exhaustion undeterred by the dampness of the floor. Neither the commotion created by the dog nor the intrusion of the python shattered their respite; Ettanu had no mind to disturb them either.

Ettanu sat watching the flood waters that menacingly rose threatening to submerge his floor. He knew he had to move out soon. Meenan's floor was the only site that had an elevation high enough to withstand the onslaught of the river for a few more days. For a change, the sun showed its face for a while. Ettanu thought it a good precursor promising a sunny day. But a bright rainbow that arched across the sky in the east was a gloomy forerunner.

In no time the sudden gust of chilly breeze turned squally. He crossed both his arms across his chest to ward off the direct thrust of the freezing air on his shivering bones, which was sure to provoke a spell of dry cough. He coughed, lapsing into a convulsive spasm with tears involuntarily oozing from his eyes.

"This rain and wind will take my life ." He muttered in silence, taking a deep breath; a little phlegm surfaced on his tongue. With great effort he spat to throw out the phlegm.

By late afternoon Meenan came rowing a canoe strenuously against the current. He brought the canoe close to the hut and stepped directly from the boat, on to the floor of the hut.

"Meena, come and see what we have here." Ettanu invited him, gleefully. The whole Ettanu family sat around their proud catch but they looked sad for their dear dog that died a martyr. The sky was still cloudy yet they had some thing to look forward to as the bright sun cheered them. Ettanu enthusiastically narrated the story of the dog and the python as in a fable and explained what he planned to do with his catch.. Pakkothi said python meat was good for consumptives, and added that she knew how to cook the meat.

"You skin the python, the rest I will do." She added with gusto.

"The children haven't eaten any gruel for the last three days."

"The python too was starving, perhaps it came looking for the dog. We were also hungry looking at the dog for an answer; now we have no dog but we have a dead python instead." Athai sounded rather philosophical.

Pakkothi thought that all was not well with Meenan. She found him worn out and drained, and she asked him:

"Meenacha, what happened?"

Athai too thought he appeared pale with face shrunk and no life in his eyes. "Ettanucha, I don't hide any thing from you. In fact I have come to tell you about the worst experience I had in my life." The Ettanu clan sat around Meenan, avidly listening to what he had to narrate.

Meenan explained to them his encounter with a drowning woman in the flooded river. He concluded: "None would have dared the formidable river at this time of the season."

"It's a great thing that you have done, and these are the things that we do for them; but don't expect anything in return." Ettanu tried to pacify him.

Meenan handed over to Pakkothi a small basket that contained what he had received from Rosma, rice and tapioca. The starving Ettanu children grabbed handfuls of tapioca chips from the basket. As they struggled to crack the hardened chips in their mouth Pakkothi took away the basket. She busied herself to light a fire in the hearth after many days; she missed the dog on the ash mound from where she had to chase him out earlier as she attempted to light a fire.

"Do you know how to cook *Kappa biriyani*?"

"It is very simple; you cook tapioca with the meat. It's neither meat nor tapioca. It's tapioca biriyani."

"The river is rising very fast; let us get away."

"Where do we go?" Ettanu asked in frustration; he knew the answer but still he asked the question,

"You will come to my hut; my floor is higher and safe for a few more days."

They moved out in Meenan's canoe.

"Ettanucha, do you know what happened to our Kokkadan?" Meenan asked Ettanu, staring into his eyes.

"No. I have no news; I am stuck with this cursed flood." He casually answered.

"He is missing for the last three days; his son came to me yesterday; he wanted me to search for him. We spent the whole night searching but failed to locate him". Meenan felt sorry he didn't get time to inform Ettanu.

Apparently, Kokkadan was caught stealing a pot of rice porridge, a kind of special feed for the cattle as monsoon rejuvenation. His family had been starving for almost a week; he knew his children couldn't endure the hunger any longer; they survived on the muddy water the river had carried down.

Few days ago in the afternoon, Kokkadan reached at the gate of his landlord; wading the flooded waters, he crossed the canal to reach the mansion where he waited for some one to spot him. The courtyard was empty though the sound of soft music that rhymed with rain wafted in the air.

Hours of waiting yielded no result and Kokkadan returned, disappointed; he felt miserable, returning home empty handed fearing his children might not survive the night. As he walked down aimlessly it began to rain, rather heavily; he took shelter in the cattle shed where he was sure he could not have been accused of polluting any one as his tribe enjoyed equality with the bovine fraternity. The rain continued to beat with no let up, tiring him physically and mentally. He sat by the half wall of the manger waiting for the rain to cease.

The cattle in the shed, a bull and a few cows, recognized him; They stood shaking their heads and constantly gazing at him with familiarity. For, he had been looking after them for years.

Kokkadan moved towards them patting some on the back and touching the heads of a few. As Kokkadan advanced further an old cow that lay on the floor rose up and stood before him, shaking its head. Kokkadan stood by its side with his hand resting on its back. He noticed iron buckets filled with thick rice gruel left over by the animals. He tried to make them eat more but none cared, apparently they had had their fill. Kokkadan knew it would be thrown out as no one drank the gruel left over by the cattle. It was the best he could take home for his children. It was thick gruel, mixed with palm sugar candy, the kind which his children had never tasted. He collected the left-overs in one bucket, covered it with a plantain leaf and walked home carrying the load on his head. He was in a hurry to reach home before it got dark; he wanted to witness the joy the faces of his children.

As he emerged from the cattle shed, a maid servant saw him hurrying out carrying a pail on his head. She thought it contained valuables stolen from the house. She immediately alerted the servants who ran after him with a vengeance and caught him red handed.

"What is it that you have stolen from the house?" They questioned him but he remained quiet; one of the servants slapped him on his face. He was forced to walk back with the pail on his head; detained until the master of the house appeared. The chief heard the matter.

"Do you know what the punishment for stealing is?" He asked Kokkadan, who kept quiet; he knew the law was very harsh. If he denied stealing he had to prove his innocence by dipping his hand in boiling oil; if he came out unharmed he could go free, if his hand was found scorched it proved the charge and the punishment was chopping off of his hand; the outcome of the ordeal was a foregone conclusion.

"We don't need any proof; we have before us the gruel he stole" One of his tormentors explained.

"It's true; the punishment is to cut off your right hand."

Kokkadan stood dumbfounded with a rush of darkness blinding him ; his head spinned in circles throwing the bucket off his head. He slumped on the ground..

"Take him away." The chief was annoyed, but he decreed a lighter punishment:

"Make him stand in the river neck deep, over night."

He directed the two men who had captured him to stand guard. Kokkadan stood in the icy floodwater; at home, he remembered, his children waited for his return at home. It began to rain again and the guards wanted to protect themselves from the rain; they erected a simple contrivance with a pole fixed firmly in the river-bed to which Kokkadan was tied by his legs and hands to ensure he didn't escape; the guards left their post.

Kokkadan stood in the ice-cold water that gradually numbed his limbs but his mind remained alert, overwhelmed by the thoughts of his children. He thought death was more honourable than torture but he wanted to live for his children. As hours passed by, with rain falling from above and waves of chilly water drowning him; he felt almost frozen.

It was quite some time since the guards had gone; it was dark too. Kokkadan wanted to make an attempt to escape. He began to shake the pole by thrusting the weight of his body against it. He did succeed in felling it but it turned out to be disastrous step. He discovered that he could not swim with his limbs tied to the pole. Nobody had since seen Kokkadan even as his wife and children waited many nights for his return.

Athai noticed his father's eyes suddenly brimming with tears; he asked

"What makes you feel sad?"

"Our fate is no different. What will we eat tomorrow?" Ettanu saw the gusto with which the children enjoyed a full meal, and he added broodingly.

"We have no tomorrows; we eat only when we work, no work means no food."

It was true; when it rained for a week or the river flooded they had nothing to eat, and their children slept on empty stomachs. If the python hadn't strayed in their way, they would have been starving. Ettanu sat quiet in a corner of the hut, and began to dose off with his eyelids drooping.

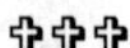

Twelve

Rain and flood had always been part of their life; starvation and death inevitably followed. The plight of the insecure never troubled the conscience of the privileged. For the abandoned, death was a blessing as it released them from eternal suffering.

When one man set out braving the adversities, many looked askance at his wisdom; many among his companions felt he was out to court disaster; but he stood unwavering. He was Rev Aaron Griffith, a missionary.

He stood amazed at the volume of water that poured down the face of the earth and the enormity of the watery expanse, since the monsoon had broken out almost a fortnight ago. The earth lay battered, trees stood with broken limbs, the dead animals were washed off; those which survived had no more cuds to chew. Men who had not hoarded grain starved, facing uncertain days ahead. The river only had the dead and the fallen for company, as living ones kept away fearing the turbulence of the water. The flood was really a great social leveller, he concluded.

Rev Griffith silently watched the deluge from the veranda of his room at the Marian church at Kudamaloor, where he was stationed. Quietly he slipped out of the room, unseen by his brother Priests who would have dissuaded him from venturing on a fearsome monsoon mission. Outside the church compound he was joined by Emmanuel, a daring Syrian Christian trader, who had offered to help him cross the chaotic river in one of his large cargo boats. A good number of men who stood idling at the flooded ferry joined him in the boat. As the boat ventured into the water, cutting across the torrential flow diagonally, the men who had gathered on both banks cheered the men in the boat.

Rev Aaron Griffith looked happy. He thanked Emmanuel for his bold feat. He walked fast, trudging the slushy path unmindful of the blinding rains and the mud that his feet got plastered with. His only thought concerned the tragic fate of the several deprived households that lived trapped in the floods, scattered in the low lying farm lands. He heard about their unfortunate lives from a worshipper in the church.

He reached the courtyard of a monastery fully drenched. He stepped onto the veranda and squeezed the seams of his wet habit to expel as much rain water and mud as possible. It was still raining outside accompanied by squalls. The sound of the rain falling on the tiled roof challenged the monastic silence the house was drowned in. He rang the bell twice and waited patiently.

"*Achho*, Praise is to Jesus." The familiar face of Ouseph, the servant grinned at him and wished him with his palms joined together under his chin.

"Now and for ever." Rev Griffith reciprocated. Ouseph ushered him into the visitor's room where he found for himself a chair, opposite the one meant for the host. He took the seat and quietly waited for the host to appear.

His mind was restless as he looked out onto the watery expanse where he saw before him the engulfed homesteads of the depressed low castes, exposed to the ravages of monsoon floods. In the initial years of his mission he enjoyed the monsoon. Once he kept a date with the great monsoon by keeping himself awake to witness its arrival at the midnight; he found it a thrilling experience. The sight of watery expanses of the flooded fallows where children rowed canoes to the rhymes of popular boat songs was captivating; he was yet to come across the seamy side of the great deluge. The seeds of misery were sowed one night at the Poovan Hills.

Rev Aaron Griffith was a Carmelite friar assigned for the mission in the East, but he personally preferred Malabar Coast where he had learnt the existence of a prosperous Christian community claiming to be Apostolic, a claim he found unfounded. On his arrival, he spent time working with different mission stations, assisting the local clergy, called the *Kathanars*. He learnt the local language and Sanskrit, the language of the gods, a command of which, he believed, would open up to him the treasure house of oriental philosophy. He did remarkably well in his endeavours, effectively communicating with the native Christians, including their Priests who knew a smattering of Syriac in addition to Malayalam. His knowledge of Sanskrit, learnt from Namboodiri teachers, was deep enough to enter into discourse with the Brahminical elites, who had laid the ground rules upon which revolved the social order of Malabar. He found the goings good and enjoyable as long as he spent his time as an unassuming learner.

He found the Christian life in the region comparatively peaceful; they were a much sought after tribe enjoying the support and patronage of the ruling class. For, in effect they constituted the wealth creators of the land, exclusively engaged in trade and agriculture, that fed the populace and filled the coffers of the rulers which included the propertied class. The Christains had over the years, become economically prosperous and socially dominant.

"Praise is to Jesus." Rev Griffith was disturbed by the familiar greetings of Rev Romulus, the Procurator of the Congregation.

"Father, your clothes look wet; I suggest you change them." He offered clothes; it was easy as the monks had their habits patterned on those of the European Carmelites.

"Never mind. I produce enough warmth to dry up my habit as well." Rev Griffith burst out laughing but the insinuation seemed to be lost on the host.

Ouseph returned with a pot of steaming coffee. Rev Romulus personally poured the coffee into a bowl and offered him.

"Just to warm you up; it's rather cold and wet outside."

He took a sip from the bowl, and finding it too hot placed it on the table.

"Now, father, our Prior General is busy with his consultants; he has asked me to find out the purpose of your visit, and I hope I can perhaps be of some assistance to you."

"You certainly can." He got up from the chair, and walked slowly towards the outer veranda where the rain was still lashing against the windowpanes. The local Priest followed him wondering what he wanted to discuss. They could see before them the inundated expanse that stayed merged with the horizon on the distant west. The torrential fall of the rain raised a glassy wall before them making the distant view blurred.

"The whole paddy land is under water submerging the home-steads of the poor who have no means to sustain themselves or even to escape from the deluge." Rev Griffith looked at his co-friar for a response. He seemed to have not noticed any thing unusual.

"Their life is really miserable." He sympathized with his guest but added quickly:

"We shall pray for them, Father."

Rev Griffith hesitated to answer him and stood with his gaze still roving over the watery expanse.

"They are accustomed to the floods, and the hardships associated with it." Rev Romulus had a leisurely view on life's tragic situations that rather irritated his companion.

"It's good that you have offered to pray for them, and I thank you but there is some thing more." Rev Griffith remained silent for a while, undecided, but added. "Those who offer just their prayers too do good as they bring the problem to God's notice so that He can, if He is so pleased, solve it by a miracle. But those who venture out to help solve the problem make themselves instruments in the hands of God to solve the matter; they pray to God to give them strength to do it on His behalf; that makes a great difference." Rev Griffith purposely turned his face away from his friend.

Rev Romulus felt his face turning red.

"When God's poor are suffering how can we remain unconcerned?" Rev Griffith waited for a moment hoping for a voluntary response from the Procurator; but he preferred not to disturb the silence that reigned between them. The rains stopped for a moment; perhaps to listen to what Rev Romulus had to say. A brief respite followed; the veil of mist that hung under the lower sky slowly melted away. The visibility from the first floor of the monastery that stood on the summit of a hill became clear, and Rev Griffith could count a few scores of homesteads lying sunk in the flood, under clusters of palms, each with men, women and children trapped inside. He was sure to find many more beyond the reach of his eyes.

"This year's flood is the heaviest in memory, snatching every thing that stood in its way. We have received news that the dykes of our farms breached at several places; rebuilding them costs a lot of money." Rev Romulus said.

The expression of his private concern was a clever attempt to put a damper on the missionary's plans. His commitment for the cause was strong and he was firm not to leave any thing to chance. He was determined to make the procurator know what he wanted him to do.

"Father, in my conscience I am committed to help those unfortunate ones who face a certain death; if nobody volunteers. I shall do it myself." Rev Griffith paused for a response from his interlocutor, who still preferred to be shifty and casual; his attitude didn't go unregistered with the Missionary.

"Now, can you give me some help to organize my plans?" Rev Romulus kept quiet with a dubious look.

"My question is very simple. I may have to pick up about a hundred people together with some of their personal belongings; maybe a few domestic animals too, if they are still left with any. I require a couple of those large cargo boats that you have moored in your boat yard, with at least eight hardy punters to go with me to collect those stranded." Rev Griffith added:

"And, you have to allow me to use your boat house for these men to sleep for a few days, until the waters recede."

Rev Romulus stood listening to him, occasionally shifting his eyes betraying a cold response. His lack of enthusiasm didnot dampen the other man's fervour; he asked, rather boldly:

"Of course, I will be asking for a few bushels of rice, to feed them immediately. The rest I will manage." Rev Griffith intently looked into his friend's face for an answer.

Rev Romulus appeared wilted and kept his mouth shut with his lips locked tightly.

"Father, what do you think about my request?" Rev Griffith pressed him for a response.

"I have an open mind." He closed his lips as quickly as he had opened it to let out the few words.

"Hope, not open at both ends." Rev Griffith's light banter induced a broad simper on the face of the other Priest. Rev Romulus knew that the request coming from a person so close to their Congregation couldn't be rejected off hand. He withdrew from the room tacitly for a discussion with his superiors.

"Father, I am sorry, I kept you waiting. I have a report from Father Romulus. I feel ashamed that we should have taken the initiative in this matter. What you propose to do is the Lord's work, which is our work as well. We will provide you with whatever you need. You please go ahead." Father Cyril the Superior General sounded more tactful.

"I thank you Father Cyril." As the two men talked, Rev Romulus stood behind them, holding his locked palms across his belly.

Next morning soon after the Mass Rev Aaron Griffith walked into the boat yard promptly; he felt relieved when he saw Rev Romulus waiting for him with a broad grin on his lips. He was glad to see two large bellied barges ready with five punters in each in place of the four he had asked for. The Procurator received him with an affectionate handshake that exuded warmth and friendship, perhaps, to atone for the indifference that he had initially shown him.

"I have the best of our punters, who are very familiar with the river, particularly when it is in spate." Rev Romulus reassured him; those were not mere confidence building words. Those men were really experienced boatmen.

"But, Father, I suggest you don't go with them; they will manage: you stay back with us. We shall have lunch together.

"Well, I am safe in their hands and we are safe in the hands of our Lord. You need not worry, lunch I'll have later."

The morning lull in the rainfall that remained undisturbed promised to be a good omen; though the face of the sky continued to be grey with pock marks of rain clouds leisurely sifting across. It dampened the enthusiasm of the men setting out on the expedition.

"Hordes of dark devils are congregating in the west for an east bound march." Ayyappan, one of the boatmen observed.

"We should make full use of the break." Rev Griffith urged them.

The barges slowly moved into the side canal and on to the shallow paddy fields where the depth of water was over a man high. They skirted the main river to avoid the strong current. Rev Griffith occupied the mid thwart and sat staring into the watery stretch that seemed unbounded. They slowly emerged out of the canopied, rain washed woodlands into the open sky; a hover of angry crows that seemed to have lost their nests in the downpour swooped down threateningly from the crown of a lonely palm where they had taken refuge.

"They too must be hungry and need to be rescued." Ayyappan observed, and what he said was true; even carrion crows were starving.

The first call of the rescuers was at Meenan's hut that stood bordering the torrential river. The water had risen up to knee deep on the floor; the occupants spent the night standing facing the misery and destruction it spewed. The wall was not long enough for all of them to make a perch. Little Chakki stayed clinging to her brother's shoulder to prevent her from being drowned in the rushing waves.

Week long starvation, despite the python-tapioca biriyani, left them scrawny and emaciated. They survived on free air and open water, polluted and unclean, yet life lingered. Ettanu sat on the wall with his feet dangling in water, leaning on the shoulder of his wife. He kept his eyes closed as if unwilling to look at the world; the recurring bouts of dry cough confirmed he was alive. The child that lay wilted and drooping too showed sign of life as the soft thud of her upper body pressed on Athai's chest ; it hovered between life and death. The sight reconfirmed Rev Griffith's faith in miracles.

Meenan was getting them ready to move to a dry spot upland. He hoped to find a place to hide their heads from the rains in the cattle shed of Emmanuel, if other uprooted men had not already crowded it. The sight of a barge approaching them enlivened their sagging spirit, though Meenan felt they might be monsoon revellers.

Meenan panicked as the waves that the large barge had provoked, knocked against the water soaked mud wall threatening its imminent collapse. As the boat neared the floor, the inmates crowded near the wall at the entrance. The wave-beaten mud wall buckled under pressure throwing Ettanu into the water. Meenan rushed forward to hold him up as Pakothi pulled him up by his arm; he got wet but saved his head.

"We should have carried at least some gruel for these people." Rev Griffith regretted his omission; the plight of the people really pained him.

"Forget the mud wall. That you can rebuild. Now try to get into the boat and get yourself saved." He urged them.

Ayyappan and Kuriakko, the punters stepped on to the floor urging those who stood unnerved to move in. It was a rare experience for them that some one had come visiting them. They thought they had a strange vision; they saw Rev Griffith sitting on the central thwart of the boat. Fully clad in the repulsive brown of his habit, they tried to steal a look at his face. Pakkothi drew back taking away the child from Athai; the child was laid on her bosom, an ingenuous way to cover her breasts; she hid herself behind the crowd. Meenan stood still in the water with one foot in the canoe and a paddle in his right hand.

Ettanu thought he had seen the strange visitor somewhere during one of his jaunts as punter. His memory traversed in time and space, his eyes hovering over the face of Rev Aaron Griffith.

"*Arthunkal Veluthachan.*" He uttered a cry of triumph in recognising the person, jumping instantly into the water, he waded towards the barge. He boarded the boat and rushed towards the central thwart and fell at the dangling feet of Rev Aaron Griffith. The Priest stood up and lifted him up gently; rather, puzzled. He placed his hand on his left shoulder and held his right arm in his palm. Ettanu stood weeping.

"*Arthunkal Veluthachan.*" He whispered to himself with his dull eyes fixed on the face of the Priest. He remembered his visit to the St Andrews church on Arthumkal shore as punter a few years ago. He had gone inside the church, as there was no barrier and remembered praying before the 'God'. He stood very close, looking at the statue intently until a deep impression of it was engraved, unknown to him in his mind. He felt sorry for forgetting the face, and the affectionate look in the eyes of the 'God', who he thought had appeared in flesh before him.

"*Veluthachan* has come to see me now." He chimed in a monotone.

A flash of the face of *Veluthachan* in the niche, and the *Veluthachan* who appeared before him in flesh alternated in his mind.

"He is the same." He reassured himself.

Ayyappan and Kochu Thomma helped the children board the boat followed by Pakkothi with Chakki still cleaving to her mother. Ayyappan asked Ettanu whether he had any personal things to take with him. As he wavered Athai said:

"Not much, except his bow and arrow, that might help him go fishing."

They went inside and returned with a couple of old mats, besides the bow and arrows. Ettanu continued to sit at the feet of the Priest still believing the man was none other than St Andrew of Arthunkal.

Meenan in his sleek canoe piloted the barge to Chathan's hut; he was anxious to help move the family to safety. Reaching Chathan's hut appeared a formidable task as he lived on the opposite bank. Crossing the river in spate was rather risky. The punters hesitated to venture out and stood wavering.

"We can't let one family perish; you are five men and now you have these young men to help you. I think we can manage; of course it needs hard work and we have God's help in plenty." Rev Griffith encouraged them.

The punters shoved the barge into mid stream but soon realized that the current was strong and their poles were not long enough to reach the river bottom. They lost control of the barge, which drifted down as the panicked punters looked on helplessly. Rev Griffith felt it was a folly on his part to have them cross the river.

Meenan handed over his canoe to Athai and took the master oar of the barge, and by manipulating it he directed the boat diagonally across, in tandem with the current. It reached the opposite bank rather down but found them safe; they slowly worked their course up cutting across the shallow waters.

"Young man, I thank you for the great feat; it was timely." Rev Griffith shook hands with Meenan patting him on his back.

Chathan was down with fever, and a part of his hut had been damaged when an old palm tree fell on the roof corner; he had a chance escape. Chitha and Kallu sat beside him with tears in their eyes as Chathan repeatedly said he was dying. Kallu had wanted to swim the river to call Meenan or Ettanu, their immediate neighbours. But Chathan forbade her.

Meenan felt sorry that he failed to look after them when he knew that the river was in spate. Kallu couldn't control herself when she saw Meenan and began to sob. Her tears overwhelmed him as he slowly nudged towards her. He stopped abruptly seeing the ugly sneer on her father's face. Instead he extended his hand to Chathan to help him board the boat.

The weather continued to be tolerable with light drizzles in between. An occasional appearance of the sun warmed the atmosphere with sweltering humidity; the recurring breeze, however, provided them with a welcome relief.

Both Ettanu and Chathan were sick, one had running fever and the other had all kinds of sickness that he was unable to describe, yet they sat aloof unmindful of each other's presence. The women and children, despite the pangs of hunger and suffering, enjoyed the ride on the unruly surface of Meenachill.

The prized find of the expedition was Accori, a lonely man found sitting on the crown of a solitary palm by a dyke. He was stationed to look after a farm, and he expected his landlord to send men to take him home when the flood situation worsened; but no one came looking for him. The rainstorm on the first night had blown off the roof of his hut, exposing him to the ravages of the weather; water stood almost waist deep on his floor, leaving him with no dry spot to plant his feet. The nearby palm was his only hope of survival.

He climbed up and perched atop the tree with the open sky for a cover. Rain fell on his head day and night and the deadly storm battered him; he clung tightly to the crown as it swayed in the storm. He survived on a tender coconut a day, and the last nut was plucked a day ago.

"Hornbills survived on rainwater, and I too may have to." he consoled himself.

Accori saw a barge moving down the canal with men on board; he thought it might be a marriage party going to fetch a girl.

"How mad can the people be? When the flood is taking a great toll they are feasting to bring a girl for some one."

Trying his luck, Accori tried to catch their attention. Sitting in mid air on a tall palm he had no time to climb down. He waved his hands and shook the crown of the tree with no impact on the boatmen; they passed, not noticing the tree or the man who nested atop.

Accori had a last option, the consequences of which he was uncertain. Slowly but carefully he sprang up on his feet and jumped into the flowing canal making sure that he plunged midstream.

✞✞✞

Thirteen

The sudden flash of water just behind the barge alerted the boatmen. Kuriacco who punted from the stern noticed merely the clash of waves that the plunge had generated. Accori took some time to surface from the depth of the canal.

"There is a man in the canal." Kuriacco shouted, and extended his pole for the man to catch on to; they hauled him in, and found him naked and embarrassed. As he jumped, the rag he had over his loin got entangled with the palm fronds. Kochu Thoma, who had a second cloth to cover his head, threw the piece onto him. To their surprise they found him dumb.

Rev Griffith added one more to his catch of eighty-nine.

The boatmen had to skip their mid-day meal but by past mid-afternoon the expedition returned to its base with ninety persons counted, besides sixteen fowls, four dogs, three cats with six kittens, all smuggled in, concealed under arms, between the folds of the scanty clothing they had on their person. Ettanu felt sorry for his dog when he saw Chathan's dog, trotting and sniffing indiscriminately, unmindful of the crowd and the noble personality of Arthunkal *Veluthachan*. They had no right to rear domestic animals in their homesteads so they had no cows or goats in the barge. A few had raised pigs in their backyards but they were frequently killed by nocturnal prowlers, and those that escaped were washed away by the flood.

Finally, the two barges with the men on board moored at the cemetery landing. The crew disembarked and tied the boats to poles. Ayyappan helped Rev Griffith come out of the boat. He stood a little away awaiting the crowd to come out. Rev Griffith watched with surprise the men sitting stupefied, making no effort to stir out of the seeming shelter offered by the boat, except Meenan who stood in the water with his hands placed on the rim of the barge expecting the folk to follow.

The children and the women rejoiced at the sight of dry land and the shelter offered by the cozy boathouse. The men languidly walked out of the boat. Meenan and Athai helped both Chathan and Ettanu climb out. The excited children gambolled in the spacious open ground, eyeing the bushy palms and marking the bunched bananas, perhaps, for a night prowl. The men looked uncertain in unfamiliar surroundings, and meekly lingered about for direction. Soon, Rev Romulus came down from the monastery and Rev Griffith conferred with him to finalise the arrangements. He announced:

"The monastery has offered to provide you with enough rice for your gruel, and also cooking vessels, fire wood and some condiments. You make arrangements to cook the rice. There are a few threshing mats available in the boathouse; you can sleep on them. Take care of every thing. I will make arrangements for whatever further you may need."

Rev Romulus added:

"Now, I warn you against any indiscipline in this compound; don't pluck nuts from the palms. If you find nuts lying on the ground promptly turn them over to the watchman. I have posted two men to oversee you, and another important matter, don't dirty the place by defecating."

"How will you solve the problem?" Rev Griffith enquired.

"Well, we shall provide them with two sheds with pits for the purpose, one for the males and one for the females."

"I do not want any fight among you. The watchmen will keep an eye on you, and any one found misbehaving will be thrown out immediately."

"And finally make sure that the women and girls sleep separately from men and boys. No mix up." Rev Romulus withdrew as he had other pressing matters to attend to. The men felt relieved as they were assured of gruel for the night. Ettanu told Chathan that it was all because of the wonders of *Veluthachan.*

"He is a God; he sits in Arthumkal church." Chathan ignored his friend's observation but when he heard him repeating it he retorted:

"How could he be a God? He has no stone-studded gold crown; no bracelets, no jewels; no silk… then how could he be a God? Not possible."

"He has every thing; he wears them when he sits in that church. You have to see him there to believe."

Chathan kept quiet, Ettanu taking this as a sign of defeat, wanted to tell him one more thing. "He doesn't wear that jewellery and those silks because of the thieves that wander about." Still, Chathan refused to believe.

Once they were assured of a meal, their next concern was the weather. Hopefully, they looked up to the sky for a sign of reprieve. To their dismay the black hordes found scattered earlier in the afternoon were regrouping on the low, in the west.

Rev Aaron Griffith returned to the camp soon after, to see the final arrangements. He was quite upset to see that there was no progress as yet. The men deputed hadn't arrived so far. The cooking vessels were not in place nor had the supplies arrived. He found the campers squatting in small groups, mostly families together, expecting some one to come with the promised gruel. The anguished look on their faces confirmed that hunger was their vital concern

"Where are those in charge of the kitchen?" He enquired from those whom he found in the camp. Nobody answered him, as they had no knowledge of the men entrusted with the management. The campers sprang up on their feet with their eyes focussed on him as they saw Rev Griffith.

"Nothing works out unless you are after them."

The camp supervisors arrived a little later carrying on their heads jointly a copper vessel large enough to cook gruel for the entire campers. Things moved faster with his presence. An abandoned fireplace in a corner of the boathouse came handy; they mounted the vessel on the hearthstones.

Pakkothi and Chitha helped by bringing firewood from a nearby dump. Some men helped to fill the vessel with water from a nearby well while a few others lighted the fire. They stood watching the flame leaping up as they pushed more splinters down the pit; soon the water reached boiling point.

Kuriacco brought in rice, and green gram that Rev Griffith had arranged with Emmanuel, washed and put it into the boiling water. The men sat around watching cheerfully, the rice and green gram boiling in the big vessel, the size of which was amazing. Frequently they looked into the vessel to see whether it was ready for serving.

"Kuriacco, have you added the coconut gratings?" Rev Griffith was observing their operations; he hadn't seen them scraping the coconuts.

"Sorry Father, the nuts are not yet grated." He was apologetic.

"What you are waiting for; hurry up."

They had a few graters, borrowed from the neighbourhood, already brought in. Pakkothi and Chitha volunteered to do the grating. Each sat on the body of the grater and did the work briskly. Pakkothi had her son Kodan sitting by her side, peeping at her. Apparently he wanted to tell her some thing but she ignored him, as she was busy. The gratings spilled over the floor tempting Kodan, who slyly gleaned and ate. The starving child found the stuff quite tasty, and in a swift move he scooped out a handful again and thrust it into his mouth before Pakkothi could stop him.

"You rascal, get away from here." The woman rebuked him with a spank.

"That brat of yours is a pilferer… kick him out." Chathan who sat watching the women at work noticed what the boy had done, and shouted aloud, besides, beating the floor with his staff to stress the misdemeanour of the boy.

It was for the first time that someone had disturbed the peace of the boathouse and naturally it raised many eyebrows. Rev Romulus who had reached the spot, heard the row, as he was watching them from outside while keeping company with Rev Griffith.

"Chathacha, better you mind your words; he hasn't pilfered any thing of yours." The accusation of Chathan provoked a strong retort from Athai. Mundan who stood feeding the fire thought what Chathan had said was true. He was watching Kodan ruthlessly pushing out his four-year-old son, who too coveted the spillings.

"Your brother did it, supported by your mother." Mundan repeatedly asserted.

"We are not filchers." Athai's riposte had a ring of derision that wasn't lost on Mundan.

"*Podaa Naari*; do you mean that I am a filcher?"

"I don't say so; but you know better." That was a provocative insinuation. Mundan advanced towards Athai with a burning splinter that he had picked up from the hearth, threateningly.

"I will thrust this staff into your foul mouth." Ettanu, who had been sitting in a corner of the boathouse slothfully, rose from his squat and rushed towards the warring youngsters, with his other children trailing behind.

"Mundaa." He let out a cry, in spite of his poor health.

Athai retraced a few steps, and stopped by a pestle that he thought would be handy in case Mundan attempted an assault on his father. When the fracas seemed to be taking a violent turn the men who stood apart moved into a circle around the brawlers either taking sides or watching disinterested. None thought of intervening to pacify them.

Meenan who was watching the quarrel thought Mundan was bent on forcing a fight. He rushed forward and jumped into the fray, took Mundan by his arm, he twisted it back and snatched the burning splinter from him.

Rev Romulus who stood engaged with the other Priest had his roving eyes on those men who had drifted into a brawl. He found the situation going out of control, and he rushed towards the hall picking up a cane from one of the side rooms. When they saw him coming towards them brandishing a cane, the motley crowd that stood watching the fray meekly dispersed, exposing Mundan who stood with a defiant expression. As Rev Romulus advanced Mundan cowardly backed out.

"You nasty rogue!" He gave him a thrash, which Mundan shielded with his hands.

"Father Romulus, please don't." Rev Griffith had rushed into the hall after the Procurator, and tried to stop him from his attempt to flog the man a second time.

Rev Romulus paused for a moment, keeping the cane down and looked at him enquiringly. His air spoke of his displeasure at the intervention by his fellow friar

"No doubt, an offender deserves punishment but before judgment he should be heard; otherwise the punishment becomes unjust." Rev Griffith tried to enlighten his companion.

Taking advantage of the brief respite following Rev Romulus' disengagement with him, Mundan quietly slipped behind the crowd, nursing the bruise the caning had left on his arm. The frightened crowd, which had stepped back, still stood gaping, uncertain as to what would follow next. They loathed the pale light of the boathouse as it exposed their ashen faces writ with panic and shame. They wished they were drowned in the darkness that smothered the earth. They would have slipped into it but for the rain that lashed outside. The two friars too stood in silence.

"Adam's transgression brought upon him the punishment of God, the Lord. But, remember before judging him the Lord asked him what he had done with His Law God pronounced the punishment only after hearing him. And, be sure that we too do the same. For this is the source of the principle of Natural Justice."

"Haven't you read St Augustine who said 'Audi Alteram Partem', meaning no man shall be condemned without being heard."

Rev Romulus responded to the homily with a brazen simper that failed to conceal the emotional discomfiture that lay buried deep in his mind.

Rev Griffith left the matter there, as a minor aberration but he thought that the hurt feelings of these voiceless men should be assuaged.

He enquired about the cause of the brawl and found the misdemeanour of a hungry child as the genesis of the incident.

"Poverty and hunger leads to transgression, but what happened here is an indiscretion only; it shouldn't have gone out of control."

"Now you get all the kids here, all under ten."

He hailed them together. Some came running not knowing what they had been called for. A few hesitated, as they feared the man behind the brown habit still had the cane in his hand. Ettanu and Munda's children too came but they preferred to stand behind their parents.

He found twelve under tens; some one pushed forward the Ettanu, Mundan offsprings making the total count fifteen.

He lifted a vessel with coconut gratings, that he distributed among the children. He knew that a pinch of gratings wouldn't lessen their hunger but it helped to bring back the lost cheer on their faces. He asked Kuriacco:

"How soon will the gruel be ready?" He moved towards the vessel to see for himself.

"You have to wait a little more."

The men looked into the large vessel with expectation as the rice-gram gruel slowly came to boil in the vessel, on low fire. The aroma and the soft bubble-boiling sound of the stuff wafted in the air. The rain and unremitting breeze chilled the atmosphere and the men jostled and elbowed one another to secure a foothold closer to the hearth to warm themselves. A closer look at the simmering gruel enhanced their sagging spirits. As the men stood around making an impenetrable fortress the children had been making unsuccessful attempts to breach the barrier to secure for them too a peep hole.

Accori had been sitting close to the vessel tending the fire; the savour of the cooked food wetted his appetite. In a swift move he scooped up in his palm a handful of the thick, steaming porridge; as he found his palm getting scorched beyond endurance, he thrust the stuff into his mouth. As it began to burn the soft skin of the mouth he shifted the sticky gruel between his cheeks. Finally he spat out the whole stuff on the floor and rushed towards the canal, keeping his mouth wide open to inhale the chilly breeze that he thought would soothe his mouth. Accori jumped into the canal and stayed deep, and occasionally surfaced, wallowing in the water that had turned muddy. Meenan and Kochu Thoma followed to help him.

Accori missed the groovy porridge; he sat in a corner of the shed for the whole night keeping his mouth open to let in the of balmy breeze.

Each person was given an earthen bowl and leaf-spoon to sup the gruel.

"It tastes very good." Ettanu remarked while eating his third helping.

"If some jaggery is added it becomes *payasam*."

They ate well, and there was enough for everybody.

As days passed a respite in the rains slackened the flow in the river and the water level in the canals receded. The men in the camp stood watching the water inching down the cobbled steps of the landing, baring the skits deposited by the flood. Rev Griffith was happy as he found them contented. For he saw the rain that lashed the land for twenty days, almost half the number of days the Lord had caused to rain on the earth to punish the sinners, had been called off, mercifully.

Slowly though the sky had changed sunny, brightening the face of the earth. The men looked at the sky and knew it was time for them to start anew. They appeared happy and contended though they were uncertain as to what awaited them when they returned home.

"Will we meet all our people alive when we return?"Ettanu wondered.

Nobody dared to answer his question. Rev Griffith met each camper personally and talked to them. They mobbed him, with the men taking his hands in their hands. He took the palm of Pakkothi who stood before him with her head bent down, making a feeble effort to wriggle out. Kallu rushed in grasping the hand that had Pakkothi's already in. A few bowed at his feet; others felt his coarse, cotton habit that seemed different. For most of them he was a living God.

"*Veluthachan.*" Ettanu mumbled as he walked out of the yard wiping his moist eyes. They boarded the barge that slowly moved away.

Rev Aaron Griffith sung: "Te Deum Laudamus Thee…"

✞✞✞

Fourteen

They too had dreams and expectations, had indulged in brawls and employed intrigues to win over and defeat as much as they tried to excel.

"Chathan, Ravunni Achan wants to replace Uthon as the head worker; he has become too old to manage the farm." One evening Ettanu confided to Chathan. but Chathan paid no attention.

"The *Thampran* asked me who was the best to replace the *Thalapulayan.* I have recommended your name." Ettanu added.

Brushing him aside Chathan walked past. A teetotaller, he believed Ettanu was trying to impress him to extract a drink gratis.

But on second thoughts Chathan guessed that he stood a chance, even better than Ettanu though he was very close to the Lord; he conjured up the vision of him self assuming the role.

The *Thalapulayan* was the first to reach the farm and the last to leave. Though he had not yet been appointed, he decided to reach the farm early and urged Athai to get the boat to move faster. Chathan himself took the paddle and rowed to make it go faster.

Chathan was happy they reached the farm even before the arrival of Uthon, the *Thalapulayan.* A few men moved towards the water wheel to see whether it was in working condition. One man tried to turn the wheel to check how heavy the load of water was. The workmen tarried around gossiping and gesticulating. Chathan didn't appreciate their conduct.

He walked on the dyke for a short distance, inspecting the condition of the embankment and checking the water level in the canal; it was about three cubits above the paddy field. He concluded that the water wheel would have a heavy load requiring more men on the scaffolding to turn the wheel. He wondered whether Uthon had noticed the difference. He moved towards him to have a word with him. Instead, Uthon asked him:

"I didn't see you yesterday. Where were you?"

"I had hurt my big toe yesterday; still it pains."

To get the sting out of the situation Chathan asked:

"What happened? You look very weak and thin."

"Don't worry; I am alright. If your big toe is hurt you could have stayed back for another day." Uthon brushed him aside and moved ahead.

Chathan positioned himself within the eyeshot of Ravunni, the landlord who had just arrived with Ettanu trailing behind. Chathan stood peeping at him to ensure that he didn't miss any call from the boss. But to his disappointment Achan never sought him.

The first day was futile with his pushy manoeuvres failing to get Achan's attention. He comforted himself thinking there was still some time for a decision. He changed his stratagem to make himself visible to the landlord. Occasionally he gave instructions to people who worked along with him. But as days passed his enthusiasm petered out with no sign from Achan's face

Though he despised Ettanu, Chathan tried to move closer to him hoping he would throw some light on the subject; but found him unwilling to open up. Every night when Chathan retired, he found his head crowded with his image as the *Thalapulayan.*

He saw Ravunni Achan constantly, calling him for information and giving instructions. He did well on every occasion and everywhere, except once when he asked a critical question just when he was bringing out the grain from the barn to measure out the wage for the workers.

"Chathan" Ravunni Achan called him. He went running and stood before him, a little closer than what the *theendal* distance had permitted.

Achan never objected, as it was inevitable while working on the farm.

"How many have worked today, and how much grain is required to measure out their wage?"

Chathan was not prepared for the question and he had no answer. He stood in front of him, scratching his pate, unwilling to meet the master's eyes.

"You haven't counted, have you?" Ravunni shot the question as Chathan stood dumbfound, at the unexpected bark; his eyes unconsciously trailed a gaggle of ducks that sailed down the river.

"Are you counting the ducks?" Achan stood riled at his reticence.

"What kind of a foreman are you, if you can't count the number of men working on the farm? Get lost; I don't want see your face." Achan walked away in rage. Chathan found himself standing alone on the dyke watching Athai's boat moving upstream with home bound workers, women giggling and men with smirky faces. He suspected that they were making fun of his woeful face. Chathan felt piqued; he ran along the dyke asking the punter to shore the canoe, believing he had the authority of the head worker. When he found the *vallom* moving upstream ignoring his yells he jumped into the canal and swam to the boat that he had failed to catch; he seized the punt pole and pulled it towards him.

"*Ayyoo*! What do you do?" Chitha who was sleeping by his side shook him off as she found him pulling her leg.

"What happened to you? Are you going to kill me?" She was upset; she feared that a fiend had possessed him. He sat up on the mat and asked for Kallu.

"Why do you want Kallu now? She is sleeping, let her sleep."

"I have some thing urgent to ask her; you call her." He insisted.

"What is so urgent that you can't wait until the day break?"

"Yesterday she said she counted up to a hundred. I want to learn counting."

"You cannot learn anything in darkness, you better sleep now."

Chathan believed her but woke up much ahead of his usual time, and sat by the side of the courtyard where it merged with the weedery. Kallu came and sat by his side still sleepy.

Chitha lit a fire in the open that he kept feeding with dry leaves and twigs, to ward off the chillness in the morning air.

"Kallu, come on, my doll. You said you could count up to one hundred." Cajolery was not his forte, yet he coaxed his daughter, patiently.

"Yes *Acha,* I can count up to one hundred and ten." His question seemed to have brightened her face..

"Can you teach me to count up to a hundred?" He looked at her imploringly.

"Why don't you ask Meenan? he can count up to a thousand."

"What is that?" He could not grasp what a thousand meant.

"That must be very big, perhaps, going up to the sky." Kallu stretched out her arms skyward in amazement, assuring that Meenan could teach him more. Her repeated taking of Meenan's name irked him.

"Stop it. Is he the only one who knows? Perhaps Chamari can teach me," he snapped at her. The angry expression on his face frightened her.

"No, I will teach you." She didn't want him to bring in Chamari, a man to whom Chathan was planning to give her in marriage.

Kallu was in love with Meenan but she knew her father had been harbouring an ill-founded animus against Meenan for a long time, even before Poomachee's death. She believed Meenan's teaching him would eventually help heal the rupture. But Chathan hacked her hope.

"Let us begin." Chathan sat like a child looking at her with admiration.

"I will tell you the way he taught me."

"*Ngoom.*" He grunted.

"Show me your head." She began formally.

"Here it is." He placed his palms on his head.

"So that is it. You have one head."

"Now you have learnt to count 'One'."

"Now it's two. Do you know how much are two? It's one and one."

"Yes, I know how much two are; it must be a big one. I heard at the ferry that lad *Mandan* Muthappa's father Mammukka telling."

Chathan's blithe reply provoked a big guffaw from his daughter.

"No wonder that guy is called a *Mandan* but his dad too is one."

"Now you show me your eyes." He bulged out his eyes for her to see.

"No. Not thus." She took both his palms and placed them on his eyes one by one.

"One, two.... You have two eyes."

"Now you have counted one and two." Suddenly she sprang up on her feet and rushed towards the hut, and came out with a dehusked coconut.

"Show me the eyes of the coconut." She placed the coconut in his palm.

With his outstretched index finger he touched the eyes of the coconut at each touch she pronouncing:"One, Two, and Three."

"So you know that a coconut has three eyes."

"Myaavoo." Kallu heard her little kitten protesting when the warm cheery fire had died out. It stretched out and arched its body to draw out the muscles, walked towards her and climbed onto her lap.

"O! Chakki too has come to teach you in time." The kitten cuddled close to her bosom with its eyes closed feigning a slumber.

"Look at Chakki. How many legs does it have?"

Chathan gazed at the kitten with fascination wondering what he was going to discover. Kallu upturned the puss in her lap where it lay with its legs drawn out.

Kallu held each leg and asked him to count.

When she grasped the first leg, he said"one."

When she grasped the next leg, he said"two."

When she grasped the third leg, he said"three."

When she grasped the last leg, he paused looking into her eyes.

"Four." She said.

"Four" He repeated.

"So how many legs does it have?"

"Four." Chathan was sure.

Chakki dashed off her lap with its tail held high as soon as she was released. It disappeared into the hut and climbed on the ash mount above the hearth.

Kallu next grasped next her father's right palm, and holding it asked him:

"How many fingers do you have in your hand?"

He counted up to four by touching each finger, and looked at her for a prodding for the last. She folded the thumb and said:"Five."

He repeated: "Five."

The session continued up to ten when they had covered both his palms. Chathan was happy he could count up to ten, and Kallu was glad that she taught him to go up to ten. She collected ten pebbles found lying scattered in the courtyard and asked him to practice counting up to ten by placing one pebble for each count.

"When I learn up to a thousand from Meenan I will teach you too." She promised him with a twinkle in her eyes.

"No. I don't want you to learn any more from him." His curt answer hurt her; she walked out of his presence, her face ashen.

A wild enthusiasm bordering on smugness pervaded his conduct. In the morning he climbed out of the boat, stood apart on the dyke and began to count the heads of the workmen as they disembarked from the boats. He counted up to ten and suddenly stopped when he realized that he had to learn more. Nevertheless, he appeared to be in a hurry to parade his newly acquired knowledge before his co-workers.

Back home at night he wanted to make use of his learning. The summer sky was clear with the waxing moon drenching the earth in gold. Both Kallu and Chitha slept on a mat with Chakki lying curled up close to Kallu.

Chathan's dream of impressing Ravunni Achan had only been a cause to stimulate his urge to learn counting. It had dismayed him many a times in his daily life. He didn't know that one could learn counting from another person until Kallu told him what she had achieved.

He was jealous of Meenan who counted up to a thousand, though its meaning was beyond his grasp. He was happy that he could count up to ten, and he was determined to go further, certainly beyond a thousand.

He couldn't sleep; frequently turning his head, looking for some thing to happen. It was past mid-night and he had become very restless; lifting himself up from the mat he sat quietly for a while watching whether he had disturbed his wife or daughter. He lowered his face close to theirs to confirm they were fast asleep. Slowly he made a stealthy exit, into the yard and moved towards the back of the hut, keeping himself close to the foot of the mud wall, where the shadow of the thatch gave him coverage. As he walked he watched for any movement around either on the ground or the river.

The whole world was in slumber, except the face of the harvest moon that glanced at him from the sky. He cursed the moon for its unwanted brightness. He squatted by the side of the wall, facing it and dug his fingers deep into the earth; the scooped up soil he deposited by the side of the wall, carefully. As his hand reached deeper he reached an earthen pot with a lid capping it, further protected by a laterite stone overlaid. Watchfully he lifted the stone, placed it a little away, and removed the lid. He sat looking into the pot

The long hands of the moon had already reached the pot ahead of his eyes. A glimpse of the contents of the pot in the moonlight lifted his spirit up. He scooped up and brought out what was inside the pot and spread them on the lid. The sight of a large number of silver *panam* forced on his visage a rare grin chasing out the abiding scowl that sat on his face. He took out a coin and looked at it intently but dropped it immediately in a reflex action as if frightened, when he saw the venerable head of the *Maharaja* engraved on it. He believed the king was staring at him as he had polluted him by touch.

He always wanted to count his hoard but could not as he had no knowledge of counting. It was unthinkable to get it counted by any other person, as he feared anybody could con him. He placed the pebbles that Kallu had given him in a row on the lower edge of the wall; counting them to ten; then he carefully placed one *Panam* against each pebble and knew that made up ten. But he was left with more coins, which puzzled him. He thought it was a waste of time to make another attempt. Suddenly he put the whole lot back into the pot and placed the lid on top with the stone over it; he covered the pot with soil and dressed the soil securely to give it the original look. When he was almost finished he saw Chitha emerging from the side of the hut. She asked him: "What do you do here in the dead of night?"

"Won't you allow me even to pass urine?" He countered her. Wit seemed to have come to his rescue. In no time the grin that had dawned on his face retreated letting the customary grimace to return.

"Why this man urinates against the hut when there is enough space out side?" Chitha wondered.

He felt disappointed at his inability to count the whole lot in his hoard, that he had diligently accumulated over the years. He didn't think it would be much as he could only put an occasional coin that came his way into the pot. Yet, he wished to know how much was in his store.

Chathan continued with his efforts to learn counting; he could go up to twenty now when he covered his fingers and toes. For further progress he imagined Kallu would make use of her and her mother's fingers and toes, and it turned out to be true.

When he covered one hundred he felt assured that he stood a chance to assume the title of *Thalapulayan* when Uthon retired or died.

Every evening before boarding the canoe homeward he made it a point to talk to Uthon to quietly assess his state of health. One evening, towards the close of the season, as they waited to get their wage measured out, Uthon's son Madari came to inform them that his father had ceased to breathe.

✞✞✞

Fifteen

Born to toil, the *Pulayas* lived wedded to work; they truly ate by the sweat of their brow. For a day's labour they earned two measures of paddy, of which a part was parted with, to buy salt and condiments to give the conji a certain flavour. The rest yielded less than a measure; as a result they lived underfed.

Weekly rest was unheard of; they worked all seven days a week and all the weeks of a month, flood being the only exception. The society treated them as untouchables and their sight and sound was repugnant. Theirs was a small world and they were a small people.

They too were human, aspiring to blossom into a full life but were denied opportunities; they lived stymied with their social life restricted and material life devastated.

With Poomachee's death Meenan felt lonely; his link to the society was restricted to Athai and his father Ettanu, a father figure in his life. One person, who unknown to him had built a nest in his bosom, was Kallu, the daughter of Chathan; Her mother Chitha, cared for him but the father loathed him.

Chathan had become increasingly remote; he ploughed a lone furrow with limited interaction with his neighbours whom he despised; he made himself hateful with a surly look on his face. Hard work and tight fisted life helped him hoard cash, making his neighbours dub him *Panakkaran,* which he enjoyed in private, a chuck under the chin.

After every summer harvest, the season that saw the *Pulayas* flush with grain, they indulged in dreaming of their sons taking daughters of their fellows as wife or giving their daughters as wives to the sons of their fellows. Naturally, Meenan and Kallu too had dreams; they felt assured.

Meenan was aware of the custom of the groom paying a certain amount of cash as bride money to the girl's father; it was intended to compensate the loss of working hands the parents suffered with the girl leaving her parents. It could be any sum bargained and settled between the parents. Greedy men had made the custom an opportunity to bleed the boy's parents. Meenan knew Chathan was no less; he feared he stood no chance of winning the girl, for he was penniless.

"I have neither silver nor gold to warm the cockles of your father; I don't know whether he will accept me without any." Recently Meenan told Kallu.

He put forward a brave face but was uncertain how to cross the bridge when he would come to it.

Sleep evaded him as his thoughts hovered over the hut across the river where a bee lived trapped in a diurnal lotus bud that had closed its petals at twilight; he heard the chirp of the proverbial bee.

The night will end soon, with the east blushing at dawn.

The sun will ride in glory, awakening the bud into blossom,
letting the bee into freedom.

The bee dwelt in the bud, stifled and suffocated, counting the moments. The sound of heavy feet stamping on the hard ground echoed in the nectary of the closed flower. A scared Meenan screamed aloud when he imagined a tusker plucking the blushing blossom. He woke up suddenly, and looked around, horrified.

In the evening Ettanu strode into Kunjan's tavern. The place was unusually crowded with the untouchables squatting in the open.

"*Pulayas* and dogs are not allowed inside." He remembered what he was told when he stepped into the tavern for a drink years ago. He found Kunjan's dog enjoying a nap inside the kitchen; perhaps it was more respectable than the *Pulayas*.

He sought a little privacy and found a quiet place by the side of a haystack that sheltered him from the crowd. He waited patiently for his turn as customarily the turn of the untouchables came after the respectable were served. Ettanu felt fidgety but tarried, scratching his back.

A hushed up conversation from behind the haystack caught his attention. As his name frequently came up in the gossip he felt compelled to lend his ears for details. He recognized Chattan's voice as one of the person's but the other man sounded unfamiliar. Ettanu subtly followed their conversation.

"When do you want Konni to come?" The other man asked.

"Chamari, let him come any day when he has twenty-five *Panam* in his hands; you too should come, besides his parents. We will decide the date for *Penn Koda*." Chathan affirmed.

Ettanu guessed that they had fixed Kallu's marriage to one Konni; he knew neither Konni nor Chamari. Ettanu thought of going closer to hear their discussion distinctly. The sight of a bearer passing the other side of the haystack stopped him from moving closer; the boy carried two bowls of toddy meant for Chathan and his guest.

"Bring two more." Chamari instructed the bearer.

"No. I don't need; you may have more." Chathan tried to dissuade him.

"No, no; today is a very important day; we have finalized a deal." Chamari insisted.

All right; I will have one more. You may go for another." Chathan knew, after all, it was for him to pay the bill; though a miser he acted liberal as Chamari was an important ally. When the servant returned he looked at Ettanu, enquiringly. He raised his index finger signalling for one bowl, for he wanted them to finish soon without finding him hiding behind. Ettanu lingered, nursing his drink to kill time, hoping the other fellows quit sooner; he ordered for another fill.

"How many have we had?" Chathan asked the bearer, apparently, to thwart any repeat order by Chamari. The bearer stood scratching his head and said: "Six."

The bearer knew the *Pulayas* were illiterates, neither able to read nor count; they usually paid without questioning what was demanded. But the boy was not aware that Chathan could count.

"How come six? It cannot be." Chathan got irritated; he objected, perhaps, for the first time a Pulaya dared to dispute an account.

"I have kept a pebble each time you brought a fill; see for yourself and count." It was almost a challenge. He showed him the pebbles and counted them one by one to prove his point; what he had learnt from his daughter had come handy.

"One." He kept one pebble aside, and asked the bearer to count too.

"One." The bearer also counted

"Two, three, four and this is..?"

"Six." The bearer foreclosed Chathan.

"No. five comes after four." Chathan asserted staring into the eyes of the boy

"It's six after four." The bearer insisted, and asked Chathan, with a scornful smile on his face:"Where did you learn counting?"

"That is none of your concern… but know that my daughter has taught me" proudly adding"she is correct."

"Chathacha, are you sure what your daughter has taught is correct?"

It was Chamari's turn to doubt his competence, and he added:

"That boy who taught her need not be correct."

"No. Meenan is right in counting." Chathan was unwilling at least in this matter to let down Meenan. Ettanu, who had been listening to their dispute, thought it the opportune moment for him to present himself before them. He emptied his second bowl in one draught, and quietly showed up before the yelling trio. Chathan turned peevish at the unwelcome appearance of Ettanu, who, he feared had heard all what they had said. Chamari looked at him stupidly.

"Why do you quarrel? Ettanu intervened with an air of geniality. Chathan didn't like his poking into their personal business; though

Chamari thought they needed a third party to settle the dispute, and asked him earnestly:

"Do you know for certain what comes after four?"

"O! It's simple. Five." Ettanu confirmed, looking at Chathan.

"I too knew it." He answered, the snide that he was born with clouding his face. The bearer sheepishly withdrew from the scene. Ettanu was happy for the discomfiture he had caused Chathan; the latter was unhappy fearing that Ettanu would spill the beans. Ettanu guessed both Chathan and Chamari were dull witted.

Ettanu returned feeling sorry for Kallu and Meenan. He was sure that Chathan's decision would cause them heartburns. He wanted to save the situation but was unsure how he could help them. He walked into Meenan's hut to see whether he was aware of the developments.

"Meenan, I have bad news for you." He opened up the topic without any introduction. Meenan looked at him for a clue.

"Chathan has agreed to give Kallu in marriage to Konni." Ettanu paused, watching the reaction on the young man's face. He sat transfixed with his eyes glued to the setting sun at the distant horizon, lost in thoughts that crowded his mind; what he heard failed to stir him up.

"Did you hear what I said?" Ettanu got impatient when Meenan responded with a listless shrug of his shoulders.

"That chap Chamari is the villain behind this." Meenan continued to tarry with his mind closed.

"Chamari has offered twenty-five *Panam*; if you offer, say, thirty *Panam*, perhaps, Chathan will change his mind" Ettanu could read Chathan's mind better.

"Where do I go for thirty *Panam*?" Meenan raised his head in desperation, and he added: "I haven't seen even one; what I have is one measure of paddy left from yesterday's wage." They deliberated together endlessly with no solution emerging.

"You have neither money nor grain to pay for a bride; you go and tell him the truth. Let him give you an answer." Ettanu finally suggested.

"An alternative is to borrow money or grain from somewhere. I can lend you five *Panam* for a year. I need it when its Athai's turn to bring a girl." Ettanu offered to help him.

"Of course, you may lend me some money but who else will do it? And, who else among us has the means?" Meenan doubted the feasibility of the suggestion.

Yet, he was ready to make an effort. He approached a few with whom he enjoyed a good relationship, explaining the circumstances. They could not help but laughed at the proposal.

"Borrowing money to pay for a bride?'

"If you have no money why should you go for a costly wife?"

"Let her be sold for thirty *Panam*." His attempt ended in a fiasco; yet he was confident.

Ettanu's offer of five *Panam* formed the core into which he visualized money pouring in. Meenan was sure he could repay the entire amount by the following harvest. With Kallu on his side they could work in paddy field during daytime, and go fishing in the nights that would double their income. He checked the sums that added upto thirty *Panam* in his hands, and felt assured that it won't be difficult to raise more, if need be.

Thirty *Panam* was a big amount for Meenan, and for that matter for any Pulaya; he marvelled at his ability to raise such a sum in such a short time. It left him in high spirits, and armed with all the cash, he dared to confront Chathan.

The sky was clear with the sun hovering low in the west; flowed river Meenachill, continuing its eternal journey. The evening breeze shied away unwilling to ruffle the silvered cloak the setting sun had laid on the breast of the river.

Meenan crossed the river and entered the familiar premises over the thorn bushes that guarded the hut. Chathan was sitting on a downturned wooden mortar, mending his old fish net that once embittered his otherwise cordial relationship with him. Kallu squatted on the ground close by, locating the holes in the net that her father had been sewing together. Chathan didn't notice Meenan as he sat engrossed in his work, with his head bent down. Kallu could not fail to notice as she always had her eyes for the man who lived across.

"Meenacha, how sweet, you thought of visiting us." She grinned at him.

Chathan lifted up his face that turned cloudy when he saw Meenan walking towards him, nonchalantly, smiling. He wondered who was he smiling at, the father or the daughter?

"You better go inside." Casting his head down again, and pretending that he hadn't seen the visitor, he waved his daughter off. Kallu failed to gauge his rage and tried to linger around.

"I tell you, go inside." He snapped at her with his eyes piercing her face.

Kallu flung the net on to the ground and strode into the hut; she took her place just behind the front screen pining back her ears, watching how her father mauled the young man.

Chathan continued with his work, not caring to lift up his face, pretending he hadn't seen him. Meenan felt uncomfortable as the girl stood troubled at the uncouth behaviour of her father. She rushed to her mother and nudged her out to ease the awkward situation. Chitha too was upset at the brashness of her husband.

Unwelcome though, Meenan squatted on the ground in front of Chathan, like a son before a father, and picked up the net looking for the holes.

"This is a lucky net, never lets you down." Meenan expected a little sweet talk would lighten the situation. Chathan restrained himself by pretending that he hadn't heard the comments.

"How long have you had this net?"

"Very old, you leave it." Chathan abruptly snapped the net while Meenan was holding it firmly in his hand, still locating the holes; the unexpected pull tore a hole in the belly of the net.

The unpardonable insolence of the young man drove Chathan into a fury. He stood up, threw the net into the thistles that grew beyond the kerbs with no effort of ever retrieving it. He shot off towards the hut.

A stunned Meenan sprang up on his feet with a sheepish demeanour on his face pleading forgiveness.

"I am sorry; I never expected you to snatch it so forcefully." Meenan followed him as the man rushed inside, without a word.

"O! That is an old net; you can always mend it." Chitha tried to pacify him.

"Why have you come now? To spoil my mood?"

Kallu, who was standing behind the screen, sneaked out of the hut as her father rushed in. She feared the mishap might spoil his chance of patching up with her father. Meenan stepped into the hut and stood face to face with Chathan, and said:"I came as I wanted to talk to you."

Meenan looked into his eyes for a response. Kallu, who still stood outside, saw through the slits of the screen the frightening capricious look on her father's face,.

"What is it that you wanted to speak about?"

Meenan stood startled at the alien expression on his face. Chitha could guess what could it could be, and Kallu was sure about the question Meenan wanted to talk about. Only Chathan pretended that he knew nothing about it. He stared at the young man, showing his tobacco stained row of teeth in a growl. Meenan knew what he wanted to ask but found himself wilting under pressure, with words sitting heavily on his tongue. A languid drawl marred his speech and made the words inaudible.

"What...?" Chathan barked at him.

Meenan looked for Kallu, and saw her standing by the mud wall of the hut like a granite statue but with live eyes that swam with tears.

"I have come to seek Kallu's hand." Meenan could only lisp but his words hit where they were intended to. An ominous silence descended as Chathan stood disconcerted with his eyes still peering at Meenan.

"How dare you ask for my daughter?" He bellowed at him.

"All the time I have heard everyone saying that Kallu and I are made for each other; and we believed it honestly."

"I never said so, and I don't care what others say."

"But we believed, and we love each other."

"My daughter has never loved you." He insisted, and added as an afterthought lest Kallu disaprove him,

"Even if she did love you I don't care; you should have no illusion." He waved his hand, scornfully, expecting him to depart straight away; but instead, Meenan decided to tarry, hopefully provoking an indictment.

"Never dare to cross the river to sneak about." Still Meenan stood unwearied, remembering the instruction Ettanu had given him.

"I will give you five *Panam* more than what any other person has offered." Meenan knew that Chamari had offered twenty-five *Panam* and his offer would make the bride money thirty.

Chathan had progressed in his arithmetic to know that thirty was greater than twenty-five. Chathan promptly suppressed a faint light that flashed across his face. He decided to probe his worth.

"How much do you have now?"

Meenan wondered whether he was seeing a glimmer of hope in his tone. Chathan pondered for a moment as the young man waited to hear him. A nagging doubt agitated him; he debated how this young lad, as penurious as any other Pulaya youth, was confident of raising thirty *Panam*, unless some one was behind him; he concluded it was none other than Ettanu; yet he decided to suffer him at least until Ravunni Achan appointed the *Thalapulayan;* he feared the man could spoil his chance.

"Make it fifty, and if you are ready, come to me next Sunday."

It was a quick decision and Chathan's face revealed a rare determination, as much as his failure to hide the wiliness that poisoned his mind.

✝✝✝

Sixteen

The hour of reckoning had finally arrived in Meenan's life. It was a quiet Sunday morning, and he had a few hours to test the waters. The prospects of winning or losing were even as Ettanu had predicted. As moments passed by, Meenan's heart began to pound violently, at times threatening to break the side open to lay his heart bare before Chathan.

"Even a blood red heart is a mere hibiscus flower for Chathan." Ettanu had warned him as Meenan set out for his encounter with him.

A low sun had floated under the western slope of the sky, the lower rim of which had the colour of fallen hibiscus that bled red. Below, a light wind shook the crown of the lofty palms. The river flowed down keeping all its woes sunk deep in its bosom.

Meenan rightly guessed that his chances were bleak; he being a friend of Ettanu disqualified him completely. Besides, his act of racing his boat against Chathan's canoe remained an unpardonable sin. On top of it Ettanu's getting posted as the *Thalapulayan* seemed the straw that broke the camel's back.

Meenan walked into Chathan's courtyard where he found him counting the mussels that he had in an earthen bowl. A few venturing creatures had toppled the lid and smoothly sailed over the edge of the bowl. Chathan forced them back. Meenan guessed there must be a special guest who feasted on mussel meat whenever Chathans cooked mussels.

Meenan searched for a smile on Chathan's face which remained dark and forbidding. Slowly though, their eyes met, yet, nobody dared to break the silence. Meenan stood in the courtyard with his arms crossed across his chest. Chathan busied himself ritually picking up pebbles that he found scattered across the yard and throwing them out at random. Finding no more pebbles to pick up he turned to Meenan with a question that sounded odd.

"Why have you come alone? Don't you know what the custom is?" Chathan's gruffish tone had a tinge of annoyance.

"I don't know what the custom is." Meenan sounded defensive.

Chathan elaborated:

"I know I can't expect you to know the customs; it is not your privilege. But bride money is always paid by the parents to the parents in the presence of the elders of the community." He stared at the young man's face

Suddenly, Meenan found himself tongue-tied. He searchingly looked at the young man but could not find him carrying any money on his person.

"I haven't come with money nor do I have any." Those words had delivered the message and relieved him of the pain.

"But I wish to speak to you." Meenan looked into Chathan's eyes. But Chathan stood quiet; the intervening silence encouraged him but Chathan's face remained stony.

"Speech doesn't compensate money." His curt reply didn't hurt the young suitor as it was not totally unexpected.

Chitha came out of the hut with a sweet smile on her face. Kallu had pushed her out to tame her father though she knew it was impossible.

"He who has no money shall have no bride," he snorted without lifting up his face. For him bride money was a matter of status also. He was convinced that his daughter was smart and beautiful, though black.

"I will work for you a year or two; you will collect my full wages. It may exceed even fifty *Panam*. I will seek Kallu only after accounting for the entire bride money." Meenan expected his offer to entice him.

"Why don't you listen to him? He is honest." Chitha tried to persuade her husband who remained unbending.

"Do you seek a bride on credit? Even cattle are not sold on credit these days. My daughter is not that cheap." Chathan ridiculed him.

Meenan wilted under the scorn he poured out.

"I have other reasons too why I don't want to give you my daughter." He kept Meenan guessing, and then asked.

"Tell me who your father is?" Meenan quivered in shame but admitted, meekly.

"I don't know." He had never heard Poomachee, who he thought was his mother, ever telling him who his father was.

"You have no father, at least tell me who your mother is."

"Poomachee." He had a ready answer that he flung at his face with a rare courage. The last question and its answer, in fact, put him at ease.

"No. Poomachee was not your mother." He was raking up a long forgotten episode.

"He too was born of a woman and a man, just like us; what more do you need to know, not known earlier?" Chitha chided her husband. She thought he was deliberately deriding the poor boy. It was true, but not known to many that Poomachee hadn't mothered him but reared him up.

Almost two decades ago, on a sunny afternoon, an enormous float of coconuts that sailed down Meenachilaar came to shore in front of Poomachee's hut in Kudamaloor, near the ferry.

Growers in Meenachill valley produced huge quantity of coconuts that found its way to oil mills in Aalapuzha. Hauling the nuts by large *valloms* was hazardous and costly too. A Meenachill man observed that nuts floated in water, and Ittan Mathan, a coconut trader thought he could float down the river all his nuts if he could ensure the nuts stayed together.

"If I can construct a base that doesn't tear apart I can throw over it hundred thousand nuts, safely." The man concluded, and his ingenuity took him further.

The fibrous husk of the nut was strong; he dug out from the husk of the nut a strip and tied it to another, making a pair; the paired nuts linked together by interlocking made a network that constituted the base. He strengthened it by adding another layer on the first. A hundred thousand nuts were heaped on, and Ittan Mathan sat on the little mountain that leisurely floated down the river.

For his ingenuous idea he thanked a petty anthill that he saw gliding down a serpentine canal, *Pannagam*, as a young boy, years ago.

Astonished onlookers on both banks of the river marvelled at the sight and hailed him; many admired his guts, a few felt he was doomed; but since the days of Ittan Mathan, cargo had been a regular sight down the river.

The punters on the float had a hard time steering clear of bunged bends and low river bottoms with projecting rocks. Only experienced men could manoeuvre the behemoth along the river to safety. And Ittan Mathan himself was originally a punter. The men had their lunch break at Poomachee's site.

"The Meenachill men eat fish like trencher men and drink toddy like fish, so make sure you have both." Poomachee warned the fishermen; she sent word to the toddy tapper to ensure that he had special toddy for them.

"Poomachee, is everything in place?" As the owner stepped on to the land he asked Poomachee. She knew what he was enquiring about; she had arranged enough for them.

"I have arranged everything."

"Good. I knew you would do it." the broad grin on his face baring the tobacco stained teeth crowding his mouth, confirmed his happiness. The owner settled down by the open yard near Poomachee's hut; his workers joined him opening their ditty bags for a tobacco session.

"Poomachee, we have brought a basket of *Paala Kappa* for you; go and collect it." One of the punters told her. Tapioca grown in Meenachill valley tasted superb.

"We will have tapioca with fish today." The punter reminded her as she walked away.

"Then, tender toddy to go with it." The owner announced.

"Sure…sure." The men joined him shouting boisterously.

Poomachee walked towards the float to collect the tapioca they had specially brought for her. As she climbed the nut hill she heard the weird cry of a baby from one end of the float; she paused for a moment, straining her ears to make sure what she heard was true . The baby cried again. Wading through the loose nuts into which her steps had sunk, she reached the corner where the cries had come from. She stood aghast, her mouth wide open, when she saw a new born baby boy, lying naked, trapped in the loose nuts, with a swarm of red ants eating into its soft flesh. She lifted up the baby, still kicking and crying, cleaned its body by wiping off the ants. She planted a warm kiss on his ebony black but chubby cheek; the little child innocently responded by exposing his amaranthine mouth.

She held him close to her breasts. The child experienced the woman's warm body, and instantly began groping for her breasts by rolling his mouth over her chest.

She ran towards the men with the baby held close to her bosom; she found them still lingering with their tobacco pouch.

"Where did you find this baby?"Poomachee asked the punters.

"Oh! He is Neeli Manka's son; they have killed his mother, Neeli,"

"Neeli Manka!" Poomachee exclaimed. She had known the *Pulaya* woman; they were friends in their younger days. The name brought to her mind awe and admiration; she had fought to defend the *Pulaya*s.

"Poomachee, you rear him up; I will give you enough rice to feed him." The owner of the float assured her.

"We shall call him Meenan as we had found him from river Meenachill." The owner said.

The punters found him lying abandoned in an ant infested, thick hanging bower, entangled in vines that almost touched the water. Uninterrupted, teems of red ants travelled down the vines, reaching the foot of the tree to feast on a pool of blood that smelt human.

"Neeli was your mother but nobody knows who had fathered you."

Chathan had an ebullient grin on his face.

"You are born a bastard; never ever cross my path to seek the hands of my daughter." Chathan hurried back into his hut.

Msgr. Aaron Micah never felt ashamed when he discovered his grandfather was a bastard or his great grandmother was a woman with an uncomplimentary past.

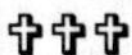

Seventeen

"With great difficulty we have recreated the story of Neeli who became Neeli Manka in her own right. She single-handedly fought against the caste lords to defend the untouchables. But she was finally felled like many who had preceded her; she left behind a son in the bosom of the river, Meenachill." Sivanandan explained. This occurred almost a hundred years ago when the haves had held the have-nots under their fist. All that remained of Neeli Manka was a pool of blood at the foot of a jackfruit tree; she had her lodge on top of the tree. She had a past that shaped her life. Poomachee remembered her, they being contemporaries, having shared experiences of rejection and deprivation. Poomachee was frail and timid; Neeli too was thin but bold and vengeful. After the death of her mother nobody had seen her. Forgotten by her kith and kin, she had become notoriously infamous. Mothers invoked her name to frighten into sleep their unmanageable kids; her story was later recited like a fairy tale.

As the coconut float sailed slowly down the river, the punters saw a gang of ferocious looking dark men carrying hog-tied on a bamboo pole the body of a woman, mangled with head broken and blood dripping down from her head. A large man walked behind the gang carrying on his shoulder a blood stained iron-clad pestle; his flawed upper lip turning his face hideous and brutish.

It was a hired gang whom the upper castes used as hatchet men in their feuds or, to liquidate those who dared to challenge them. The carriers knew that Neeli was of their own blood; but they were helpless as disobeying the order endangered their own existence.

Neeli was a young, ugly looking, ferocious woman, heavy built with a dark skin. Her jaws when opened revealed a cave like mouth, reddened by chewing excessive quantity of lime daubed betel leaves, and hedged by a row of black teeth with a thick coat of tobacco stains. Nobody knew where from she had come from. None dared to pass the mud road that led to her abode after the night fall. Most of the day-time she confined herself to her sky borne perch watching the unwary pedestrians on the road or the jostling and shoving schools of fish that collected under the peephole of her lodge, awaiting the crumbs of food that she would throw at them in her pastime.

Neeli was associated with a dare devil gang that had organized themselves into a secret resistance group, known as *Pulapedies* to avenge the atrocities committed by the powerful against the oppressed castes. The gang lurked by the deserted roads or on the banks of rivers that carried much of the traffic. The gang physically harassed their victims; to frighten and pollute them. Daring men among them kidnapped upper caste women, raped and threw them into swollen rivers or gorges to die, as *Pulayas* would in the hands of their oppressors.

Neeli was the victim of sadistic justice, the trauma of which refused to die down even after a long passage of time. It happened when she was about seven, a few months after a great flood; flood always brought misery and suffering.

She lost her father when she was an infant and the mother raised her; the mother was lame limiting her capacity to earn. Hunger and disease left the child frail and emaciated. Early mornings the mother left for work leaving the child behind to fend for herself.

One morning Neeli woke up late and sat on the floor rubbing her eyes. She was surprised to see her mother still lying on the floor, shivering; she struggled to ward off the chill by crossing her arms across her breast. She lay shaking violently. Bouts of malaria fever that attacked her regularly tormented her. They had no gruel for days, as the woman could not work.

Neeli got up from the floor as the sun had risen over their roof; the day had become hot and humid. She sat aimlessly under the shade of a cashew tree, fatigued and hungry; she searched whether the tree had the season's first crop of cashew apple to relieve her hunger. The tree bore blossoms that hosted the bees. Across the paddy field she saw a sprawling orchard bearing palms and mangoes. She knew mangoes shed tender fruits early in summer and palms dropped nuts at random, if not plucked when ripe. She sneaked into the compound looking for anything edible. Luck was not in her favour; she found nothing safe to eat on the ground; a few tender mangoes putrefied lay scattered. She aimlessly walked out of the compound; she was not in hurry to return home but the thought of her mother hastened her steps. The orchard merged with a small hillock that was home to an unimpressive, tile-roofed temple. She stopped by a pond by the side of the temple, covered with thick, mossy floatage.

Neeli, watchfully, stepped into the cool water, cleared the moss from the surface, and threw a few scoopfuls of water over her face; she felt fresh and revived. A shoal of fish rushed towards her and mobbed her shanks in a rare show of piscine camaraderie. She stood excited as a run of portly fish jostled against her slender calves. It was really a tempting sight, and she wished she had just one fish to survive on. She stood still, intently watching the unsuspecting shoal, and slowly lowered her torso, arms thrown down and palms cupped to scoop up the big one that had nearly nipped at her ankle. Instantly, she closed her cupped palms around the fish. She lifted herself up, holding the fish in her palm by its tail. The fish, choked of breath, quivered in her hand; it gave a sudden jerk and slipped back into the safety of the pond. Neeli, shocked at the unexpected slip, leaned forward in an effort to hold the fish back, but ended up with fisherman's luck.

As she struggled out of the pond disappointed, she saw a small crowd walking towards the temple, apparently to perform certain rituals.

Fishing in the temple pond or an untouchable entering the pond was a sacrilegious act inviting severe punishment. She knew she had defiled the pond and would be killed, if detected. She ran away in panic and took shelter behind a thicket of thorny, screw pine bushes that grew behind.

The temple mount had become noisy with the Priest ordering the men about. A solitary crow that found a perch atop the dome of the temple strained its neck to survey what was happening below. Neeli saw a young man, after a dip in the pond, standing in front of the temple, with his eyes reverently closed and hands folded across his bare chest with water dripping down wetting the ground.

The young man was the descendant of a departed ancestor; the small crowd had gathered at the temple to propitiate the departed soul. The celebrant had placed three large balls of cooked rice on a plantain leaf as a ritual feed for the soul of the ancestor. The spirit never appeared in person to feed on the rice ball; it was given to the black crows to peck the balls. Neeli thought, instead of feeding the black crows they could have offered the rice balls to her; she too was black. She wondered whether a black girl was less honourable than a black crow. For a moment she wondered why her mother hadn't borne a black crow in place of a black daughter.

"Clack...clack...clack." The man clapped his palms together, inviting the soul to descend and feed on the offerings. She had seen the ritual earlier but largely ignored it. As an Untouchable, she was forbidden from entering the premises. She knew the crows feasted on the rice balls but scattered much. She walked towards the temple stealthily and hid herself in a ditch behind. Hunger incited her to rush forward and grab the balls but the fear of her being caught held her back. She tried to count the balls but she realized she could not count beyond three. She figured out how she could share the balls with her mother. The one on the right was for her mother; the one in the middle was for herself, and the one on the left was for her to share with her mother.

"Maybe the whole for my mum," she concluded as she remembered her mother's wretched face.

She gazed at the sky and the treetops; there was no sign of crows except the lone one that continued to perch atop the temple dome. She thought of shooing it away, a potential rival for the rice balls; but she dared not. The young man clapped again as instructed by the Priest. In response, the crow descended, hovering over the roof and the crown of the palm apparently to partake of the offering. Some more flew in and perched on the tree-tops, a few landed on the ground, and trotted towards the rice balls.

Neeli thought she stood no chance now. She waited. A few that sat on the tree-top uttered a strange cry and took off unmindful of the offerings; the rest followed the leaders without a second look at the rice balls.

The man stood with his head down cast as he realized that the crows had refused to break the *Bali Pindom*. The birds had disappeared in the distant sky, except the lone one on the temple roof.

The refusal of the crows to break the *Bali Pindom* had painful consequences; it dishonoured the family, scandalizing the society. The man looked skyward for a sign. Every tree top was devoid of birds; the young crow was still there brightening his hope, agile and active with its neck swinging left to right, at times focussing on the rice balls; the other one as black as a crow, stood craving with folded hands behind the temple, unseen.

The lone bird took a sweep down and landed very close to the rice balls; hesitantly though, it hopped closer with its head moving alertly.

The crow suddenly stopped short of the balls and looked upward distracted by the raucous caws of a throng that suddenly hovered over the palm.

The man clapped again as a fresh appeal, and waited for the guests. The one on the ground moved forward again with its beak aiming at the rice ball. The birds from the palm top swept down to the temple top with a cacophonous yelling at the lone crow that dared to violate the apparent ban. The swift descent of the crows saddened Neeli who was sure of at least a share of the rice with one bird breaking the ball; she stood cursing the crows and the gods.

In the twinkle of an eye, dashing the last hope of the man, the single crow took off, not breaking the rice ball. Soon the crowd too disappeared leaving the sky empty.

The men stood under the blue dome of the sky stupefied, unable to fathom the mystery of the crows' refusal to partake of the *Bali Pindom.* The young man looked into the eyes of the Priest who had been gazing at the sky for a prognostic omen to explain away the incident. He found nothing ominous in the sky. He searched the earth for a sign. He hobbled across the open ground, over to the rivulet.

Neeli saw from her hide out the Priest at a kissing distance. Sheburied her face in the mother earth. She lifted up her face as she heard the retreating footsteps of the man and wiped her face. He turned right at the corner of the lime-daubed. She sprang up on her feet and remained firm, holding onto a screw pine for support.

She tore herself away from behind the thorny thicket, bruising herself by the teeth of the thorn that cut her skin deep; it failed to produce any blood, and she ran forward taking shelter by the wall; each step was put forward cautiously, holding on to the wall by her right hand.

She paused for a moment where the wall terminated and put forward her head. She saw the last man walking down the slope of the mount, vanishing beyond the rivulet; she mustered enough courage, and dashed towards the plantain leaf that held the rice balls, invitingly.

The leaf was wet with water sprinkled in a purificatory rite with red blossoms of *Thetti* and hibiscus scattered over. A brightly polished bronze vessel with a spout on the belly, filled with water stood on the right of the leaf. She took no notice of the gleaming vessel as she concentrated on the rice balls. She squatted facing the leaf, broke one ball, and swallowed a few mouthfuls in quick succession. She was happy she had found some thing for her starving mother.

"Two balls I will take home for my mum." She kept apart the two on the left half of the leaf. She gobbled the rice with determination yet fearing that she might be detected stealing the sacred rice, the rice she had shoved into the mouth choked her throat and blocked her breath.

She sat wriggling in agony, dropping on to the leaf the rice that she had forked up into her mouth; her eyes bulged out and became wet. The sight of the golden vessel with water eased her tension; she lifted the vessel, brought it to her lips and drank some water that cleared the tract. She forked up another mouthful in her fingers.

It was the Priest. As he walked home, he remembered that he had left behind the golden vessel near the pond. He turned back immediately and doubled up the steps to reach the temple yard. He stood stunned at the sacrilegious sight of an unwashed *Pulaya* girl eating of the *Bali Pindom*, and drinking from the sacred vessel.

Stealthily, he moved behind her. She felt the pressure of hands on her neck lifting her up. He slapped her on both her cheeks, unmindful of defiling himself. The girl stared at him open mouthed, the rice dribbling off her mouth on to her chest. The chewed rice with spittle landed on his hand, provoking him to brutalize her.

"You filthy pig! you have polluted the temple and defiled the gods; your presence chased away the soul for whom the rice balls were offered, and scared away the crows that had come to eat the offerings." He hit her on her head with the golden vessel; and pushed her down on to the earth.

"You will never do it again.... I will kill you." He shouted at her looking into her eyes, intimidating. The men who had left for their homes returned and stood by the temple yard, gaping at the sight of the Priest grappling with an Untouchable girl in the precincts of the temple.

He held her by her arm and dragged her towards the live fire pit. Neeli, cowed and fatigued collapsed by the edge of the fireplace. The fiery-eyed man pulled out a smouldering splinter from the pit and thrust it against the soft flesh of the little girl's cheeks. Her shrieks and the nauseating burning smell wafted in the air.

He threw the burning splinter back into the pit and dragged the hapless child by her legs, out of the holy precincts, and threw her beyond the thorny hedges, into the rivulet. He walked back nonchalantly into the temple yard, picked up his vessel and walked down the steps into the pond. He took three deep dips in the water, and came out, cleansed. He Priest returned home satisfied that he had protected the gods and punished the offender, rightly.

Neeli survived, with the wounds healing; but the incident continued to haunt her and he cried for revenge. When she lost her mother, Neeli found herself freed from all bonds.

On a summer evening, in the light of the setting sun she walked down the slopes of the hillock that had been her abode, for an unknown destination. She walked along the dry bed of the creek sheltered by the shrubs that still flourished on its banks.

She had gone there to meet a man whom she had never met before; she hoped that he would chart out her future as a member of the gang *Pulappedi.* Kodari, was there waiting for Neeli.

He was big built with long arms and longer legs, the bones of which sheathed in flesh. The mesomorphic manifestation of the man coweredher in frozen panic tending her to withdraw her steps. But she stood still watching him emerging in the gloaming out of the screw pines. But she stood still watching him emerging in the gloaming out of the.

Neeli entered the gang called *Pulapedi*; they instilled fear in the minds of the caste hierarchy; they retaliated the crimes against the untouchables. They believed and practiced the maxim, kill the killer and rape the raper's kin. Neeli's world had expanded as she became a symbol of the untouchables' resistance against oppression.

Neeli had become Neeli Manka, Neeli the dame; her eponym was the present Neelimangalam, a sleepy hamlet of yore on the banks of river Meenachil.

Chathan was aware of the story that proved Meenan was the son of Neeli Manka, the outlaw murdered by the caste hierarchy.

And the bishop designate was her great grandson.

✞✞✞

Eighteen

It was the interlunary night, the *Karutha Wavu;* the old moon had just exited; the ceremonial appearance of the new moon, just a glimmer, went unnoticed. The dark night of *Karutha Wavu* was inauspicious to commence good deeds.

Meenan, sought shelter in the dark night; perhaps to bury his woes and shed two drops of tears, unseen and unheard.

When Chathan had shown him the door it crushed his hopes. The revelation that he had no father to own traumatized him. The disclosure that the woman who had raised him hadn't borne him wounded him not. For he knew he had grown up sharing the warmth of her body; she had nurtured him. He wondered what testimony he needed to prove whose son he was. He had lost Kallu as he had failed to raise fifty *Panam*; if he had the sum Chathan wouldn't have unearthed the skeleton in his cupboard; he guessed it was no use crying over spilt milk.

Ettanu had mobilised the community elders to canvass support for Meenan; they spent the whole night arguing and debating. They argued that a boy had the right to seek a wife from his own community. Chathan alleged that under the guise of a new ruling they were trying to support Meenan. Chathan didn't contest their proviso; but insisted that his right to demand bride money be conceded to.

"Your right to seek bride money is agreed but it shouldn't be unreasonable, beyond the ability of the boy." Ettanu intervened, adding:

"Remember, the boy has neither father nor mother."

"Do you suggest that I provide them too?" Chathan pooh poohed.

"My daughter shall not be available for a petty sum." Chathan trooped out of the meeting.

"Don't dream big; even for a hundred *Panam Kallu* won't be his," he declared.

For Meenan, it was the last nail in his coffin.

Meenan continued to sit in the darkness; quiet flowed the river before him. He sat, throwing a random pebble into the river.

Suddenly, he noticed a *vallom* slowing down when it neared his hut. The punter berthed the boat and walked towards him. Meenan wondered who the visitor was and what was his business.

"Meenan...." The punter called softly.

"I am Kochai; I come from Paala. Anthayose directed me to meet you. Don't you remember him and his wife Alma?"

"Yes, I remember them; how are they?"

Kochai explained that he was carrying a load of Paala pepper to Alleppy to be delivered at the port town by the morning. He said it was his maiden venture to cross the Vembanad Lake and he was scared.

"Why did you undertake a job you are unfamiliar with? Crossing the Vembanad is not an easy task. Besides, I am not well." Meenan explained.

Kochai found Meenan reluctant but he persisted.

"In fact, Anthayose was to punt the boat to Alleppy, for some reason he couldn't make it. He asked me specifically to meet you and gave me the exact description where to find you and what to tell you." Kochai spoke well and Meenan failed to discern how well the messenger was coached.

"What did he want you to tell me?" Meenan enquired.

"He told me to offer you five *Panam* to help the *Vallom* cross Vembanad. He told me that you are in need of cash to pay the bride money; five *Panam* is a tidy sum." Kochai paused and asked, solicitously:

"How much does the girl's father demand?

"He demands a hefty sum, fifty."

"Hoi...it's a huge sum...... but perhaps Anthayose can help you."

"How?" Meenan was excited, though he wondered whether Chathan would come around even for fifty. Meenan looked at the man for an answer.

"Now, listen, every week we deliver four loads of pepper at the sea port. We will entrust the transportation to you. You earn twenty *Panam* a week and sixty *Panam* in three weeks.

"Really?"

"Yes, really."

"Okay, I agree. I will come with you right now."

With Poomachee gone Meenan was free. He thought of Ettanu his mentor, but decided to inform him on his return. He planned to visit Chathan along with Ettanu to tell him:

"Now, here are sixty instead of the fifty you had demanded. Please give me Kallu."

Meenan boarded the Vallom, stood at the helm with the punt-pole which he checked and found strong; he pushed the pole against the bottom of the river. The boat raced ahead gaining speed Kochai sat drowned in the darkness, avoiding any talk with the punter.

"Kochai, what did you say the cargo is?" Meenan casually asked the man as he lazed the pole for a while.

"Eh... pepper. "Kochai answered, as if woken up from a dream.

"But it doesn't exude any fragrance?"

"Oh! That's because it's fresh, not yet dried." Meenan believed him. He continued with the pole earnestly dreaming of the *Panam* and its use. True to his promise he berthed the boat at the canal jetty before dawn. Kochai appeared happy; they came out of the boat.

"Meenan, here is some cash, two coppers; you go and have some breakfast. Return leisurely. We have plenty of time." Meenan was happy. He had a quick break-fast, took rest and promptly returned to the canal.

He found the boat missing; There was no sign of Kochai. He was puzzled and searched for the boat and the man both missing. He sat by the canal waiting for hours, guessing Kochar might have moved the cargo to the godown of the trader and would come back soon. Soon he noticed that the load he had carried was left piled up, rather abandoned by the canal. He discovered that it contained river sand instead of pepper. He knew he had been conned but failed to understand why. He found himself stranded with no money to pay his fare home. He waited the whole day, resisting his need for sleep, to find an upgoing boat needing a helper; he found one late evening.

He rushed to Ettanu's home. "It's good that you were away." Ettanu heard his story and made a cryptic remark.

"On the night of *Karutha Wavu* Chamari had schemed with Chathan to carry Kallu away. They tricked you into a journey offering a tidy sum to keep you off the scene; you succumbed to their trick charms." Meenan sat glum.

The night when Kallu was carried away she requested a common friend, Manka to be Meenan's wife in her place. Kandan, Manka's father, conceded to the proposal as mooted by the community which admonished Chathan for his greed.

Meenan had become a successful punter of cargo boats to Alleppy. One night, almost a year later Meenan was ready to depart. A stranded passenger approached him for a lift to Palachode; Meenan accepted him.

"Some thing is floating on the surface." Iraman, the passenger noticed a large bundle drifting almost touching the belly of their vallom.

"Hope it's not a dead body, again." Iraman shuddered at the thought of another corpse within a few days of an earlier one. He was scared.

"Gods are out to wreck vengeance on the wicked." Iraman said.

"It's the carcass of a cow." Meenan pushed it farther with his paddle.

"Dead bodies floating in these canals are very common." Iraman narrated the drowning of a man.

"Konni was my neighbour, mad but healthy. A few days ago, he went out fishing at night. Nobody saw him for a couple of days. His wife thought he might have gone visiting relations, as was his habit; but he never returned. Later, some fishmongers saw a dead body floating in the canal with his canoe drifting with the ebb and flow." Iraman briefly described the incident.

"He was struck by *Padachamundi*." Iraman added:

The name Konni was familiar and Meenan was anxious to identify the man.

"Is he a relation of one Chamari?"

"Yes, he was, though not exactly. Do you know him?"

"Yes." Meenan stopped with that short answer, as he feared more questions would lead to complications. Iraman too appeared wary taking the matter further. An uneasy silence followed. Meenan was reasonably sure that the dead man was the Konni for whom Kallu was procured by Chamari. He was scared, yet he wanted to visit Konni's home; his heart began to beat rapidly.

Iraman got off the boat on the left bank. Meenan moved to the right bank where the lamp-post stood by a coffee shop nearby. Meenan thought the man could give him more information about Konni but he was uncertain how to proceed. In the dead of night, a stranger, enquiring about a young woman, whose husband had just died, would certainly provoke suspicion, perhaps elicit more embarrassing questions.

He moored his boat a little away from the coffee shop and remained in the shadow of a palm, making up his mind. Gathering all the courage he could muster, he walked towards the hut, where he found the man wrapped up in an old cotton shawl sitting on the floor, leaning against the mud wall. Meenan woke him up. The man responded promptly.

"Do you need some *Kapi*?"

"Of course, I will have that, but tell me whether you know one Konni."

"Konni, the loony?" Meenan didn't answer him, he waited to hear more.

"Yes, but he is no more; his wife lives nearby."

Konni's hut was in a sprawling compound filled with palms and mango trees. Darkness and an eerie silence prevailed.

No sign of life was evident in the hut; not even a traditional oil lamp flickered for the dead soul. A young wife whose husband had just died could not have gone to sleep so early. Kallu wasn't asleep either.

She sat crouched in the open, under the canopy of the tree. She had her chin turned left, resting on her shoulder with her arms firmly entwining her folded legs. A black cat sat quietly, perched on a low branch of the tree, its attention focussed on a tiny nest not far from its vantage position. The nest had a young bird sitting over two precious eggs.

Unnoticed by Kallu, Meenan stood in the courtyard. The presence of an intruder deflected the attention of the cat. It jumped down from its perch to be at Kallu's feet faithfully. It pressed its body on to Kallu's bare calf meowing softly.

Meenan found himself bereft of words. He tried to clear his choked throat by a low cough, a normal practice to invite attention. She was slow to respond, and rather reluctantly looked up. For a moment she failed to recognize him, as she hadn't seen him for several months since that fateful night; nor did she expect him to visit her. She just saw a man standing quietly by her side; she continued to sit unconcerned, a habit that she had learnt since her moving to Palachode.

It could not be Chamari, for quietness was not his habit.

"It cannot be the dead man coming alive, either; then who?" She looked at the man, straining her eyes.

"Meenacha, you have come." She mutely pronounced his name and started to cry. Meenan and Kallu stood still, gazing at each other. Meenan decided to break the silence.

"I was returning from Aalapuzha; a local man told me all about it casually. I guessed it was some thing that concerned you." He stopped for a breath but failed to resume, instead he called her out.

"How did it happen?

"I don't know much. I heard from others."

She felt quite relieved; at least some one had strayed in to speak to her.

"Meenacha, please come inside." She invited him to come inside as she walked ahead. She lighted a wicker lamp from the embers in the hearth.

She had nothing to offer him to sit on except a small square, granite block flattened on the surface that Konni used to sit on whenever he was at home. He hesitated to occupy the stone that was Konni's. But he did as Kallu sat on the bare ground. They sat facing each other but their eyes strayed, unwilling to face the reality.

She had no idea of what had happened to Konni; she could only piece together whatever she had heard from others. She didn't even see his dead body.

It was almost a week ago; the evening was quiet as usual. A small patch of dark clouds grew into a mighty rain cloud in no time. They ate the gruel together with broken chilly as a side dish, leftovers from their midday meal. Konni appeared unhappy as there was not enough for him in the bowl, and Kallu emptied her bowl into his.

She spread a mat on the dusty floor and lay down. The cat that sat on the hearthstone was restless, as it had nothing to eat, and it was disturbed by the fury of the rain that lashed the roof. It briskly walked towards Kallu and lay close to her. She loved to have the cat close to her bosom; its claws never hurt her. Konni was sitting on his stone smoking his last beedi of the night. He was agitated as he had been in recent nights. He felt incited when he saw her fondling the cat keeping it cozy. Konni snuffed out the beedi butt in the dust and moved his mat closer to Kallu's; as he lay close to her he placed his hand softly over her shoulder.

Kallu was cold, pretending to be asleep. He lowered his palm over her shoulder seeking her breasts. With a jerk of her arm she threw his hand off; he was angry but kept quiet. Konni was hurt; it pained him, he loved her.

"Kallu, please?" He begged.

"You better sleep; you have work in the morning." She admonished him, and continued to pet the cat. Konni snatched the cat from her side and tossed it across the hut. Konni tried to hold her in his strong arms.

"Touch me not, you cruel beast." She yelled and sneered at him, pushed him aside and jumped up from the mat.

"Why do you trouble yourself? It's not in you, and I am not your wife either."

"But I love you, Kallu."

"Yes true. I love you too but not as your wife." What she said silenced Konni. For she spoke the truth, and he too knew it. Kallu sat on the corner of a grinding stone, crying, as had been her fate every night since she had stepped into the hut. Her subdued sobs merged with the beating of the wind on the broken thatch.

"Meenacha, you don't know how much I have suffered from the day I was seized by Chamari and brought here. "

"This is the man you shall live with hereafter; take care of him. I shall come back but tonight, you take rest." Chamari gave his commandment as he stomped out of the hut where Konni the man whom she had to live with, slept.

Kallu sat disconsolate when she found the groom (Chamari had trumpeted aloud and her father had bargained for) lying on the bare floor, scantily clad with his palms thrust between his thighs to warm himself up against the biting cold. His face was turned away from her. She had no more tears to shed; a rare determination to face life as it unfolded before her strengthened her will to survive. Tired and exhausted she slipped into a deep slumber, though disturbed by the heavy snoring of the man who slept next to her.

Konni continued to sleep and snore.

He was a strong man, short and bushy with clusters of thick hair dotting his limbs. His protruding belly drove him into a rage when empty. The sight of the man was revolting and his habits nauseating.

Kallu abruptly turned her face away from his facade as he slowly began to open his eyes. He pinched his nose and wiped the mire on his fingers in the dust of the floor. He saw a strange woman squatting on the floor with her legs doubled up and head resting on her knees.

He gathered himself up and sat quietly looking at her, straining his neck for a glimpse of her face that remained hidden between her knees and arms. A broad grin brightened his face.

"And, you have come now." He spluttered in disbelief.

Finally, their eyes met as she lifted her face up. Intrusive stare frightened her. She sat watching him, forcing a smile on her lips too.

"A m m a...?"

"*Amma, Amma*, you have come. Where were you?" He looked excited. Konni sprang up on his feet and dashed towards her extending both his arms to embrace her. She stood up too, embarrassed. She grasped his arms and held him back to abort the hug he had, perhaps, intended. Konni was neither disappointed nor annoyed.

"*Amma, can* I touch you?" He stared into her eyes.

Placing both his hands on her upper arms he shook her violently.

"I know you are my mother whom that man had killed." He began to sob, his eyes brimming with tears. He took her face in his and kissed her profusely on both her cheeks.

"Who killed your mother?" She intently looked into his eyes for an answer.

"I won't tell you. No. I won't tell you. If I tell he will kill you again."

She noticed his face becoming cloudy. The sudden change in his face was really fearsome. For Kallu he was not Konni the loony, people talked about; he was a big man physically fit to be a husband. She wondered whether his behaviour was feigned, intended to disarm her.

"*Amma*, I am hungry; give me what you have." He looked at her, head to foot, enthusiastically, expecting her to respond.

"Yes, you have the boiled tapioca; eat it,"

"No no tapioca! I want your milk, will you not give me?" He grasped her breasts as they stood closer and before she realized what he planned; she couldn't wriggle out of his hold.

Kallu looked at him aghast as he slowly tightened his grasp on her breasts. She was incensed by the brutish conduct of the man. She almost decided to knock him down by a kick on his big belly. Tiny beads of sweat sprouted on her forehead as fear and grief agonized her. But she remained calm with no effort to overwhelm him. She watched him for any sign of erotic upheaval, normal in a man when holding the breasts of a young woman.

She found him cool and unstirred. She quietly said.

"Konni, I am your mother, am I not?"

"Yes, you are, you are." He affirmed.

"Then believe me, there is no milk in these breasts." She calmly pushed his hands off and got her breasts released from his grasp. Konni believed her. For a moment he looked askance at the distant sky, gloomily but soon he remembered that his mother's breasts were very large when full.

"When there is no milk the breasts become small." He concluded.

"Then who drank all the milk?" The question agitated him, and he still wanted to find out the truth from Kallu, whom he firmly believed, was his mother come back alive.

"Amma, don't allow that man to enter the hut." He paused with a piercing look. "Who?"

"Chamari; don't you know? He will drink all your milk." It was a stern warning and he rushed out. Kallu stood watching him trudging for an unknown destination carrying an axe on his shoulder.

"I felt safe as long as Konni hated Chamari and he believed that I was his long dead mother; once he died I don't know whom to turn for protection, I am doomed." Kallu stopped, looking at the dark sky.

"Perhaps I have to follow Konni." Her words stirred him.

"No, You shall go with me," he assured her rather impulsively.

Suddenly he remembered that he had taken Manka as his wife as decreed by the elders. He wondered how Manka would react and how the community would respond. He believed that Manka would be happy and he felt assured that he could convince the elders; for he had rescued Kallu.

✞✞✞

Nineteen

"Ravunni Achan is stabbed to death."

"Meenan the *Pulaya* has murdered him."

"No; it's Kocharayan, the mahout who has committed the ghastly murder."

The news spread like wildfire.

'The *Pulaya* youth couldn't have committed the crime; for to carry out a murder one needs a lot of guts which he lacks, being rather timid." Men who had known Meenan doubted.

Besides, they had other reasons too. They knew he was Ravunni's favourite errand boy and Ravunni was to him a patron. They doubted he would kill him with no apparent motive. They believed that Kocharayan had committed the crime, for Ravunni had snatched away Kocharayan's wife, an incident that the mahout could never forgive.

It was an enormous crime committed against a very influential family of a dominant community; the police necessarily acted in tandem with their dictates.

Meenan had to run for his life. He ran fast, never looking back, unmindful of those he passed by. The high castes squeezed themselves out of his path to avoid getting polluted. Even though he guessed he had no escape, he looked for a place where he could lie low for a while before they set out the dogs on him.

He failed to find a safe hideout as every spot seemed vulnerable. Finally he reached an abandoned well atop a hill which he thought would be a safe haven. He found the well kerb smothered with over grown grass and gnarled shrubs, all under the hood of a great *Anjili* tree. The kerb was well built with cut laterite rings leading down to its bottomless bottom.

Without a second thought he lowered himself into the well stepping down, holding on to the protruding roots and overhanging branches, until he touched water. An exposed trunk root of the tree served a comfortable perch, and he sat on it stretching out his legs.

Below the water was bluish-green but placid with lots of dry leaves floating over it. A darkness spread a pall of gloom with the sun never peeping into the depth. The measured chirps of the little birds that had made the well their home, occasionally broke the spooky silence. Night came and time stood still. A tiny squirrel that had popped up its head from a dead stump sat watching its strange neighbour, amused. Meenan too sat still observing the little one. The squirrel reached his foot and began to nibble his toe with no inhibition. Meenan kept his foot taut, a confidence building measure that encouraged the squirrel to advance further, eventually they became friends.

His attention was distracted by the sound of dry earth falling into the water; he saw a snake slithering along the trunk root that he sat on, crawling over his shanks, perhaps taking him for a statue. Its head entered a hole, leaving behind almost half its body. The snake had frightened him but he stayed quiet least he provoke the reptile into an attack.

It was past midnight; he was hungry but the prospect of a meal seemed bleak. Slowly he climbed up the well. He stood in a palm grove with young trees producing nuts, and a few yielding toddy. He clambered up a tree with bunches of nuts, with a couple of earthen pots placed inverted over the shoots of inflorescence. He carefully lifted up a pot, almost half filled with sweet, tender toddy; he inhaled the sweet aroma of the liquid which he found irresistible. He brought the pot to his lips, took a sip and a long draught. The liquid rolled down sweetening his mouth and lifting his spirits.

The liquor had gone to his head and stray thoughts began to rush in to his mind. A feeling of floating in the air keyed him up. Suddenly he remembered his wife wanting to share a secret with him; when he insisted she shied away. He could guess what the good news could be.

"Will you bring me some sugar candy in the evening?" She asked him

He knew when a young wife craved for this. He returned home.

The sight of his hut consoled him; he believed his women would have cried themselves to sleep not knowing his whereabouts. He wanted to spring a surprise on them.

The hut was still, merged with darkness but the silence was daunting. He waited hoping they would to wake up. He peeped inside to see whether they were sleeping but the sight of the pots and pans lying broken on the hearth shocked him. He imagined his wives might have been maimed, burnt or killed as had always been the upper castes' method of chastising the under dogs. He feared that some one might be lying in wait for him behind the hedges.

"The palm too is cruel."

He heard the faint sound of snoring from inside; he moved closer peeping inside. What he saw stunned him. A policeman, slovenly dressed in his uniform, lay sleeping on the floor, he was certainly expecting the fugitive to return.

"I will kill him." Meenan resolved in agonized frenzy.

He looked around for a weapon and found nothing a honing stone. As he slowly he raised it up to his chest, he put one step forward, he felt a strong hand pressing his shoulder down. Meenan panicked and looked back still holding the stone aloft. It was Ettanu.

He dropped the stone and as they stood embracing each other.

"No talk; follow me." Ettanu walked out signalling him to follow.

Ettanu told him to enter the canoe and lie down at the bottom; an old threashing mat was thrown over him, covering his head to toe. A few blocks placed over the mat ensured it was not blown off.

"No talk until I lift off the mat." Ettanu warned him. He rowed the canoe silently, occasionally casting a furtive look in around.

"Stop. Who is there?" The constable, woken up by the disturbance at the river side had reached the landing shouting:

"Shore the canoe and show me what the cargo is." He demanded with his lathi raised over his head.

Ettanu was caught unaware; he sat at the stern keeping the paddle idle over the water, groping for an answer that would satisfy the constable.

"My Lord, please don't insist on my shoring the canoe before you. I am carrying the body of a man who died of small pox" a blatant lie but he risked it.

Ettanu knew that the very name small pox was awful and frightening. He paused for a moment, pretending that he was taking the body for him to verify. The man in the uniform looked nervous.

"*Maari Amma,* small pox?"

"Lord, shall I bring it to you?" Ettanu insisted,

"No…no, rascal, you get lost immediately." The constable withdrew cursing both the dead and the undertaker, invoking the names of all the gods.

They believed that small pox was the presence of the naked goddess *Maari Amma* in another person; she pervaded the humans who chanced to see her bare; running away from the victim, dead or alive, was the sole remedy to escape from her embrace.

"Meenan killed Ravunni." Konna Kaimal declared. He was the Grand Sire of the renowned Mankott *Tharawad* with extensive landholdings enjoying unrestrained authority over the *Pulayas*, the farm labourers; they worked their land and raised the crops for them.

Ravunni was Konna Kaimal's bastard and *Sambandhakaran* to his niece. Under the Matriarchal system the estate belonged to the females of the family but was administered by the eldest brother. Connubial ties remained restricted between cousins, brother's son rightfully securing the hands of sister's daughter. The bond was confirmed when the man handed over to the woman a *Pudava,* a length of cloth to clothe the woman. Ravunni had given *Pudava* to Nangeli but the woman loathed the man shunning him. Frustrated, Ravunni developed a relationship with another young woman, no less attractive; with her he had begotten three kids and the relationship continued with no questions asked. But the illicit liaison hurt one man, Kocharayan, the mahout of the family; he had given *Pudava* to the woman. It was no secret that Kocharayan waited for a chance to regain his woman; he was willing to go to any extent to gain this end. Naturally Konna Kaimal was unhappy at the tardy progress of the police investigation.

"None be spared." Konna Kaimal thundered in rage, as Sub Inspector Ramdurai explained why the police couldn't apprehend Meenan. Head Constable Keshu Nair and Constable Kuttan Pillai avowed their Chief's explanation. Kocharayan, who acted as a private eye in the investigation, ventured no opinion.

"The police will catch him, no matter where he hides but we have no witness to prove that he committed the crime." Ramdurai tried to convince the *Karanavar*.

"Kocharayan is a key witness to prove the crime." Konna Kaimal assured, looking into the eyes of the Sub Inspector. He was not impressed.

"He is not enough; a good lawyer can easily negate him."

"Who else do you want?" Konna Kaimal was impatient.

"It's not whom we want; we need one whose evidence the court will rely upon, don't you know that? " The Sub-Inspector coolly asked.

"Who could be that person?" The *Karanavar* demanded of the police.

"There is one person, rather there are two." Kocharayan intervened.

The policemen and the *Karanavar* turned towards him, pinning their hopes on him; his revelation brightened Konna Kaimal's otherwise drab face.

"Who are they? Come on, bring them." Konna Kaimal jumped up in excitement.

"It's Parvathi and her son Veeran; both were present at the scene."

"True…true." The Sub-Inspector exclaimed,

"Kocharayan, you are really intelligent."

Konna Kaimal also knew there was no better witness than Parvathi; but getting her on his side bothered him. He reasoned that the murder of Ravunni was a blow to her and it was her need too to get the murderer punished.

"I'll speak to Parvathi to see that she testifies." Konna assured the police as they took leave of him.

Konna was determined to get Meenan stringent punishment, for he firmly believed that Meenan had killed Ravunni though he could not attribute any mot, and the *Pulayas* respected him too.

"Why should a Pulaya youth kill a man who was sympathetic to him?" He could not find an answer to the question, and he left the matter at that. But he had other reasons, equally strong, to be vindictive.

He found Meenan a rebel, questioning traditional rules and values, unwilling to pay obeisance's to the caste lords. He seemed to have been impressed by the pernicious missionary ideas that all were equals being the children of the same God, and untouchability was a sin against humanity. Konna Kaimal was troubled that the younger generation of the *Pulayas* were stealthily rallying behind him. In fact he had warned Ravunni to throw him out. The *Karanavar* had other charges too against the Pulaya youth.

A scion of the family, Gopikrishnan, whom the *Karanavar* had sent to Madras for higher studies, had returned with an Irish wife. Bumping off Gopikrishnan's wife was the *Karanavar's* decision to protect the honour of the *Tharawad*. Kocharayan was deputed to execute the order. Meenan's intervention to frustrate the act was sheer arrogance. In the process he had broken the right arm of the mahout. Konna had reports that Meenan had his wives going around covering their breasts violating the prohibition on Pulaya women. He thought the Pulaya youth had become a liability, his actions fomenting discontent among the *Pulayas* on whose sweat and toil thrived the great *Tharawads*.

"He should be reigned in."

"One murder and another murderous attack; it calls for stern action."

"Parvathi may not testify before the police; she said she would speak the truth. I think her truth may not be what the police want to hear." One evening Kocharayan briefed the *Karanavar*.

"How do you know?"

"I spoke to her."

"You, ass! you have spoiled the game. Are you so much enamoured of Parvathi?" Konna Kaimal was annoyed when Kocharayan reported the failure of his self appointed mission. He feared that she wouldn't come to give evidence before the police. But she did come, accompanied by her children who looked puzzled and scared at the sight of the big house and the still bigger men who strutted across.

The sight of the woman ravished Head Constable Keshu Nair, who had come to record her evidence. Kocharayan stood in the courtyard, hoping to see a thaw in her face while Konna Kaimal tried to be unusually warm with her. A bevy of women who had collected inside the hall stood staring at the rare visitors. Konna Kaimal tried to be informal to relax her.

"You are visiting the *Tharawad* after a long time." Konna Kaimal observed as if making a genuine complaint. She paid no attention, stood composed, wiping off the tears that wetted her cheeks. She remembered that the sprawling compound was once a calf-ground where the blissful siblings of the *Tharawad* gambolled around. She was one among them, always a prima Donna, though junior.

"Parvathi, forget what happened between us; you are my niece." Konna Kaimal said in an effort to mollify the alienated niece. She stood quiet, declining to be drawn into the niceties. He had learnt for once that cajolery was more effective a weapon than threats.

"Uncle, you haven't told me why you have called me." Parvathi felt uncomfortable, in an apparent, hurry to depart.

"We shall have lunch together before you return home. Today is your aunt's birthday; we have *Payasam* for lunch." Konna was still unsure on how to tackle the woman who was at odds with him. Parvathi ignored his suggestion.

"You have not yet answered my question." She reminded him frankly; her blunt manners displeased him.

"Haven't you heard from Kocharayan?" Konna Kaimal too was getting worked up, and his voice quivered as he spoke with displeasure.

"I don't go by what he says; you may please tell me what it is." Obviously, Parvathi wanted to hear straight from the horse's mouth; and he spoke.

"The criminal who stabbed Ravunni to death should be punished." Konna declared vehemently, staring into her eyes. The stoic expression on her face angered him.

"Didn't you see Meenan stabbing Ravunni?" He bellowed in disgust

"No. I didn't." Parvathi remained unprovoked.

"You didn't?" He almost shouted; he was getting worked up.

"No?" the policeman, Keshu Nair sprang up on his feet, walked towards Parvathi in style and asked. "Do you know that he was stabbed to death?"

"Yes.... I was told." She began to sob, as she could no longer stand their questioning.

"Calm down. We want to help you and punish the culprit." Keshu Nair tried to reassure her. Parvathi wiped her face with the corner of her *mundu*; she remained still, her right hand resting on her son's head.

"Tell me.... Who told you that he had been stabbed?"

Parvathi appeared undecided, wavering and unwilling to look into his eyes. The Head Constable concluded that she was evading his question. He moved closer, his eyes feasting on her unencumbered breasts and seductive face. He whispered,into her ears.

"You are trying to hide the truth; give a straight answer or else we know how to extract the truth from you, it may hurt you a little." The crabbed expression on the constable's face was intimidating.

Parvathi drew back, shielding the little kids under her arms. He repeated.

"You haven't answered my question. Who told you that Ravunni had been killed?" he demanded, tapping his palm with the baton as a less obtrusive act of coercion to convey that the police meant business.

"I have nothing to hide. It's my son who told me; you may ask him." She nudged Veeran forward in case they decided to question him. What she had said stunned them into silence.

"Veera sonny, come tell me; did you see some one stabbing your Achan?" Konna Kaimal asked the boy pretending to be solicitous. Veeran stood confused and hesitating, looking at his mother and the men around him. Parvathi encouraged him to speak out.

"Yes, I saw."

"Good boy." Keshu Nair complimented the boy with a wink at his mother. Kocharayan, who stood behind the policeman slowly went out unnoticed towards the ghat.

"Who did it?"

Veeran again looked into the face of his mother and the policeman who stood beside him.

"That man who goes there." He raised his hand, pointing his index finger at Kocharayan who had disappeared down the ghat. Keshu Nair was angry. He shouted at the boy shaking his head.

"You are lying. Who told you to tell a lie?"

"No one; I saw it with my own eyes." Veeran asserted as he drew back, hiding his face in the safety of his mother's *mundu*. "Some one might have tutored the boy, very cunning." Keshu Nair observed adding: "Let them go. You have to come to the station whenever we call you."

Konna Kaimal looked at the policeman enquiringly, as Parvathi trooped out of the room leading her kids.

"No criminal goes unpunished for want of an eye witness; circumstantial evidence is good enough." Keshu explained.

"I know that much." Konna Kaimal, a former policeman himself, was irritated. Keshu missed the ugly sneer on Konna's face as he dismissed his explanation.

The police came up with a proposal to launch a hunt for Meenan. They needed Konna's support in providing them with a boat with an awning and two punters.

"Ravunni's boat is free." Kocharayan had informed them in advance.

Konna Kaimal summoned the mahout and advised him to hire two punters, not *Pulayas*, either Christians or Ezhawas, by the evening; he told him to ensure that the mission remained secret.

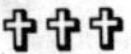

Twenty

The policemen arrived at Mankott, three in mufti and two, the Sub-Inspector and a constable, in uniform. The men in mufti wore only loincloth with liberal of oil on their body to make it slippery in case they had to wrestle with the *Pulayas*; at least a few of them were known to be big built.

"Be careful; they are beef eaters and hefty." Kocharayan had warned the police.

The uniform had always been an instrument of intimidation. The police theorized that Meenan would not have gone very far off as he had two young wives, one pregnant; the women were known not to be on good terms with their parents, depriving them of the usual parental support. However, it was certain that his community would harbour him.

"Chathan and Chamari would have been of much help but you have foolishly rendered them dead," the Sub-Inspector observed as he entered the vallom; he sat under the awning on a wooden seat specially erected for its former owner, Ravunni, whose murderer they were out to apprehend.

"Ravunni was lucky but unfortunate too," Ramdurai thought as he sat on the howdah like seat under the canopy that very few could aspire to enjoy.

Their first port of call was Ettanu, whose protégé Meenan was. H0is attempt to smuggle him out had come to the notice of the police.

The Sub-Inspector stayed back, sending a uniformed man. Pakkothi was sitting in the courtyard weaving a basket with her daughter helping her. Seeing the strangers she sprang to her feet and ran into the hovel, with her daughter following.

"Where is your man?" the Constable shouted. The terrified woman could not utter a word; as she stood stupefied the policeman yelled at her, annoyed. "Haven't you heard? Where is Ettanu?"

"He hasn't returned." She sounded feeble and choked in her throat, frightened.

"It's late night; where does he go in the night?"

"He doesn't go anywhere."

"Then where is he?"

"He hasn't come back."

"I want to search your hut."

Pakkothi came out of the hut as the constable rushed in, swinging the baton. A couple of her children who were inside the hut ran out as they saw the policeman. He broke with his baton an earthen pot found in a corner, covered with an old mat, spilling the grain they had saved from their wages, some thing for a rainy day.

"Where is your eldest son? What is his name? Oh, Athai?"

"He has gone fishing."

The Constable, Kuttan Pillai, asked her the last question.

"Where is Meenan? Do you know that he has killed Ravunni?"

"No. I don't know where he is; must be in his hut."

"Oh! Well said. Ask your husband to come to the station tomorrow. If he doesn't I will return." Kuttan Pillai walked back and reported to the boss.

"Let us go to the other chap, Chathan; he is Meenan's father-in-law."

They saw him lying flat on the floor with his wife sitting silently by his side, massaging his neck. . He struggled to lift his face up when he heard footsteps; his wife pressed his head down as lifting the head strained the wound on his back. A sudden, sharp, piercing pain made him flinch.

"*Aaraa*?" He enquired, keeping his face down but turning his eyes towards the visitors. Chitha raised the kerosene lamp to catch a glimpse of the unusual night callers.

"*Ammo*...police." She uttered a cry, as she sprang to her feet, instantly dropping the lamp and spilling the oil on the mat, which unnoticed caught fire, as she stood gaping at the men. Chathan lay with his eyes closed, unwilling to face the man in uniform.

The kerosene spattered mat flamed up instantly, scorching Chathan's skin, forcing him. Chitha swatted out the flame with her hands and crumpled the mat scorching her hands. The wound opened up letting out blood.

"Why have you come, to kill me?" Better, you kill me; I can't suffer any longer."

Frustrated, Chathan rattled.

Kuttan Pillai stole a close look at the man. The broken flesh, twelve whip blows one after another across his back, had festered from his buttock to shoulders. A putrid smell fouled the air. Chitha stood dazed.

Kuttan Pillai made a quick round of the hut to see anyone hiding, but returned empty handed. When he turned Kocharayan came looking for them. His presence frightened Chathan, who conjured up a vision of being burnt to death by the mahout. Both Chathan and his wife refused to look at him; they remained silent resigned to their fate. In an unusually generous gesture, Kocharayan moved closer to Chathan, braving the nauseating stink and forcing a compassionate grin on his face. For, he knew that Chathan would be useful in the coming days even as a witness against Meenan.

"Chathaa, are you angry with me?"

He refused to answer him; he lay sobbing with his eyes closed.

"Are you listening?" Chathan's silence dampened Kocharayan's zeal; he used another ploy.

"I have arranged two measures of paddy for you; send some one to collect it." The mahout suddenly turned generous and concerned, but Chathan refused to bite the bait. The mahout walked out without another word. As he walked out Chathan hailed him:

"*Thampra... Aanakaran Thampra.*" To address a high caste man by his occupational name was offensive. Yet Kocharayan tolerated it and looked back, retracing his steps.

"Even my dog won't come to collect your two measures." A stunned Kocharayan quietly followed the Constable who had gone ahead of him.

"We shall search all the *Pulaya* dwellings tonight; look into all the boats that pass by." Ramdurai didn't want to miss any chance.

"We shall go to Kandan's hut next." Keshu Nair asked Kocharayan to give the punters direction to Kandan's place.

"What's that big flame there? There are a good many men around. Let us close in on them." The Sub-Inspector noticed leaping flames ahead with men moving around busily. He came out of the awning and stood screwing his eyes to catch a clear view of the site.

"That is where Kandan lives." Kocharayan confirmed.

"Half of you land by a dark corner of the compound and wait there; the remaining will land on the opposite side. Both the parties shall sweep down on the crowd as I whistle you into action," the Sub-Inspector instructed them. He suspected that those men were engaged in clandestine activities. The first batch with Constable Kuttan Pillai landed on the eastern side of the compound and waited for the whistle. The boat moved forward with the rest. Kocharayan accompanied the Sub-Inspector's team. Ramdurai sent out Keshu Nair on a reconnaissance mission to ascertain what the men were up to and whether Meenan was with them. If he was among them the Officer wanted to target him personally. Kocharayan went with the Head Constable to identify the men, particularly Meenan.

Keshu Nair didn't encounter any problem; he went go near the fire and counted nine men in the group. Meenan was not among them. The report shattered the Sub-Inspector's hopes of catching the absconder.

"What are they doing there?" He demanded.

"We couldn't see; the men stood in a row hindering our view.

"*Widdikal.*" He cursed himself for his fate in leading a band of idiots.

The Sub-Inspector blew his whistle signalling his men to fan out. They ran towards the site, instantly. Ramdurai kept pace with them while the mahout followed him unhurriedly.

The whistle of the police went almost unheard by the men who were busy with the task at hand. One man heard the strange sound across the night sky.

"It's the squawk of a hawk for its missing mate."

"It might have smelt flesh; be watchful, it might swoop down on." Athai warned them, unaware that the police stood ready to swoop down on them.

Covetously enthusiastic, the men engaged themselves in chopping and cutting the carcass of a heifer they had killed. Pakkan, an expert butcher and Ettanu, together skinned the animal; it was left to Pakkan, who wielded the cleaver to cut and chop the beef into equal shares for nine of them. The entrails were given to the butcher free as wage for his labour, in addition to one share. The head was for Ettanu who had secured the carcass from its owner. He was also responsible for selling the hide for a good price and hand over the money to the owner, who refused to handle the business in public, the act being considered repugnant to his caste status.

The *Pulayas* were excited, their joy unbounded. For, each one's share was a substantial quantity that would last them for days. Ettanu thought he would send a cooked portion to Chathan, even though they were not on good terms; of course, with a warning to Chitha to not disclose who had sent it.

Athai collected two shares of the meat in the small basket he wove out of a frond-end; for himself and his father.. The rest of the men looked around for plantain leaves or palm fronds to wrap up their shares. Pakkan was busy cleaning the entrails.

"Stop. None shall move." The Sub-Inspector roared, blowing a whistle, springing a surprise on the men. Petrified with fear, they stood dazed for a moment, as the policemen converged on them. They ran helter skelter fearing reprisal at the hands of the police. They left behind

Pakkan who was busy with the entrails, and Ettanu who never thought he had violated any law.

Six of them escaped, jumping into the river; which they believed would protect them and she did. Athai could have escaped into the river, but for his father's sake he stayed behind, hiding himself atop a palm watching the goings on.

Keshu Nair caught hold of the two easily as they made no attempt to escape. Kuttan Pillai and the bare bodied men covered them, promptly. The Officer felt nauseated at the sight of Pakkan with splotches of blood all over his body.

"Put down the cleaver, immediately." The Sub-Inspector ordered Pakkan, hitting him on his head with the baton. He dropped the cleaver down, gnashing his teeth silently to assuage the pain.

"You have slaughtered a heifer; the cow is our mother and killing her is a sin and a crime. And, you have stolen the animal, haven't you?" Ramdurai stared into the eyes of the men, swinging the baton in his hand. He directed one of the Constables to tie their hands behind their back.

"Haven't you heard what I asked you? Where did you steal this animal from?" he demanded.

Ettanu looked at Pakkan. Though he knew the truth, he feared that the police wouldn't accept his truth.

"Why do you look at him? Did he steal the cow? I have other business; hurry up."

"No, he didn't." Ettanu mumbled, his original courage washed-out

"Then who did ? Did You?" He jabbed the baton under Ettanu's chin forcing it up, bellowing: "You, look here, at me, at me."

As he repeated his words he pushed the baton, thrusting at his prominent adam's apple.

Ettanu ssaid,

"No. Sir, he didn't."

"Then who? Did you?"

"No Sir, neither did I."

"It's astonishing. Did the heifer come to you and commit suicide?"

"Tell me, yes or no." Ettanu's silence enraged the Officer.

"No, Sir."

"You are lying." Ramdurai, who stood in front of Ettanu, pushed the Constables aside, and kicked the man on his right cheek with his foot; it left him with a thick livid scar on his cheek. That was his notorious way of whacking the untouchables, whom he refused to touch with his hands. Ettanu tasted blood in his mouth, and as he spat, he lost his first molar in sixty-one years.

"As my tongue was polite my teeth remained unbroken." Ettanu remembered his having said a thousand times when people complimented him for his good row of teeth, though tobacco stained.

"Keshu Nair, take them to the station for questioning."

The Sub-Inspector suddenly remembered that he hadn't come to recover a lost heifer. He was out to arrest Meenan, who was absconding. He turned back to Ettanu.

"Hey… you… tell me where is Meenan? Tell me soon, if you don't want me to break your bones," he warned him, and then he suddenly remembered what Kuttan Pillai had reported a few days ago. He asked Ettanu.

"Did you carry in your canoe the body of a man who had died of small-pox?"

"Yes Sir."

"Was it the body of Meenan?"

"No, the dead body was not of Meenan."

"Is it true, Kuttan Pillai?" The Sub-Inspector verified from the Constable who was on the night watch, and he affirmed that it was not, though he had not checked the boat to ascertain whose body it was.

The search continued long after mid night; the boat carrying the police party criss-crossed the river and the side canals, detaining cargo boats that sailed down the river, and awned *valloms* carrying passengers

Last, they entered Chappan's hut at the extreme end of the land stretch beyond which it lay the green expanse of the paddy fields. As they shored the boat an old dog began to howl in protest but it retreated quickly as the police stormed in with their batons. The dog bit Kuttan Pillai on his calf. Keshu Nair, who walked behind, hit the dog on its leg with his baton, sending it limping on three legs. The mournful howl of the dog evoked no sympathy.

They surrounded the house, yelling for Chappan to come out but the faithful dog, though crippled, reappeared at the door to defend the house. An enraged Kuttan Pillai picked up a pestle, found lying on the courtyard, and hit the dog on its head. The dog died instantly, splashing the mud wall with blood. Kuttan Pillai entered the house.

"Nobody inside Sir," he reported to the dismay of the Sub Inspector who had expected a catch. For, beyond this there was no place for a runaway to hide himself. They decided to call off the search. Ramdurai occupied the royal seat, and the rest found place on the thwarts and edges of the boat. Ettanu and Pakkan lay dumped in the hold with their arms tied together. The Sub-Inspector was in a dilemma; he had not arrested anyone as he had hoped to find Meenan in one of the huts. However, he had a strong feeling that at least a few of them knew where Meenan was hiding. He kept the matter for the next day and turned to Ettanu.

"You don't want to tell me whose cow you had stolen, eh?"

"Sir, we haven't stolen the heifer nor did we slaughter it; it was sold to us by the lord of Elaymadhom. The calf ate tapioca leaves and died." Ettanu told the Officer, pleading;

"Sir, please let us go; I am the *Thalapulayan* of Mankott *Tharawad*."

"I don't care what you are and where you are from; you have caused me enough trouble for the night." He abruptly dismissed them.

Ettanu and Pakkan could not be lodged in the lock-up room, where a criminal caste occupant, would be polluted by the presence of untouchables. "Keep them chained to the palm in the courtyard." He instructed the constable on duty before he left for home. The Constable locked them two legs, one of each, together and let them crawl in the courtyard. The chain was not long enough to go around the palm tree. That was how they always treated the *Pulayas*.

✞✞✞

Twenty One

"Meenachaa....Kalloo."

They stood still, looking deeply into each other's eyes. The feeble quiver of a life in Kallu's womb had them wonderstruck.

"Meenacha, when will you come to see our baby?" Finally, she asked him pressing her face into his breast.

"There is time, I'll come soon; you know I am innocent." He tried to comfort her, passing his hand over her hair tousled by the evening breeze. The sun had already sunk behind the long line of palms that loomed on the western horizon; the night had just arrived; they remained merged in its grey ambience. *Uma Thamprati* was soon to return home; she expected Meenan to travel with them as their punter.

Taking advantage of the night's darkness, a quaint looking fisherman's canoe rowed by two men berthed beside a cluster of screw pines; the men in the boat waited as Meenan stepped into the water, followed by Kallu close behind. They exchanged few words; each knew what the mission was. Meenan held Kallu's arm and helped her wade the shallow water to board the canoe.

The boatman signalled her to lie on the floor of the canoe, as they threw a roll of fishnet over her. A powerful dip of the oar into the water sent the canoe a darting across the water. In no time the canoe disappeared from the eyes of Meenan.

Once again he found himself alone. He had enough to eat and plenty of time to sleep but he could neither eat nor sleep. Loneliness and fear tormented him; he spent his days dreaming of the pleasant time he had had with his family.

"Will I ever return to them?"

That was the question he had been asking every night as he sat leaning against a palm trunk awaiting sleep. He had news that Athai's marriage was after the harvest when the baskets of the *Pulayas* got their annual fillings. He was marrying a Christian girl, though *Pulaya.* He thought it augured a change for good; he vowed he would be with them. Marriages had always been occasions for great feasts.

He was determined; "I'll give them a surprise."

The night was long and the darkness was blinding; he knew the fishermen had a long tract to row up and Kallu had a lengthy journey. Kallu slowly slipped into a slumber despite the damp fishnet she was covered with.

The boat reached its destination and Kallu let out a wail of anguish as she lifted her head. She stepped out of the canoe and stood hidden behind a bamboo thicket; she feared some one might pounce on her. The night was cool and quiet with no sign of daybreak in the east. The men shoved the canoe away and quickly disappeared beyond the fisherman's cove.

She walked some distance cautiously searching for her hut but could not locate it. Stealthily, she trudged the beaten mud path that stopped in front of the courtyard where the hut once stood. To her horror she realized that her hut was no longer there.

Kallu panicked, as she stumbled upon the wreckage of the hut that lay strewn on the floor. She groped in darkness, lifting broken thatches and and palm-fronds, fearing her mother and Manka might be trapped in the debris. Finding no sign of life, she sat alarmed, awaiting day break to resume the search.

At dawn Manka came running, her face exposed the fear and anxiety that overawed her. Manka appeared tense while Kallu looked nervous.

"Where were you; where were you?" Both asked, looking into each other's eyes, eventually clasping each other into an embrace. They had a lot to talk about but remained confused. Tears streamed down their cheeks.

"Manka, what happened? Where is Mamma?"

"Chithamma is safe; she's just coming. She is scared to walk in the twilight." Manka assured her, adding:

"She is very sad, talks seldom. Even her eyes are dry with no more tears to shed." Kallu sighed deeply, pained at the plight of her mother and the sight of their wrecked homestead.

"What happened to our hut?" Walking around the roof that had crashed on to the floor, Kallu noticed that an attempt was made to set the hut ablaze.

"Fire was more merciful; it refused to catch on."

"Nobody knows who did it. One night when we returned to sleep we found the hut razed to the ground." Manka looked at her helplessly.

"The *Aanakkaran Thampran* came to the hut a few times with a policeman. Some one said they came looking for Meenan, not finding him, they pulled down the hut."

"Ettanucha came with Athai and took us home where we have been sleeping. Every morning and evening we came here looking for you; we had a very hard time with no news from you." Manka sounded unhappy.

Meenan's women had no idea where he had gone to escape the police dragnet; though Ettanu knew he refused to divulge it. It was on the evening after Athai's marriage with Maria was fixed and Kallu was about to return home after some work at Emmanuel's house; she tarried behind with a woebegone look that caught Rosma's attention.

"Kallu, I know you have enough reason to be sad but I know some thing torments you; what is it?" Rosma felt sorry for the young pregnant wife.

"Rosma, please help me. Yesterday I had a dream that the police had broken his head; he is lying in a pool of blood in a ditch. I want to save him. Will you please help me? Please tell me where he is."

Kallu's request disconcerted Rosma, she stood in the veranda looking into Kallu's face, but slowly withdrew into her room debating how to handle the situation. She knew for certain where Meenan was but feared that any indiscretion on her part could endanger his safety. Her husband had offered to help Meenan, as he was certain the *Pulaya* youth was innocent. He sent him hiding to gain time so that he could seek bail from a court.

"If Kallu visits him, the news will gradually spread alerting the police. I won't do it." Rosma concluded, and told Kallu firmly.

"Kallu, I'll find out whether what you had dreamt is true or not. If it's true we'll go together; now you need not worry about him." Rosma believed it was better to tell the truth rather than telling a lie, and added:

"I understand your anxiety as a young wife, carrying a baby but his safety is more important. Don't you think so?"

Kallu agreed. But Rosma's balanced thinking failed to brighten her ashen face. A few drops of tears rushed down her cheeks; she quickly wiped them off with the back of her hand making an attempt to regain composure.

"Kallu, would you like to have some thing to eat?" Kallu never said 'yes' but her being quiet always meant 'yes.'

"You eat one and take the rest home." Rosma gave her three sweet 'jackfruit *ada*'. She went indoors to get the dinner ready. Kallu lingered around, undecided; finally she sat by the corner of the veranda wondering whether she should make one last. Her passion for being with her husband was so strong that no amount of reason would dim her urge; the realisation that she was helpless frustrated her.

"Perhaps, I am born to cry; if so I have to face it." She tried to console herself and decided to face it. She broke a piece from the *ada* and ate it; she was hungry and it was tasty.

Uncertain and undecided she continued to sit in the corner of the veranda. The night had advanced and the pall of darkness it cast on the face of the earth was daunting. She waited patiently for Rosma to return after her chores. Fatigued by anxiety and fear she slept.

Words between Rosma and her husband coming from their bedroom startled Kallu. She heard Rosma taking Meenan's name.

"Meenan is safe in your father's farm house; why should she worry about him? I had news this afternoon." Emmanuel explained to his wife, adding:

"Tell her that dreams are unreal products of a disturbed mind."

What she heard soothed her mind; as she had learnt where he was; she thought she could secretly visit him soon.

In the night as they lay side by side, sharing the same mat, without the man who had his permanent place in between, Kallu whispered in the ears of Manka: "Manka, I know where Meenan is hiding. Shall I go and meet him?"

Manka was unsure whether it was the right step, fearing the risk involved.

"It's a far away place, very hazardous to journey; if you are caught his life will be in danger and ours too." Manka cautioned her.

Kallu waited for the dusk to set out on her journey. Travelling by boat was unthinkable, as it would expose her, a stranger to public view inviting inevitable questions. Walking across the dykes and bunds of paddy fields posed still formidable problems. A lonely young woman, black yet comely, trudging wearily was invariably a prey in the eyes of hungry men.

She deliberately shunned riverside pathways to skip manned ferries to avoid being detained or questioned. She called off the walk at day break when men began to come out. Wayside thickets or abandoned farm sheds offered her shelter during the day. She had no meal to eat except the three jackfruit *adas.* She ate one in the morning and kept the rest aside for Meenan. The meandering water courses and deceptive mud bunds skirting extensive paddy farms often frustrated her; she found herself stranded at a cross junction where a mud path ended at a ferry with a light house.

"It's Palachode; oh God, it's where Chamari lives." She exclaimed, panic sweeping over her, she took a left turn to avoid the ferry.

Cutting across the slushy paddy land, she walked, finally reaching a woody compound, with no sign of life. She still had two loaves of *ada* and she broke off a piece from one and chewed it leisurely.

"One more night to go and by midnight next I'll be with him." She mused as she lay on the sand mound, stretching her legs. She recognised the compound where she had lived with Konni.

The man was dead but she refused to stay there any longer. She wanted to undress and swim across the canal. Stripping off posed no problem for she was scantly clothed. Slowly, she lowered herself into the canal; the water was cool and clear, flowing silently.

Her palms rested on her bulging lower abdomen to feel the life that pulsated inside.

Her progress on the road was slow; for, the stretch was hazardous and wearisome. The bund had frequent wide and deep breaches that she forded, one by one, with rare determination and patience.

Long before daybreak she found herself standing deep in the cool waters of Meenachill where it gently entered the lake Vembanad. Kallu stood watching the early breeze stirring a chain of waves.

"It's now or never." She thought; she knew that the last quarter of the night would usher in a flurry of activities, fishermen and shell miners with their boats and nets crowding the lake making her attempt futile.

Kallu dived spreading her legs and arms kicking vigorously forward, tearing apart the glassy sheet of water.

She tarried for a moment, keeping herself afloat by flippering with her arms and legs alternately letting the limbs loosen up.

"Will I reach the shore? Suddenly she realized she had lost her loin cloth and the sweet *ada*s that she had saved for Meenan.

✞✞✞

Twenty Two

Jayanthan was in mourning; he spent his time indoors refusing to meet any visitor. Eachara Warrier, his steward, sat on the edge of the veranda, with his left leg resting over the right, eyes closed. Occasionally, he swapped his palm across his face to chase away a housefly that persistently hovered there.

Rev Aaron Griffith walked into the courtyard unnoticed by the steward.

"Good morning Mr Warrier." Failing to locate Jayanthan, Rev Griffith decided to wake up the steward.

"I don't think the *Thirumeni* will receive you. Don't you know that he is in mourning?" "His wife passed away about ten days ago; don't you know?"

"Did she, really? It's news to me."

"Yes, she is no more. So you may come another day."

"But that's exactly the reason why I want to see him," he insisted.

Eacharaa, who is there?" Jayanthan heard him talking to some one. He walked up to the porch, looking for the visitor.

"Oh reverend, you have come. I am glad; at least I can unburden my mind. You know I lost my wife." He struggled to speak.

"I can't believe that your wife is dead." He stared into his friend's wet eyes.

"You don't believe? You can see the mound of earth, still fresh in the burial ground."

Jayanthan thought the Priest regretted his inability to attend the burial.

"The burial was, strictly a private affair, late in the night with minimum rituals under compulsive circumstances." Jayanthan sounded apologetic.

"The condition of the body was ghastly, pocks eating up the flesh."

"You didn't see the dead body, I suppose?" The Priest posed a simple question.

"None of us attended the burial, custom doesn't allow us to; it was all managed by the servants. Poor things they had a very hard time." He explained, struggling to suppress his angst.

"You know how nauseating it is to handle a rotting body, that too of a smallpox victim." He sympathized with the servants who, he believed, had really helped to bury his dead wife.

Rev Aaron Griffith was away in Kochi for almost a month; on his return he resumed his regular walk of the country side accompanied by Kuriacko. His walk took a long time since it was the first after a long break; he had to stop and talk with many, unmindful of the fact that night was approaching.

"We should hurry back; the sky is getting overcast." Kuriacko reminded him.

"We should have called on Jayanthan… his wife is sick I heard."

"Father… I am afraid… she has smallpox, rather virulent." Kuriacko cautioned; he was as afraid as any body of small pox.

"All the more the reason why we should visit him," the Priest insisted. His companion was unhappy but walked behind him silently .

It began to rain. They looked for shelter and took cover under the nearest gnarled Pipal. The rain battered the earth and the tree could no longer provide them refuge to hide their heads. "Father, perhaps, you could borrow an umbrella from Jayanthan *Thirumeni*; we are at the back of his compound." Kuriacko expected no respite from the rain.

"Why don't we walk in? We shall look up the patient as well; you come, we'll go." Rev Griffith walked into the rain, pulling his cowl over his bald pate. Kuriacko preferred a detour.

"Kuriacko, where do we go? The path seems to end here." They had reached the end of the compound where the path merged with a wooded strip of thickly hanging vines and boughs that shrouded a building with no sign of life.

"I am sorry; I have missed the route,"

"Come on, let us return home."

As he turned back Kuriacko moved closer to him and whispered into his ears.

"Father, I think it's a devils' hide out. I saw two of them…there." He pointed his finger towards the house. Kuriacko made a sign of the Cross and stayed behind the Priest.

"I am here; you go and find what they are up to." Rev Griffith thought either it must be his weird imagination or some night prowlers caught in the rain. Kuriacko put a few steps forward cautiously but turned his face back, hesitating. Rev Griffith signalled him to go, showing him a crucifix that he held high in his hand. It strengthened Kuriacko's will to move forward. What Kuriacko narrated on his return was shocking.

He had recognized the men, Kolappan and Changu, cousins, descendents of a former State hangman, wily men, they were undertakers living by knavery. If death was by smallpox they buried the body after mid-night. Their presence confirmed death and Kuriacko concluded that the Namboodiri's wife was the victim; he suspected possible foul play; he decided to listening to their conversation.

"Even in death, she looked ravishing." Kolappan affirmed as he stood handing over a scoopful of *Panam* to his partner, that being half of what they had collected from Jayanthan as their wage.

"Why do you say so? She is not dead, she is still alive." Kolappan overruled him.

"She'll be dead by the time we return, I am sure." He assured.

"If not we may have to employ our hands."

"Why employ hands? Dump her into the pit and throw the wet earth over. I felt sorry when she protested as we wrapped her up in the mat."

As the undertakers entered the room holding a wicker lamp Uma opened her eyes. The swollen eyelids pained her. She wanted to send a message to her husband; she was thirsty and wanted some water. Seeing the strange men, she hesitated and closed her eyes; she asked:

"Will you… will… you please… give me… some… water?" Her tongue was heavy and dragged inside her mouth; her request for water fell on deaf ears. They spread a mat on the floor, lifted her up by her legs and arms from the banana leaves on which she was lying, unmindful of her groans and cries for mercy; they laid her on the mat; she lay writhing in agony with blood oozing from the full-blown pocks, broken afresh by the strain and stretch the skin was subjected to. "She is still kicking and alive; our job is not so easy." In the faint light of the lamp Kolappan surveyed her body that appeared strong despite the long illness.

"The body will not release the soul effortlessly."

"And that's what you are paid for exactly."

The undertakers collected money from the family confirming the victim was dead; if it turned out to be false, the consequences were severe, grimmer than losing the money; it was in their interest to see the victim dead. They understood that they stood to lose a lot of money.

The broad seams of the mat were suddenly drawn over her body; she protested making an unsuccessful attempt with her hands and legs to cast off the mat. They overpowered her. She lay immobilized, only her head remaining free to shake and cry. Quickly, they passed a rope closely around the wrap, binding her into a bundle.

"You wait here; we shall return soon." They rushed out of the house and ran towards the tavern for drinks that would harden their mind. Soon they disappeared into the darkness.

Kuriacko rushed back to the Priest and explained to him what he had seen. Rev Griffith was shattered. It was the first time that he had come face to face with a life and death situation; he debated.

He knew he could easily walk away, unmindful, leaving the woman to her fate, no questions asked. He also knew he could, perhaps, save her or make an honest attempt to save her, God willing. The first option was simple but dishonest; the second was overwhelmingly tough and challenging. He might even be called upon to answer a few unflattering questions; he decided to settle for the latter.

He walked into the hall with Kuriacko following.

In the insipid light of the wicker lamp he saw the woman lying bundled up; the only sign of life being the faint gasp that escaped through her half opened mouth. He asked Kuriacko to throw open the tiny windows to let in fresh air.

He was aghast at the mindless brutality the men had committed on a hapless woman. More heinous was the mindset of a learned man, her husband, who blithely dumped her in a dingy house, into the hands of merciless butchers with no qualms. Rev Griffith was confused and wavering on how to handle the delicate situation; it involved a woman, wife of a well known person, daughter-in-law of a high caste family whose inner rules of conduct were honour.

He thought of waking up Jayanthan in the night to apprise him of the outrageous crime. But he was not sure how he would respond. The woman was on the verge of death and her tormentors were due to arrive soon. Time was running short.

"Kuriacko, cut the rope with your knife; do it quick we have no time." The Priest instructed his assistant.

"Please… don't… kill me; please." She craved for mercy.

"No, not to kill you; this is Father Aaron to help you." Kuriacko assured her. What she heard lifted her spirit up.

"Father… my father… you are late; why have you come now? Why have you abandoned me? she lamented.

"No I have come to take you out, to save you."

"She sees in you her own father." Kuriacko explained.

"Yes, I guess so. I shall treat her as my own daughter." He turned to Kuriacko. "You rush to Emmanuel; take his boat and return. Get one or two men also on your way back. Get Meenan and his wife too."

Rev Griffith squatted by the side of the patient, deftly removed the mat. She lay shivering in pain as he tore off the mat. He noticed her making unsuccessful attempts to wet her parched lips. He found no water in the hall, or a tumbler to fetch water. He tore off a piece from a corner of his scapula, soaked it in rainwater and wetted her lips.

The wicker lamp was slowly dying out and he feared it might go off soon. He saw an earthen fire-pan sitting in a corner of the hall with tinder strewn around; he collected the tinders into the pan and lighted a fire.

Outside, the rain continued after a short respite. In a brief flash of lightening he could see a freshly dug grave by the side of the coppice. Puddles of rainwater overflowed into the grave filling it almost half. Further away everything was quiet in Jayanthan's house.

"Perhaps, they planned to drown her in a watery grave." Rev Aaron Griffith was getting impatient; he felt time was running out and there was no sign of Kuriacko with the boat. He was unsure whether the servant would show the wisdom to bring an awned boat with more men to help out. He fretted, pacing the hall.

It was dark outside and raining too; he heard the guffaw of the two men as they came up to the door.

"It's past midnight; we still have half a night to enjoy…ha…ha…ha."

Rev Griffith stood deeply distressed, not knowing how to deal with them, particularly if they turned violent, which he assumed they would. Grappling with lumpen characters was an absurd situation for the missionary. He waited patiently behind the door that he had closed; it was dark inside. They entered the veranda where they stood groping for the door.

"We had left the door open. Who locked it? Has she done it? Impossible." They argued as they stopped by the door, pushed it, and finding no response began to knock on it.

"Some devil might have gone in to suck her blood, I am sure." Changu asserted as he stood leaning against the door. Rev Griffith had an easy solution before him.

He pulled his dark-brown cowl over his head, covering his face up to his eyes. He lifted the fire pan that had glowing embers and removed the door latch; the door opened felling the man who had stood leaning against it, breaking the arrack bottle and spilling the liquor over the floor. As the man tried to spring up on his feet, the Priest threw the embers in the air. As they fell on the floor, they inflamed the liquor spilled over there. The rapid flash of the flames blinded the men who ran helter-skelter shouting in panic: "ghost…ghost." They had seen a ghost.

Rev Griffith stood in the veranda in the bright light of the flame that still lingered, covered head to toe in his garb, the horrifying vision of his dark, ghostly silhouette looming large in the night. They ran for their life. Rev Griffith was sure that the pair would never dare to return.

Finally, Kuriacko arrived with two additional men, and an old widow Innachi, who was herself a survivor of a smallpox attack. He had brought in a lamp also.

"Kuriacko, you have done well, intelligently too. Very good, I thank you."

The man stood gaping at the Priest unable to grasp what he had said in so many words. They entered the hall, led by Rev Griffith.

"Her feet are turning cold; it's a bad sign."

Innachi sat on the floor at the patient's feet. She lifted Uma's cold feet and placed them on her lap and began to massage the soles vigorously. Uma began to respond by moving her legs, though still unconscious. Kuriacko returned with a fairly large, coir net that he had picked up from Emmanuel's yard.

"It's not safe that we continue here; if detected it can trigger off a storm." Rev Griffith observed. For the first time he appeared troubled as he had no definite idea where to give Uma a safe sojourn, hopefully, for a few days. He had a couple of sites in mind; he preferred one far away from the crowd but easily accessible. He consulted with Kuriacko.

"Why don't we go to Rosma's father's farm house? "

"It's away from the public eye, on an isle with plenty of clean air and shine; that's what the patient needs."

The four men stood by the patient's sides holding the net in their hands. Innachi, though old, was well built with a steely frame. She lifted up the delicate body of Uma along with the mat that remained stuck, in her arms and placed her gently on the net. The men silently moved out into the veranda, holding the patient. Innachi followed. Mercifully the rain had ceased but the boughs continued to shower heavy drops.

The boat was ready with the awning in place. The net was tied by its four corners on to the roof of the awning; it lay sunk with its precious load curled up snugly inside. Kuriacko shoved the boat away from the shore with a pole; the other men joined him with their paddles rowing. Rev Aaron Griffith sat with his head still covered by his cowl. Innachi sat inside the awning. Uma's feet remained warm and Innachi believed it was a promising sign.

Eventful weeks passed. Uma appeared hale and hearty but she looked depressed.

"Why all these black spots? Many look like tiny pits on my skin." She removed with her fingers the scales from a few pocks on her thighs; the pits that emerged abhorred her.

"Do I have these on my face too?"

"Not many, a few; those will disappear pretty soon, don't bother, you are alone and you will return home soon." Innachi who had nursed her back into life assured her.

"I thank you, Innachi Amma for all that you have done for me. Where is Kallu? "

"I am here." She stepped into the room with a tender coconut; its water, poured into a tumbler was handed over to Uma.

"Thank you, Kallu." Uma didn't say so but the smile on her lips said more.

Left alone she sat moodily and the night turned out to be frightening. She lay on the cot by the window, looking. The sound of waves breaking against the shore echoed across the sky. Uma had a disturbed sleep that left her wearied.

She was hurt that her husband hadn't visited her even once, hadn't sent a message or enquired about her. But then, for him she was dead and buried. She believed he might be lighting a lamp every evening by her grave to keep her memory alive.

"Will he accept me when I return?" The question frightened her. She wondered how her own kith and kin would react once they learnt that Kallu and Meenan, the *Pulaya* couple had nursed her back to life. And Innachi was the one who fed her the food cooked by Kallu. She imagined her husband might be busy in hosting a feast for the Brahmins to atone for the defilement caused by a small pox death in the family. She could imagine the commotion her return would cause.

It was true; for the second time in a month Rev Griffith had walked into Jayanthan's house. He saw the grief stricken man sitting alone in a corner of the courtyard, his eyes frequently gazing at the small mound, her grave; he had a few men engaged to erect a *pandal* over the courtyard.

"Tomorrow is the thirtieth day of her demise; custom demands I feast a few Brahmins."

Rev Griffith was taken around to view the rain beaten grave, the top mound sunken with rainwater seeping down. Jayanthan stood at the head of the grave, looking down silently; the Priest remained less solemn, watching his friend slowly walking away wiping his eyes. Rev Griffith followed him silently.

"Jayanthan, if your wife comes back to you, will you accept her?"

The question baffled the Namboodiri; he wondered how the Priest could pose such a childish question.

"Perhaps, this man is testing me." He preferred to evade the question.

"How could that be? She is dead and gone."

"No, you haven't answered my question. I expect a straight answer." Rev Griffith insisted, repeating the question.

"Reverend, why do you torture me? I lost my wife; please leave me in peace. It's a hypothetical question that you ask me. I have no answer." Jayanthan turned back and Rev Griffith followed him wondering how he could let him know that his wife was alive.

"Jayanthan, could you please come with me for a while?" Rev

Griffith beckoned him and he followed, both stopping by the squatty house where the pox victims were isolated. Jayanthan stood baffled, wondering what awaited him.

"Is he trying to trick me in?"

"Madonna… my Uma…." He rushed towards the bosk, excited.

"Jayanthan, wait; Uma is the new *Ushus* in your life, you take care of her." Rev Griffith said as he walked back signalling Innachi and Kallu to leave the couple alone.

Twenty Three

The harvest over, a festive mood pervaded the *Pulaya* households. Ettanu was home; he was free though the fear of a sudden call for *oozhium* service haunted him constantly. The untouchables were duty bound to render free service whenever requisitioned by the Sarcar or the landlords under whom they lived.

He sat shattered in flesh and spirit.

His wife had been pressurising him to arrange their son' Athai's marriage. In fact this was the subject of discussion in the harvest field. The marriage broker Peter alias Piton had several proposals, among which Maria, the daughter of Simeon was found most attractive. The only problem was that Simeons, even though *Pulaya*s were Christianised. Ettanu feared the alliance might turn out to be unequal. The broker's glib talk about the girl and Ettanu's fascination for Veluthachan, the Christian missionary whose love for the untouchables was unparalleled, persuaded him to agree. But he hadn't yet asked them to visit him to finalise the proposal; yet unannounced, Simeon came along with Peter. Their unexpected arrival flustered Ettanu.

"Ettanucha, I guessed you would be home." Simeon, as usual well dressed, grinned; he helped Peter unload the bundle the broker had on his head. Ettanu wished his wife wouldn't make a sudden appearance before the guests, for she always walked topless.

"Ettanucha, there are a few points that need clarification; we only have a few weeks left for the marriage." Peter said.

"But we haven't given our consent." Ettanu protested.

"Well, nor did you say no." Simeon argued.

"That's true." Ettanu mumbled.

"Whatever is true is true always." Simeon insisted, and Ettanu had to agree.

"Marriage is on Monday after Easter, and Easter is on the Sunday, following the Sunday after the full moon."

Ettanu looked puzzled at this riddle.

"All right, when I sight the full moon I'll let you know."

Simeon had a more important matter to clarify.

"You know we are Christians; we do not intermarry with non-Christians. How do we solve this problem?"

"I don't know; it's your problem." Ettanu expressed his helplessness.

"Your son has to be baptized to become a Christian."

"What is that? I don't know how to baptise my son."

Peter intervened; he wanted Ettanus to visit their church two days later for the baptism of Athai. They agreed. They stood up to go; he followed them up to the river front.

He was worried as he realized that marriage celebrations ruined the poor. The grain that he had stored was not enough to feed the guests. Besides, he had to buy gifts both for the bride and groom's parties. The bride's father had sent them one dozen new mats, and mundus and jackets for every member of the family.

"Mat, of course, we can sleep on but when do we wear these clothes, and where do we go wearing them?" Pakkothi asked him as she unpacked the big bundle the bride's father had brought in. For she knew wearing clean mundu or covering the breast was frowned upon; it invited the wrath of the high castes; aping them was always considered insubordination.

As the parents debated the Ettanu kids were busy examining the clothing, selecting one for each. Chennon and Viccon fought between them for a jacket, and in the melee Chakki was knocked down; she rushed to her mother whimpering

"Stop, you brats; the clothes are to be returned except one for Athai."

"Why Athai alone? I too need one." Viccon protested.

"Athai is getting married and so he gets one." Ettanu told them.

"I am also ready to get married; so I can keep one for myself." Viccon asserted, snatching a jacket from his elder brother.

"I think we have to buy some clothing for Kallu and Manka, and Chithamma too." Pakkothi suggested, adding: "Something for Meenan as well."

"Yea, poor lad. I wanted him to be with us at Athai's wedding but how, I don't know." Memory of Meenan spread a pall of silence over their thoughts.

"Now, where has Athai gone? It's past midnight. Marriage is usually a bad time; one should be careful." He felt annoyed at his son's absence from home at a time when he was needed most.

Ettanu was confused; he had to meet people, get supplies for the feast, erect a pandal and a lot of other petty but important matters.

Athai returned home in the wee hours of the night and sneaked into the hut unnoticed; he never expected his father to be awake.

"Where were you, the whole night?" Ettanu barked.

"I didn't go anywhere, was around here." Athai was casual and cool. Ettanu didn't want to rake up a quarrel.

"I have been to Meenan." Athai whispered, taking care that nobody heard him.

"... I guessed so." his father acknowledged quietly.

"Will he come? I want him by our side....poor kid."

"He said he would try...but I am sure...he'll... keep it a secret."

Meenan was keen they join the church together. He honestly believed that joining the church would render them as touchable as the Christians were.

"It is not riches that we seek but social acceptance." He believed that once baptised they would receive the same status the Christians enjoyed.

"I don't know. I am not sure." Ettanu sounded vague though he had faith in Veluthachan.

"We shall go to the church properly dressed." Athai reminded them just before he retired; it was obliquely meant for his parents who fought shy of dressing. His siblings were agog with the idea of donning their new dresses; his parents preferred to remain silent. Chakki slept by her mother still holding her jacket close to her chest.

Athai felt unsettled with no one to consult; he wondered whether it was an unequal alliance that he was rushing into. He wished he had Meenan by his side; his absence hurt him.

In the morning they boarded the boat on their way to the church.

"You children go inside and sit with your Amma." Ettanu ordered them as he shoved the boat mid stream but no one cared to obey him. They preferred to sit outside the awning watching the landscape.

Pakkothi changed her loin cloth for the new mundu but was reluctant to slip on the *chatta*; she thought it was cumbersome. Her sagging breasts conspicuously dangled inside the jacket as she walked. She had carefully folded and kept the chatta by her side to wear it when they reached the churchyard.

"Be sure that you wear it." Athai insisted.

Simeon and his people waited for them at the church; he felt relieved that his guests had arrived wearing the new clothes befitting the occasion; they led them into the church. A Priest, in ceremonial attire stood in front of the altar facing west. Athai stood in the nave facing the altar, confused and worried. Both his parents and half a dozen Ettanu kids stood restless. Chakki stood close to Athai holding his hand.

The Priest beckoned Athai to move forward.

After a reading from the Gospel, the Priest asked the young man what name he wanted to take.

"Athai." He replied believing the Priest had asked for his name.

"No, you are Mathai hereafter." The Priest corrected him.

"I baptize you in the name of the Father and of the Son and of the Holy Spirit," the Priest uttered solemnly, making the sign of the Cross.

"Amen." Simeon, Martha, his wife and Peter proclaimed in unison. The Ettanu gang remained silent, unable to understand anything. The Priest. "Mathai, you are no longer Athai, you are Mathai hereafter, which means Mathew, meaning Gift of Yah. Do you understand what I said?"

"No." Mathai answered bluntly.

"Doesn't matter. You are a gift from God to your parents and your siblings. Is it clear now?"

Mathai said 'yes' as he lacked courage to say 'no' again.

"Mathai, you may go in peace."

Pakkothi rushed ahead of others and boarded the boat; her first act was removing her *chatta* that she found suffocating. She stood by the awning exposing her bare bosom. Ettanu shoved the boat away from the shore, punting it upstream. Ettanu hadn't removed the new clothing.

The boat slowly skirted into the cove off Neelimangalam ferry. Ettanu found the spot changed from a sleepy ferry point to a beehive of activity. What was unusual was the raucous yelling of men, whose hoarse voices reverberated, holding in leash the protestations of '*oozhium*' servers; they were forcibly brought to the site to carry loads of granite blocks. Ettanu recognized the servers, many his friends and acquaintances; he dared not look into their faces. He manoeuvred his boat quietly to pass by unnoticed; but the boat attracted the attention of the supervisors. He saw them rushing to the river bank hailing him to anchor the boat. Frightened, Ettanu punted the boat off the scene.

Ettanu found himself overwhelmed as the wedding day neared; he visited his fellow men to invite them for the wedding. Quite a few wanted to join him at the nuptials, fascinated by the church ceremony; a few regretted as they had been summoned for the *oozhium* which they dreaded to skip, afraid of the consequences. For many the sumptuous lunch the bride's party would provide was a lure.

Ettanu remained worried. He stayed alert, with an eye on every passer by. He warned his wife of the possibility of her too being captured for violating the diktat.

"Will they come to take us?" Pakkothi panicked at the thought of them in the police lock up when their son entered wedlock. They had promised to attend the *oozhium* but they failed to present themselves.

Finally, the day arrived. People began to appear from early afternoon, they felt disappointed at Ettanu's sullen posture as the man sat on the edge of the floor refusing to look into the face of the guests; they lingered in the courtyard, sans a word of welcome. They found even Pakkothi rather reticent.

"Kandacha, in case the police arrest us you should take my place and see that the marriage is not abandoned." He called in his son and briefed him too. Mathai was upset, and almost rebelled against his father's decision.

"Why don't we postpone the wedding? It's only a matter of a few days." He tried to reason with his father but Ettanu remained adamant.

"Too late to postpone; we have already made the arrangements and the bride's party too is ready. It's not possible."Ettanu asserted.

"Ettanucha, you and Pakkomma can go into hiding; we'll manage. Our people are not strangers; they will understand the circumstances. If it works out you may join us in the boat." Kandan suggested.

"The plan is good but…." Ettanu still hesitated

"But… what…?"

"By hiding I may escape the police but I will be in another lockup made of bamboo thickets or snake infested jungle. Does it make any difference?" The question Ettanu posed was real; hiding provided him with physical freedom but offered little to mitigate anguish. Ettanu asked for his wife who came along with Kallu. Kandan explained to her what they had planned for them. Pakkothi stood calm, listening to what her husband had to tell; she aired no opinion.

Ettanu seemed to have relented.

"We have little time to deliberate; get ready; hand over the kitchen to Kallu and Manka. Kandachan is here to do the rest." Ettanu urged his wife.

"I am not coming; let them take me." She declared showing rare determination, stunning everybody around.

"If they pick you up, it's bad." Kallu tried to reason with her

"No…Kallu; it's my son's marriage; come what may, I want to be with him." It was a mother's wish that strengthened her resolve to defy the authority. Ettanu wavered before his wife's tenacity; fear of police or the torture in captivity bothered him not. What troubled him most was the social disapprobation his absence from his son's wedding would causel.

"Ettanucha, let Pakkomma stay behind, the police may spare her; you may keep off for a while." Ettanu, hesitatingly agreed to their suggestion.

The last vestige of the setting sun lingered on the horizon, and approached night. The household lacked the nuptial cheeriness.

A batch of three men who had left Ettanu's hut in their canoe saw a man being hauled up by the police in a boat that stayed under the cover of the canopy of boughs; the dark and thin man failed in his attempt to make a dive back into the water.

"He's caught. Ill luck…he's caught." The men sadly observed.

"But who could that be?" Their question echoed breaching the peace of the night.

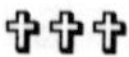

Twenty Four

The night had passed into the second quarter; the Ettanu household remained alive, refusing to retire for the night. The waning moon that hovered low over the western sky appeared slothful and niggardly. Lingering vestige of darkness still covered the face of the earth.

Ettanu defied darkness; he had his hut basking in the brilliance of kerosene lamps planted in every corner of the hut. His wife dared not extinguish them to save on oil, as was her habit. A huge bonfire lit the courtyard, the homestead regained much of its lost cheeriness.

Ettanu sat on the edge of the floor as usual dangling his feet. The bride and the groom had returned by late afternoon. Ettanu had asked Kandan to join in but Peter alias Pitton, the marriage broker, came uninvited.

Kandan noticed that Ettanu seemed quiet; he missed the usual vigour that dominated his personality on festive occasions, as if he feared some danger. Even half a bowl of liquor that Kandan had served him, failed to lift his spirits.

"I am happy the police spared me the disgrace." Ettanu said, taking the last draught of the bowl, which he placed on the floor. He racked his brains to unravel the mystery behind their leniency to him.

Nobody had told Ettanu of the police sweep on his hut the previous night; the men who faced the police kept it a secret.

It was almost midnight. Kandan had allowed the men one more round. A few of the guests preferred to stay behind, as it was late; the rest slowly proceeded homeward when the two constables suddenly appeared before them, swinging their batons.

"Where is Ettanu? We have come to pick him up." Keshu Nair roared silencing the men.

"Haven't you heard? Gone dumb?"

The menacing police frightened Mathai who watched them advancing towards Pitton. Mathai rushed out of the hut, promptly pulling off his jacket lest it offend them. He had the jacket rolled into a ball and tucked under his armpit. He stood cringing before them. .

"Where is your *Thantha*?" Mathai wavered, his tongue cleaving to the roof of the mouth.

"You won't tell?" His silence angered the constable who poked at his chin with the baton.

"He's absconding from *oozhium;* ask him to report at the Station tomorrow morning. Don't make us come again." The Head Constable issued a stern warning and turned back. Piton followed them up to the river bank unnoticed and stood behind the hedge watching where they were heading for.

"Sir, he is not at home." Keshu Nair reported to the Sub Inspector.

"Well, we have a prize catch today; let us return soon. We have to see that he confesses the crime."

Piton's recounting of the events of the previous night upset Ettanu more. He had news that the police had, the previous night, picked up a man who had stayed hidden in the water. Ettanu remembered that was a subject of discussion among some of the guests at the marriage. Apparently they had gone fishing in the night and they themselves were hiding as they sighted the police boat.

"Did you see the man by any chance?" Ettanu enquired trying to conceal his anxiety.

"No, we didn't; it was a quick action by the police. They might have been on the look out for some fugitive."

Nobody could see his face clearly. No sooner did he take a deep breath for a dive, the police helper cast his net trammelling the man in. He was hauled up and thrown mercilessly into the boat. A faint growl of the man was subdued by the uninterrupted chortle of the uniformed men on board the boat. They hog-tied him along with the net, to prevent him from escaping.

"Who must that man be?" The fishermen asked Ettanu.

"I don't know." Ettanu disappeared into the church, where he stood behind his son throughout the ceremony.

"God, the Father, Who has just joined you together as man and wife will be with you always." The Priest chanted concluding the ceremony; Maria bowed her head solemnly as the groom stood silent.

Ettanu looked frantically for God everywhere for he wanted to ask him whom the police had picked up from the river.

"Is it my son Meenan? No...he cannot be."

"Why do you look so sad on this auspicious occasion?" Pakkothi asked him as they returned home along with the couple.

"Me? No... I am not... not at all." Ettanu asserted, pretending to be in high spirits. He was putting on a false front; Pakkothi knew that but she didn't ask him. Even in the midst of merriment he stood moody and distracted. Pakkothi thought he needed a good night's sleep.

"You better sleep; you have the *oozhium* duty tomorrow morning that you can't escape. I don't want the police to come again." Pakkothi warned him. She feared the consequences of the police spotting Maria.

"She's a veritable tinderbox, looking so attractive in her milky white wrap."

Pakkothi believed she had the responsibility to protect her like a fowl that gathered her chicks under her wings against dangers. Ettanu lay on the mat and beckoned Kandan to share it with him.

Those who lived in huts never bothered who slept where; parents and children squeezed themselves wherever they found a little space. The bonfire that blazed in the courtyard slowly died down. Finally, Pakkothi extinguished the kerosene lamps.

Maria had been sitting by the hearth the whole afternoon smothered by the affectionate, juvenile pranks of the Ettanu siblings.

Mathai was restive. He was a just married young man. He found himself lonely among the crowd in his own home. For him Maria continued to be his dream girl but the irony was that she was elusive, denying him even a vision of herself. To him, the parting advice that Myrtle gave as the couple boarded the *vallom* on their way home, seemed rather intriguing.

"It's your first night; together make it great." Mathai was curious as to what she had meant by the 'first night'.

The realization that he had received scant attention in his own household hurt his ego; certainly not even half of what Maria had merited. Within a few hours of her arrival she had become the most important person and the cynosure of all eyes; his mother had been bestowing great attention upon her, solicitously sitting by her side, fondling her shoulders and feeding her bits of delicacies that she had specially bought. His siblings never left her alone and she seemed to have been enjoying their pranks.

"What business do you have here where we, the women sit? Go and sit with the men." Pakkothi admonished him as he nervously ventured in by the hearth.

"It's strange that my presence is harmful." Mathai meekly withdrew abashed at the sniggering face of the youngsters. Maria hid herself behind Pakkothi.

He snatched a mat from a corner of the hut and spread it on a haystack. Though it exuded warmth, for him the night was cold, as he lay forlorn and wakeful.

Pakkothi woke up long before dawn; she too had a disturbed sleep. A weeklong *oozhium* duty stared in her face. Leaving the hearth in the hands of an uninitiated girl worried her.

"Athai… *Edaa*… Athai… oh! Mathai…." She hailed her son; initially forgetting that he was no longer Athai. Mathai heard her shouting but cared not to respond to register his protest over his mother's chasing him away the previous night. Annoyed at his silence she screamed, waking up the household except Chakki who slept near Maria's. Maria patiently disentangled herself from Chakki's arms and came out to join her mother-in-law.

"Child, where is your man?" Pakkothi asked Maria though she had no reason to believe that the woman had known her man during their first night.

"I don't know *Amma*.... I'll find out." Maria volunteered. She knew her poor husband was sleeping on the haystack braving the chill of the night.

"*Dhe... Amma* is calling you." She moved closer to him as he lay still, pretending asleep; she stood by his side bending over him, repeating loudly"*Amma* wants you."

He grasped her hand and pulled her down.

"*Amma.*" The sudden appearance of the mother-in-law chilled her heart as it froze Mathai's limbs. Maria ran away into the opposite direction holding but instead ran into Ettanu who had emerged into the courtyard looking for Mathai.

"*Amma* told me that devil would come to devour me on the first night if I slept in the darkness." Maria told Mathai as they returned after reaching his parents at the site of *oozhium*.

"Hope the devil doesn't torment us at least on the second night," Mathai consoled himself.

✞✞✞

Twenty Five

The camp was set up in a strip of land by the riverside with the sky for a roof and earth the floor. The original claimants of the tract, frogs, bandicoots and snakes obstinately stayed back, yet were wary of the human encroachers. Perhaps, the camp was a precursor to the late century concentration camps, short of barbed wire fencing. For the timid inmates, all *Pulayas*, never dared to run away from the camp for fear of reprisal; their timidity made life easy for the thick whiskered camp managers whose intimidatory tactics and occasional lashes rendered the men docile, forever.

As the day broke out, the camp became a beehive of activities; men and women scrambled for rubble heaps or rocks to crouch behind, to answer the call of nature and as they returned they picked up tinder and fuel wood to light the hearth. The women cooked the gruel that the men ate standing to save time, promptly presented themselves before the foremen for the day's task.

The system of *oozhium* was instituted to ensure public work executed by voluntary service but the burden exclusively fell on the untouchables. The bridge proposed at Neelimangalam required huge quantity of granite blocks.

At the first bell, the labourers lined up at the entrance; one by one they walked out, dropping one pebble into a basket to ascertain the total number present to ensure that none had deserted during the night. As they entered the mud road they moved in single line. Divided into two halves forming a relay system; the first half assigned to carry the load up to the mid point of the road where the second half received it on their heads and carried to the bridge site.

"When a load arrives at mid point there should be a person ready to take delivery." Neelakantan, the chief, explained to the workers, warning them:

"Any one causing a disruption shall be dealt with suitably."

Neelakantan was deputed to supervise the construction of the bridge across the river Meenachil; he was a tough guy and a hard task master who instilled fear and hatred too in the minds of those who worked under him.

The Ettanus found their place in a fresh batch on their first work-day; everyone slogged on willingly to please the masters. The day was hot and oppressive; few ate any breakfast except a bowl of watery gruel.

Unlike harvesting or tilling, the *oozhium* was hard labour, carrying heavy loads of granite blocks on head lumbering long stretches of bumpy road. The load was always heavy with no leniency shown towards women. None had the nerve to slug as stringent supervisors sat armed with lashes, along the route. The front man set the pace and the rest followed compulsively.

"Ittatha, your loincloth is falling down." Ettanu warned a man, who walked before him unaware of his loincloth slipping down. Ittathan could not pick up the rag to tie around his waist for fear of dropping the load on his head; he walked naked, unnoticed for every one had his eyes set on his job.

"No talk," the supervisor shouted at Ettanu showing him the lash. By mid morning, the crushing weight of the loads exhausted them. Still they carried on fearing the lash.

In the evening Neelakantan visited them; he looked unhappy; he guessed one had to be harsh to extract work from a lazy lot.

"What you have produced today is less than half of what the previous batch had produced; this is totally unacceptable." His remark, a ploy, was greeted by stony silence. Tired, many squatted on the ground.

"You may go now but tomorrow you shall do double the work; otherwise you will have to work for another week to make up the deficiency."

"Oh! ... no." An unknown voice protested from the rear, and a few mutely supported him. The dissenting voice jolted Neelakantan; that was his first experience when the *oozhium* workmen dared to challenge him.

"Who said no?" Neelakantan, annoyed at the impudence of the men, stepped a few feet forward and asked. His shout cowed them down; Neelakantan, added:

"No nays, after all, this bridge will benefit you also." Neelakantan's words did little to enthuse the workers.

Back in the camp, a night Ittathan came to invite the Ettanus, offering to share his gruel with them, for Ettanu hadn't brought any rice when he reported for work. Being a widower Ittathan came alone for work with enough rice.

"Good that I lost my wife earlier; she escaped the torture." Ittathan mused.

"But the *Thampran* said the bridge is for us also." Pakkothi, who sat by, pointed out. She added: "Those who sweat today will eat the fruits tomorrow."

"Oh no, not for the *Pulaya*!"

The *Thampran* was trying to mollify us. I heard that doing this bridge by *oozhium* means more money for him and a bigger job in the capital."

"But it's not going to be easy for him." Ittathan added averting his eyes from Ettanu's face. Ittathan took Ettanu aside, and they strolled, together reaching the granite heaps that hedged the swamp. Away from the crowd, they stopped behind a pile of rocks where the men used to come for defecating. Ittathan thought it was a safe spot to exchange confidences for they were strictly forbidden from congregating in the camp or discussing any matter. Timid as they were, they purposely shunned even their acquaintances.

"Ettanucha, what I tell you is very serious and secret too."

"*Ngoom*.... what's it?" Ettanu asked.

"You remember I told you that the work is not going to be easy. He has a problem; the bottom of the river rejects the footing of the bridge."

"I don't understand what you mean by footing and rejection," Ettanu scratched his head confused.

"They failed to erect the pillars to support the bridge." Ittathan explained to him. "But why? They have a hugh stock of granites"

"Granites don't frighten away the powerful spirit that dwells at the bottom of the river. She fears that the bridge will disturb her peace. Every time they try to erect the pillar she tumbles it down."

"She? Who is she?" What Ittathan said sounded like a riddle to Ettanu.

"She is none other than our Neeli Manka whom they had killed and dumped in the river; she still lives at the bottom of the river."

The masons whom Neelakantan had brought were untrained for under water erection of pillars. When the stones they piled up collapsed repeatedly, they concluded it was the handiwork of a ghost that haunted the river.

Neelakantan created a scare among their fellow workers; a few among them deserted fearing possible reprisal by the demon.

Kocharayan was sure it was Neeli Manka, the ferocious *Pulaya* woman who haunted the upper castes when she was alive. He remembered how in a pre-dawn ambush she was captured and killed. He argued that her thirst for revenge remained unquenched.

"Who can tell us precisely who she is and what will appease her?" Neelakantan rushed to an astrologer of repute. After a lengthy investigation spread over three days, he concluded that the ghost was, untameable.

"Not exactly but it can create obstructions; however we can bind her." The astrologer had drawn his own conclusion.

"Propitiate the ghost with human blood; it thrives on blood. We will chain it at the moment when it comes to drink the offering."

"Do you mean to say a human sacrifice?"

"Yes, human sacrifice at the site of the bridge." The astrologer confirmed.

Neelakantan was a man of determination, and was willing to go to any extent to accomplish his goal.

"Let one man be sacrificed for the good of many; but where am I to find the one?" Neelakantan mused.

"Well, there are plenty who burden the good earth but the earth can do well without them." Neelakantan argued to convince himself, and he confirmed to the astrologer.

"You prescribe the time and date. I shall make available the victim but make sure it's confidential."

It was the penultimate day for the last batch of the *oozhium* labourers, the men consoled themselves as they returned to the camp at night. For them the dawn of the following day promised freedom and an end to their ordeal. Several went to sleep without the usual gruel as they had exhausted the paltry amount of rice they had brought in when they joined the camp. Ittathan's pot was empty, as he had voluntarily shared his stock with the Ettanus. Pakkothi felt bad that because of them Ittathan too had to starve.

"Never mind, hunger and starvation are our inseparable companions." Ittathan tried to rationalize though he had never slept on an empty stomach.

As he lay awake he heard a hushed conversation from behind the sentry post. He concluded it was unusual for Neelakantan to stay back late in the night.

"There must be some thing fishy." Ittathan thought, and he slowly crawled towards the sentry post and lay on the ground with his head kissing the wet earth. What transpired between Neelakantan and the sentry shocked Ittathan.

"You listen carefully and do exactly as I tell you."

"Tomorrow you detain one person from among the men."

"Just any one?" The sentry asked, not knowing the purpose behind the idea.

"Any one who walks on two legs. Do you understand?"

"See the women leave the camp ahead of the men; let the men walk down the gate in single file after the women have left."

"When the last man reaches the entrance you promptly close the gate, simultaneously felling him to the ground. Arrange two men ready with rope and wads of rags, tie him up and leave him under a mat. If any of the labourers looks back or returns chase him away." Neelakantan's instructions were always thorough.

"If you need any clarification ask me right now; no bungling and no excuses."

"No Sir… yes Sir." The man sounded confused yet pretended he understood the instructions thoroughly.

"As soon as the task is accomplished report to me at home." Neelakantan returned home; the sentry remained at his post. Ittathan rushed back wondering who would be the last man stepping out of the camp. Many faces flashed before his eyes including his own.

Twenty Six

Neelakantan paced impatiently in the courtyard awaiting news. The glimmer of an oil lamp, ceremoniously kept at the sill of the main door, cast a glow. His wife, Thulasi, was annoyed; she showed her face at the door to remind him that the night was quite advanced, and it was time to retire.

"I'll join you soon; I have urgent business." Thulasi knew her husband never retired until he had finished the day's task.

He sat on the edge of the veranda facing the gate to ensure an unhindered view of the visitors. Astrologer Rama Kurup was the first to arrive along with a well-built man who preferred to stay behind in darkness.

"Whom do you have with you?" Neelakantan asked the astrologer.

"The one to do the job." The meaning was not lost on Neelakantan.

"I have made arrangements to procure the sacrificial victim; confirmation is expected any moment."

"Well, I have done my part of the job." Ramakurup handed over to him a folded paper scribbled in pencil. As Neelakantan sat straining his eyes in the pale light of the lamp, the astrologer intervened to say:

"It lists the articles required for the sacrifice."

"Don't you need a sacrificial stone too?" It was not an omission; he had reason to omit the traditional platform.

"Here, we perform the *Bali* on a boat which is a floating platform," the astrologer clarified, and Neelakantan asked no further questions.

"Come and see the man whom I have hired for the job." Ramakurup walked ahead and Neelakantan followed him. Hewas introduced to Pushkaran, the hatchet faced killer. The man stepped forward and stood before Neelakantan for a while making his obeisances. Neelakantan found him fit for the job and asked him:

"How many have you slaughtered on the sacred stone?"

Pushkaran looked at the astrologer and a bundle of professional weapons that he had deposited, behind the nearby shrubbery. He thought the blood stained sword and the chopper, which protruded out of the bundle, testified to his expertise.

"Plenty Sir." Pushkaran muttered without lifting up his eyes. Ramakurup promptly confirmed:

"Yes plenty; look at his weapons, they reveal a lot."

Pushkaran had no remorse over the ritual slaughtering he had committed, for he believed it was for a beneficial cause, to propitiate the gods. It was, after all his profession that earned him a living. Neelakantan stayed at the gate.

"Do you have the boat ready with a reliable punter?" Ramakurup enquired of him; he too was becoming impatient. He thought they were getting late for the ceremony. Time was an essential factor for rituals; the auspicious time never waited for anyone.

"Yes, of course! Kocharayan is ready with the boat and two additional men, in case some force is required."

Neelakantan knew that no victim submitted willingly. Defiance, struggle and even violence had marred such rituals. He always had a couple of strong men around him to take care of any eventuality.

"But where is the victim?" The astrologer insisted, his voice impatient.

Finally, Mathevan Pillai showed his face reluctantly at the gate wavering whether to enter the courtyard or not; he had his assistant lurking behind him, both stood timorously, unwilling to look into the boss's eyes. Neelakantan feared that the mission had failed.

"What have you come to tell me now? The man has escaped?" Neelakantan barked at the sentries showing his extreme displeasure.

"Sir, I couldn't catch any, please forgive me."

"Forgive you? I'll kill you. You shall die in his place, now and here itself." Neelakantan lifted the bundle that Pushkaran had deposited by the foot of the tree, and drew the sword as he advanced towards the servants menacingly. Cowed by the threat, Mathevan Pillai stood shivering, raising his hands over his head in an effort to protect himself; his assistant quietly slipped into the darkness and ran away leaving Mathevan exposed.

"No… no… don't do any thing in haste." Ramakurup cautioned him, and Neelakantan stopped short of striking the man; reluctantly dropped the sword. Pushkaran immediately picked it up and put it back into his bundle. Mathevan eased off slowly as he sensed that the immediate threat had receded. He felt assured that he stood acquitted if Neelakantan cared to listen to what he had to say.

"Sir, I could have captured not one but half a dozen if only I had a few in the camp. Not a single man returned after the day's work; we combed the whole area, roads and the quarry with no luck; they seemed to have escaped."

Mathevan had made careful plans to trap the last man; he had called two extra assistants to overpower the man in the event of his making an effort to escape.

"As the last man reaches the entrance you call him back as if wanting to give him some thing; greedy as they are, he will rush back to you. The rest I'll do," he had briefed his assistant. He had, in a corner of the sentry post, hidden a roll of coir and wads of rags. He waited for the return of the men, as usual at dusk; but nobody showed up. Late in the night he thought he could catch any man who sneaked into the camp but none strayed in. The camp remained deserted.

The camp had a lot of small things that the workers had brought in, earthen utensils, ladles of coconut shells, mats of screw pine leaves, rags of cotton, sun dried tapioca chips, red chilli and salt; rice was not much but tobacco and beedis were in plenty. Mathevan was sure they would not abandon their meagre possessions under any circumstances. But they never came to retrieve any thing.

Ittathan had avoided an open discussion on the matter that troubled him. They knew if a *Pulaya* was caught nobody would ask a question. Ittathan kept the matter a secret as he feared a unanimous decision was unlikely; instead he expected commotion in the camp. When consulted, even Ettanu was lukewarm; he sat brooding. After much debate Ittathan decided to tell the labourers the truth. He met them one by one and told them what awaited them if they returned to the camp on the last day.

"He who wants to save his life, let him act with no loss of time."

Surprisingly, they responded positively; it was like a minor exodus with men and women walking in panic down the hill slopes to reach their homes, not knowing that even them own home guaranteed them no security. To Neelakantan, courting defeat was tantamount to dishonour; he appeared crestfallen. He walked the courtyard aimlessly, his face cloudy and eyes red.

"Someone might have leaked the secret," he asserted, looking at Ramakurup for confirmation.

"Quite possible... but now let us not cry over spilt milk." The astrologer tried to pacify him.

"How to overcome the situation? Shall we abandon or defer it?"

"I don't know... I am in the dark." Neelakantan looked at the man helplessly, perhaps expecting that he had a suggestion. The astrologer too showed no confidence, and he said: "We are short of time; no way of finding an alternative."

"No... no... there is enough time and I have an alternative." Kocharayan, who was asked to bring the boat, was witness to the events of the past half an hour. He had been standing outside the gate behind Mathevan's assistant. He wanted to make sure that Neelakantan's prestige was retrieved.

Brushing aside Mathevan, the mahout hurriedly stepped forward moved closer and stood before Neelakantan blocking his way.

"I have news for you." Kocharayan said, "Yes… sure… tell me what it is." Neelakantan forced a smile on his face.

"There is a *Pulaya* criminal picked up under suspicious circumstances, languishing in the police lock up; nobody has come to claim him." Neelakantan stayed unimpressed by what he had been told.

"Sir, what I mean is that perhaps the Sub Inspector will hand over the man to you, if you approached him; you may tell him what the purpose is."

"Oh! That is an idea." Neelakantan exclaimed.

"The Sub Inspector will oblige; for both of you live by the coppers thrown from Sri Padmanabha's [meaning the state] treasury."

Neelakantan agreed to meet the Sub Inspector of police. He asked the astrologer and Pushkaran to accompany him to the police station. Mathevan jumped into the boat uninvited. Neelakantan asked his aides to join him.

The previous night the police had caught a man in a trammel net; it was Meenan, the man who had absconded after allegedly committing a murder.

They walked him blind folded, hand cuffed to the foot of a coconut tree by the side of the station yard. The ground was wet and slushy.

"You better sit down; it will cool your bum." The constable pushed him down by pressing his palm over his shoulder. To make sure that he didnot escape his leg and arm were tied to the trunk of the palm.

It was quiet in the police station with the guards sleeping. The Head Constable laid himself on a table with his legs resting on the back of the Sub Inspector's chair . The Constable sat on the floor stretching his legs and leaning against a gunny bag filled with stolen coconuts.

"It might rain in the night." The Head Constable observed looking at the sky.

The oil lamp in the inner room died out; the earth stood silently wrapped in darkness. A light wind that passed overhead swayed the tree tops and the palm at the foot of which the prisoner.

"Rain is imminent; let us decide something before it showers," the mahout urged them. The astrologer repeated that the time was appropriate with the officer away and the men on guard asleep.

"Yes… I think we should go ahead." Neelakantan finally gave his assent.

Kocharayan led Pushkaran towards the palm, the rest following. It was quiet except for the snoring of the untouchbale prisoner and the surly wind that continued to blow.

Pushkaran cut with his chopper the rope that had tied the man to the palm; as the taut rope eased, the man made an attempt to stand up but Pushkaran pressed him down, close to the earth. Kocharayan carefully hooked both his legs at the ankle into a knot.

The man captured the police from the river Meenachill was on a journey to an unknown destination. He was lowered into the boat with the man lying on the wet floor.

Sailing down the stream was less tortuous for the punter, Kocharayan; the boat ran down along the flow. He manoeuvred the boat towards the right bank near the site of the bridge at Neelimangalam, and waited for further instructions from the astrologer.

"We have reached at the right time." Ramakurup confidently observed searching the sky for a sign though the dark night concealed every thing.

"Where is the Priest?" Neelakantan demanded; he too had become self-assured with the victim in their custody.

"Don't you know that the Priest doesn't officiate personally when the victim is an untouchable; it defiles him." Ramakurup explained further:

"He has given us time. At that moment he sits before the sacred fire with all the sacrificial offerings that he burns in the fire. The ritual is complete when the victim is offered at the specified site, spilling blood."

Pushkaran and Kocharayan together lifted the man and placed him upright; the boat was held firm on the river.

"Why do you keep me tied?" Meenan protested as Pushkaran passed the rope around his torso; his head jetted out into the water, slightly drooping. Pushkaran took the sword from the bundle, placed it on the victim's body. He touched its blade with both his hands and placed his palms over his forehead, standing still for a moment with eyes closed.

"Pushkaran, it's time to act." Ramakurup whispered after gazing at the sky.

"Do you need my assistance?" Kocharayan asked Pushkaran.

"Who, the *Aanakkaran Thampran*?" The victim on the platform recognized the mahout's voice.

"*Athhayda* Meenan, its Kocharayan, the mahout." He lifted in a quick flourish his incapacitated right arm that Meenan had broken. "*Tha...mpr...*"

Before Meenan could complete the word a splash of red emblazoned the breast of the river as it flowed.

When he finished reading the chapter Sivanandan looked into the face of Pathrose Micah; the veteran shifted his eyes to prevent his tears wetting the page.

"After my grandmother that was the fate of my father."

✞✞✞

Twenty Seven

A small canoe, rowed solo almost bumped into their boat but for the alertness of the rower. The sudden sighting of a canoe jolted the group that was retuning jubilantly, with their mission accomplished.

Kocharayan shouted aloud, "stop."

Ettanu's son Mathai, who recognized the voice, had no mind to stop; he sped away, knowing well that if caught his refusal would cost him dearly. Kocharayan saw the man in the canoe outmanoeuvring him.

It pained Mathai that Meenan failed to attend his marriage; he was sure Meenan would keep his promise; but news of the police catching a man from the river upset him. Mathai wanted to unravel the mystery of the black man the police had caught in the net.

He was returning after a nightly foray when the mahout challenged him. He had heard about their plan for a human sacrifice and the presence of the mahout on board the boat intrigued him; yet he didn't believe that Meenan was the victim; he returned home heart-broken.

Mathai shored the canoe inside a thicket to prevent it from being spotted by any one who cared to follow him. He waited behind watching for the boat that he had encountered. With no sign of the pursuers, he silently walked up. As he stepped into the courtyard, four women who had been keeping a vigil the whole night sprang up on their feet and rushed towards him, asking in unison.

"Have you met him? What did he say?"

"Mathai, tell us, where is Meenan?" Kallu shook him by his arm and demanded, looking into his eyes. He had no answer, the tears in his eyes speaking for him; he broke down.

"I couldn't find him; he's not there." Mathai took time to utter the few words that turned the world upside down for them. Mathai had guessed what he would find; yet he ventured up to the isle in the midst of the lake to confirm.

"Only death can stop me from attending your wedding." He remembered the parting promise Meenan had made. He was keen to witness a Christian wedding and to take up the matter of the rest of the *Pulayas* joining the church, hoping that would lead to their emancipation.

"At least our children will get education and our women can cover their bosom with no fear of someone breaking their bones." Mathai remembered him saying when he told him of his decision to marry a Christian, Maria. But he never came.

'True to his promise death stopped him from attending the wedding.' Mathai silently concluded.

Kallu collapsed suddenly with a howl, beating her chest. Maria, who stood by, caught hold of her restraining her hands. Manka crouched on the ground whimpering silently, as Chitha sat looking at them in disbelief unable to grasp what had gone wrong.

"Kallu, what I mean is that I could not meet him; that doesn't mean anything else. You calm down; we'll look for him further." Mathai tried to pacify them; his soft reasoning failed to assuage their grief. They refused to believe that Meenan had deserted the isle on his own.

"He might have been caught by the police." Manka began to cry aloud, taking Kallu's hands into hers; they sat embracing each other, wailing for the missing man. Late in the night Ettanu came accompanied by Ittathan on their way back from the bridge site. He tried hard to calm himself lest he drove the girls into panic.

"Kallu." he called as he entered the courtyard.

"Ettanucha, do you have any news of him?" Both Kallu and Manka stood up anxiously. Ettanu stood shivering unable to share with them what he had witnessed at the bridge site. He stood debating how to console the young women.

'The truth is devastating,' Ettanu concluded; for, he had seen a man being slaughtered on the thwart of a boat.

'The mahout *Thampran* too was present.' He heard him speaking, and his voice was familiar.

'If the mahout was present the victim could be none but Meenan.' Ettanu concluded.

Ittathan and Ettanu had gone to the bridge site, watched from behind a granite heap whether a human sacrifice was performed at the site. They were certain that none of the *Pulayas* had fallen into the trap; the timely warning had alerted them. What they had witnessed at the site was really shattering.

"Who is the man? Could it be Meenan?"

"Ettanucha, won't you tell us, please?" As the women besieged him he stood quiet but his silence spoke more than what he wanted to suppress. He lacked the courage to tell them what he thought. He had no proof that the man they had sacrificed was Meenan, but if he told them that he had seen a man being butchered they would conclude it was Meenan.

He looked up to Kallu and Manka.

"Kallu, Manka, my daughters, "What is fated is fated; none can change it." Ettanu walked out silently, Ittathan followed him but Mathai and Maria stayed back.

"Mathai, will you please lend me your canoe for a while?" Kallu asked.

"Sure, I don't mind but where do you go so early?" Mathai demanded.

"Where do you want to go, Kallu?" Manka too felt that the woman was rather impulsive and acted brazenly.

"You seem to have forgotten that you are in an advanced stage; you need to be extremely careful; the time is bad for us." She warned her.

"It cannot be any worse." Kallu heaved a long sigh as she searched for the paddle in the shrubby hedges.

"At least tell us where you are going." Manka followed her up to the riverbank for an answer; she didn't look into Kallu's eyes but knew her eyes were brimming with tears. Kallu moved towards Manka, clasped her arms and said.

"Manka, it's not that I don't want to tell you where I go but I don't know whether it will do any good.... I am going to meet... Uma *Thamprati* to request her to help us find Meenan.... My mind tells me that something terrible might have happened." She rushed towards the river. Kallu boarded the canoe and sat on the stern; it moved forward as she began to strike the water with the paddle.

Manka stood panicking; looking at the full-blown abdomen of her companion. No one was sure about the date but by the size of her belly it appeared that time was near.

"Kallu...listen...stop...I'll come with you... you take me too," Manka pleaded, trotting along the bank to catch up with the canoe; she found Kallu unyielding as she commenced to row fast and the canoe began to move faster.

"Better you stop; else I'll jump into the river to stop you." Her threat worked. Kallu eased the paddle over the surface of the water and sat staring at Manka, still undecided.

"I don't want to meet the *Thamprati*... you go and talk to her... I'll wait in the canoe; sure I won't come with you up the steps." Kallu thought it was a good idea. "After all she too is his wife."

Manka stepped into the canoe and sat on the prow facing her.

"Kallu, you take rest; you are tired. I'll row." Manka took the paddle and rowed forward.

Kallu feared a few morning bathers still at the ghat; but the landing was almost deserted. The paved steps were nearly dry.

They berthed the canoe a little away from the cobbled steps. Manka stayed behind watching Kallu climb up the steps. She noticed her faltering; unmindful of the strain, kallu forced her steps up. The climb was rather steep and she stopped for breath before she could touch the top.

"Do you want me to come?" Manka asked from the canoe.

"No." A wave of her hand and a shake of her head conveyed the message. At the top she looked back and signalled to Manka that she was alright.

Kallu saw the courtyard empty, without the usual crowd that waited for the Thampran to appear. She stood in the morning sun looking for the steward; she feared her presence would enrage the old man.

"Why have you come again? Do you know how much the family has suffered because of wretcheds like you and the Padre?" Eachara Warrier stepped out of the veranda and stood in the courtyard, keeping a measured distance to ensure no defilement happened as he was on his way to the temple.

"Why have you come now? Who called you here?"

"I want to see the *Thamprati.*"

"No…that's not possible, you get away…dirty pig." He stood waving his hand threateningly. Kallu stood firm, refusing to be intimidated; undaunted by his bullying tactics she moved towards the veranda. The steward thought that was an attempt to trespass into the house. He picked up a stick and rushed towards Kallu, who stood by the floor of the veranda, straining to see whether Uma was in the hall. He stood behind her unnoticed and his first strike, hit her on her belly.

"*Ammo…. Thamprate…*" She let out a loud scream.

Unabashed, he continued to smite her blindly; she turned supine shielding her belly with her hands, which suffered cuts and bruises that bled. The steward's yells and Kallu's cries stirred Uma out into the veranda, where she stood frozen at the brutality of the steward.

"Eachara, stop it; what do you do? Killing a woman in this courtyard?"

Eachara Warrier stopped instantly as he knew Uma never condoned such brutality.

Uma ran towards the woman who lay sobbing on the ground with blood oozing from her hands, lips and forehead.

"O! God. It's Kallu. How come you are here without telling me?"

To Uma, the ghastly sight of a pregnant woman being beaten and thrown into a welter was revolting. For a moment she remained dazed, overwhelmed by conflicting emotions, taboos of caste defilement that invited social sanctions, and a sense of personal gratitude that finally won. She sat by her side, took her in her arms and wiped the tears and dirt off her face; she turned towards Eachara Warrier, asking him:

"Eachara, do you know what this woman is to me?" Her anger was against the man but she restrained herself, as was her tradition. He hesitated to answer and averted his eyes.

"Look here, if I get you thrashed the way you have done to her, how will you feel about it?"

Eachara Warrier remained sweating under the stare of Uma's eyes; he stepped back shamefacedly, wiping his face with the corner of his *mundu* in an effort to hide himself from her gaze.

"Haven't you noticed that the woman is pregnant? And yet you didn't show any mercy."

Eachara had his own reasoning; he believed she had violated the sacred law against defilement.

"Violation of caste rules invites stringent punishment." Eachara enlightened her, quoting from the scriptures for he knew that she and her husband had become pronouncedly deviant.

"Kallu, can you sit up? I shall lend you a hand to rise up."

Uma extended her hand, slowly helping her to get up with her other hand around her back; but she found the woman too heavy for her to prop up.

Kallu sweated profusely and began to groan with her hands pressing down on her abdomen. Uma feared the bouts of pain were sure signs of child birth. She was scared and confused, with no support available to help her handle the situation. Eachara was the only person who could be counted on in this emergency but being a male, and a born enemy of the untouchables, she had no confidence in him.

"Eachara, please come." Uma, however, summoned him.

Kallu's breathing was uneven and her limbs had become rigid. Uma sat massaging her. Eachara feared the woman might die in Uma's arms, an event that would create a scandal. He feared that her death would entangle him in a crime; a sure escape was to drag her away from the courtyard and throw her into the river, but as long as Uma stayed by her side this was impossible.

"*Kunjathole*, is she dying?" He asked Uma nervously.

"Not sure… perhaps…why? You want to see her dead?"

"O! No…. I didn't mean…." He pleaded, pretending innocence.

"If anything happens to her, you shall be responsible," Uma warned him.

"*Ammay…Narayana…Bhagavathee….*" He recited the names of gods and goddesses to save him from this dreadful situation.

The extra long time Kallu took prompted Manka to go looking for her. She stepped out of the canoe, walked up dragging her feet, fearing someone might frown upon her, reached the top flight where she stood carefully examining the sprawling compound and the courtyard in front of the mansion. She didn't find Kallu anywhere but saw a young woman squatting on the ground and an elderly man looking over from behind.

She stopped fearing her detection at a forbidden spot but resolved to remain there hoping to see Kallu, who, she guessed would have gone inside the house with the *Thamprati* who liked her. Manka remained undecided whether to retreat or advance.

Uma felt it awkward to allow a woman to deliver her baby in the open; nor was the woman in a condition to be lifted to a secluded place. The least she could do was to provide her with an improvised shelter and some mats to place under her.

"Echara, you bring half-a-dozen mats and a few poles; we shall make a small enclosure around her; hurry up."

Taking umbrage at the mean task he had been assigned to, as it was for the sake of an untouchable woman, he stood wavering but a stern look from Uma propelled him into action. He ran for his life rather than for Kallu's, and, accidentally, ran into Manka who tried to hide behind the hedge when she saw a Thampran charging towards her.

"Stop…wait," he barked at her, "Do you have some more of your tribe hiding around?" Manka stood still, blinking at his question.

"No hiding; go there, the other woman is dying. Better you take her away, and free us of this nasty job."

She failed to grasp even a word of what he spoke; she remained unmoved averting her face. Enraged, he picked up a stone and threw it at her; it missed her as she skilfully dodged.

"Go there quickly if you want to see your companion alive."

He wanted this woman to attend on her own kith So that he could spare himself the unpleasant task of taking care of an untouchable woman in the process of childbirth. Manka dashed across the courtyard and stood behind Uma, panting. Eachara too returned with a roll of mats and a few poles that he erected around the woman. He fixed the mats erecting an enclosure of a sort.

"You wait outside, we will manage."

Eachara Warrier stayed outside and both Uma and Manka remained inside.

"Kallu, what happened to you dear? Have you been beaten up?"

Manka sat by Kallu's side as she lay struggling with the pain of childbirth. She held Kallu's hand in hers and cried.

"Calm down, don't make her panicky; the baby's head is just popping out; a sudden spurt of emotions can arrest the process." Uma carefully loosened the *mundu* that Kallu had worn rather tightly round her waist. Thick blotches of red began to wet the *mundu* and the mat tucked under her. The women, both inexperienced, became nervous.

The first cry of the baby alerted them; they both simultaneously extended their hands to pick up the baby from the mat but luck favoured Manka who received the new born into her hands, as Kallu lay sighing with the pain abating and a faint smile blossoming on her lips.

"What a cute little thing, dark though." Uma whispered to herself.

"His nose is Meenan's and the big eyes are Kallu's. Manka said as she tried to calm the crying baby, who struggled in her hands exposed to a hostile new world.

"Kallu, you have a son." Uma announced, handing over the baby to its mother; she came out of the enclosure looking for Eachara whom she found missing.

He had gone to the river, and taken three quick dips for the second time that morning not caring even to remove his clothing that dripped water as he emerged from the river; he rushed to the temple reaching there just as the morning rituals were concluding. Hestood with his eyes closed and the hands joined palms placed vertically over his head, apparently seeking atonement for the sin of defiling himself by serving an untouchable woman.

"It's not my fault… I was helpless before the *Kunjathole*."

He protested his innocence before the goddess, hinting it was the fault of the young *Antharjanam* that caused the defilement.

✞✞✞

Twenty Eight

"Meenan was caught by the police in a fish net," the local men explained to those who had come from far off places. Death of a *Pulaya* had no news value; even unnatural death evoked no sympathy. The police refused to take note of their complaint; they made no effort to investigate. The fact that the person had disappeared from their custody did not bother them.

The men talked little but the women wailed loudly. Kallu and Manka sat facing their kinsmen, in their courtyard. The newborn was laid on a new mat wrapped in swaddling cloth.

Ettanu appeared and as his eyes met Kallu he broke down, sobbing wildly. Chitha alone sat on the floor of the hut unmoved.

"Ettanucha, what is this? Hasn't Meenan come yet?" She asked by grasping his hand.

"No Chithamma, Meenan will never come to see us; they killed him, spilt his blood, like his mother's." Chitha didn't understand what Ettanu had said; she continued to sit dazed.

Ettanu slowly lowered himself and sat leaning against the wall. They sat crying, wiping their eyes and blowing their nose! all that they could do against the most atrocious crime committed against them.

Slowly, the men turned restive, each thinking of his own affairs.

"The man is gone; what do we gain by sitting here?"

"It's a sheer waste of time." One by one they whispered into the ears of the men who sat next to them. One man who sat in the back row stood up and signalled to his companion to follow him, and together they sneaked out.

Simeon, who sat watching the crowd, felt that the men were like drift wood with no direction.

"Brothers and sisters, including those who are in a hurry to return home, will you please lend me your ears for a while." They looked at him; some knew who he was, those who didn't, asked their neighbours. A few recognized him as Mathai's father-in-law; still others recognized him as Issac's son. Issac was the man who dared the State power to liberate a group of *Pulayas*, brought to be sold to a public auction at a slave market in the nearby town. He freed them and got them resettled in a colony; finally the government agreed to leave them unmolested.

"I wish to ask you one question; why have all of us come here? Just to cry with our beloved daughters Manka and Kallu? Or else, merely to dangle in our hands the little baby for a while? Of course, our presence and sympathy will give them strength to overcome their grief." Simeon paused, looking into their faces; their response was largely casual. A few sat looking into his eyes sharing his thoughts; some others could not desist from yawning and stretching their limbs. Simeon understood their mood and said:

"I guess you are all tired but I wish to continue. May I?" He paused for their response; he wanted to hear from their mouth.

"Yes, go ahead." One of the two, who had attempted to sneak out but since returned said.

"Do you believe that, Meenan was innocent?

"Yes, he was certainly innocent."They sang in unison.

"Yes, you are right he was blameless, yet they killed him and spilled his blood." Simeon stopped, letting out a heavy breath, asking:

"Do you think they have any right to kill anyone of us or commit atrocities against us and get away with it?"

"No, no, they have no right." Just one person who sat in the front row answered with the rest of the men parrying the question. Simeon was not surprised, and he observed.

"Most of you are not sure and probably unconcerned until you become a victim."

"Don't you know? They pay us poorly; they extract from us compulsory free labour. They prohibit us from walking through public thoroughfares where even dogs are free to roam about and defecate."

"They treat us as untouchables and even inauspicious to look at. They claim the right to kill any one of us for no reason. And now they have killed our Meenan for no offence." Simeon stopped again, and asked with an emphasis.

"Do you think what they did is right?" Nobody answered for or against as he waited to hear from them. After a brief pause a few of them said 'not right…not right.'

"So what should we do?" None from among the audience ventured an answer; it was a question that never crossed their mind; they guessed they had no choice; reprisal was totally unthinkable. A few turned their face towards Simeon for an answer as he stood looking into their eyes hoping to hear their views; they sat ensconced in a weird silence.

"What do you think we should do?" Simeon turned to Kandan.

"What can we do? We are helpless, poor people. Let God punish them." Kandan thought he had given a precise answer as nobody else had offered.

"Yes, leaving our problem to God is good, but whose God?" Simeon knew that those men were timid, afraid of their masters; time had stilled their conscience to a condition of accepting eternal suffering without protest. They had no dream beyond what two measures of paddy could buy them in their lives. Simeon asked his last question.

"How many of you think that we should protest so that violence is no more committed against us?" The question provoked no response like all the other questions; many thought what he hinted at was a necessary step but they themselves ended with another question:

"Who will do it? Who will bell the cat?"

"No one will do it on your behalf; you have to do it if you want a change."

He looked into their eyes for a response but no one answered him.

"You have an opportunity now; the harvest is at hand. I tell you, refuse to reap and see what will happen."

"If we decline to reap they will refuse to give us the two measures. How will we eat our gruel?" Simeon knew it was a very relevant question and concluded that they were not ready to go to that extent. He changed his strategy,

"My friends, at least you should tell your masters that they have wronged you and you are aggrieved at what they have done in killing an innocent man." Simeon believed it would be a good beginning, at least.

By midday, a company of *Pulayas*, the majority being men with a few woman including Maria, Manka and Kallu holding her baby close to her bosom, landed at the *Pulakadavu,* to seek an audience with Konna Kaimal, their landlord and master. A sense of fear gripped them at the very thought of facing the most dreaded man in their lives.

"He may think us rebellious and react violently; set the elephant on us."

"To displease him is a fatal mistake," a few had warned them before they had set out from their homes.

"Simeon can escape to his home but we are to live under the *Thampran*, eating his rice and salt." They argued among themselves.

"If they killed Meenan they have the right to do so." Theyyathan's wife, unsuccessfully though, tried to influence her husband, who ignored her advice and joined the crowd.

"You move forward." Simeon exhorted them. Evidently, the crowd lacked will, and the dread of being identified unnerved many from walking ahead. A few who had stepped forward at Simeon's nudging, quietly drew back to a hind row. Those who found themselves exposed in the front line retreated, creating confusion of backtracking men jostling and pushing.

As a reluctant tide, the throng inched up, stopping at the *Pulappad*, a line beyond which the untouchables were forbidden to enter, leaving Kallu in the front line conspicuously dressed in *chatta* and *mundu* with the babe in her arms. She was almost alone, with others covertly preferring to expose less of their faces. Manka rushed forward to give company to Kallu, with Maria following. The men stood scattered and distracted, a few cursing themselves for their folly in joining the crowd and still others damning Simeon for their misery. Everybody was in a hurry to end the ordeal and return home. Many had no idea why they had come or what to say if the lord asked why they had come. A few hoped that the lord wouldn't visit them at all.

The *Pulayas* waited patiently, honestly expecting Konna Kaimal to come out to ask them why they had come in numbers. None in the house seemed to have noticed their presence and the long wait began to frustrate them. A few tired men slowly drifted away to escape the hot sun, to slouch under the shade of trees; more joined them leaving the few women in the front line. Simeon feared his mission would collapse.

He knew their silent presence wouldn't send any message to the masters. He himself was not sure how to make their presence felt indoors. They were forbidden from entering the premises; violating the rule was insubordination and clamouring for attention invited reprisal. Simeon too was in a dilemma and the crowd that stood tired turned restless.

Simeon concluded that the *Pulayas* could legitimately grieve the murder of their own son before their masters. He managed to gather the crowd together.

"We are here to lament the murder of our son before our master; let him know our grief." There was no precedent of the *Pulayas* rushing to the mansion whenever they lost a soul; yet they found Simeon's idea good.

"Our son is killed," they wailed, beating their chest. Those who had emerged from the dining hall heard the high decibel lamentation of the crowd; it was immediately reported inside.

Konna Kaimal had almost closed his room for a nap after lunch when a maidservant knocked at his door. He saw a frightened woman standing before him apologetically.

"Yes, what's the matter?"

"A horde of our *Pulayas* has assembled at the Pulapad wanting to see you."

"Our *Pulayas*? We have no *Pulayas* of our own. There are *Pulayas* who work for us, and they receive wage for their work, that's all. Of course, they live on our land, but they don't pay any rent therefore."

"What do they want?" He snapped at the servant.

"They are in good numbers; they seem to be determined." The woman walked away without waiting for any instruction. Konna Kaimal was not in a mood to oblige them, either. But the news had shocked him; he could never imagine the *Pulayas* barging into the *Tharawad* compound demanding to see him. He guessed that times were changing.

"It's an act of revolt, totally unacceptable."

Never in the past, had the *Pulayas* aired their grievances in public, that too collectively. Whenever the farm hands felt hurt they waited on Ravunni at the end of the day's work to unburden their woes. The man stood behind his lord, scratching his head and keeping his head wrap rolled under his arm, symbolically cringing for mercy. He never dared to open his mouth until asked.

"Yes, what are you hanging around for?" That was the signal for a worker to present his problems. The master either agreed or disagreed and dismissed him peremptorily with an appropriate word, and the matter ended there.

'How come, they have become so arrogant to challenge me?' Konna Kaimal sent for Kocharayan, the henchman.

"I know why you have summoned me." The mahout said.

"Yes, those men have become rebellious; it should be suppressed."

"I know; they deserve no leniency." Kocharayan looked at Konna Kaimal for further orders; Kocharayan suggested.

"Shall I let the elephant loose on them? He will do a neat job."

"No…no.., we need men to work the farm. No farm hand means no crop raised." Konna Kaimal warned him, adding:

"Only maim them so that they stay away from work for a few

weeks, with no wage to take home; let them starve."

"You take a couple of men with you equipped with *lathis* and charge them mercilessly; but remember never look into their eyes as you begin the assault." That was how the policemen were trained to be effective.

He knew that tiring them was the best way to dispose them of. And it was true; the indefinite waiting tired them; hunger and thirst drained them off their enthusiasm.

Kocharayan emerged from the courtyard with his tackles and four men walking behind him wielding *lathes*; they took position facing the *Pulaya* crowd. The sight of Kocharayan with his armed retinue sent shivers down their spines; they remained unarmed and unprepared for a physical confrontation. Their honest intention was to represent their grievances before their lord and let him know their angst at what had happened.

Kocharayan stepped forward, surveying the crowd; he counted them-around thirty with five females occupying the front row. He found the women in a rebellious mood with their breasts covered in violation of the law. He summoned Kallu by a wave of his rod; she stood still, unmindful of his diktat. Her refusal provoked him; he barked his command:

"Kallu, you devil, come here." She refused to budge and said aloud:

"I haven't come to see you, the *Anakaran*; I have come to see our *Thampran*."

Kocharayan felt her snub; he stroke towards the crowd, targeting the women, who he thought, would collapse at his first charge; but they stood huddled together, determined to face the mahout.

"I am the *Thampran* here; tell me who gave you permission to cover your breast? Mind you, none of you will return home alive."

"I order that you remove your *chattas*, forthwith."

Kocharayan ordered, but the women stood their ground; he felt humiliated again. He hooked Kallu's *chatta* on his rode and pulled it out ripping open her breast. One of his armed companions snatched the breast clothe and threw it up in the air. The *Pulayas* stood unnerved, looking for a breach to run away from the melee; but Simeon stepped forward daringly, donning Kallu with his own jacket to protect her honour, instantly. The *Pulayas* by and large remained unconcerned at Kocharayan's disrobing of the young woman. To many, Kallu's act to cover her breast was rather daring. But Simeon who had been standing at the rear came forward crying:

Save, we shall our honour, the right from the Lord.
No, no you shall not violate our breasts in gaping:
Vested as we walk in, who on earth can stop us?
Protect we shall always the honour that's ours.

It was a Christian chant yet they sang in unison. Kocharayan's gang looked dumbfound for a moment as the *Pulayas* repeated it more daringly. The electrifying effect of the chant was that the *Pulayas* came forward, rallying behind the young women who stood in front, with Simeon urging them on.

Ettanu found himself between the devil and the deep sea; timid as he was, he shunned violence; it hurt him the way the high castes had treated them. He never claimed that the *Pulayas* enjoyed equal rights with others on this earth but he expected they be treated humanely.

An uneasy silence descended on the crowd. Simeon thought the crowd needed efforts to keep their spirits up; he shouted.

"We want to meet Konna Kaimal."

"We want to meet…Ko…."

The crowd stood thunderstruck; they failed to repeat the slogan. It was unthinkable for them to take the name of their lord. Simeon looked askance at the sudden silence of the throng; they stayed looking at each other at the apparent impudence of uttering their lord's name.

"Charge." Kocharayan barked and let loose his goons on them instead of the elephant. They had a free hand; they mercilessly beat up the front liners. Kallu had her head broken but she boldly saved her baby by covering him with her body. The lathe fell on her head and back. The men took to their heels and women lay prostrate on the ground with their faces kissing the earth. There was great wailing and gnashing of teeth, the most the *Pulayas* could resort to. Finally, Kocharayan chased the protestors off the compound and called back his accomplices.

"This is the first warning; they will never in their life make another attempt." Kocharayan triumphantly announced as he lifted up on his hook a torn and blood soaked *chatta* of one of the women.

The agitators quietly boarded the vallom mourning their ill-fated protest, nursing their injuries and cursing their fate. They sat gazing at the distant horizon avoiding each other. More than the physical pain it was the humiliation that wounded them most.

They thought Simeon was the cause of their humiliation. Simeon was not unhappy at the turn of events, and he told them frankly when a few in the boat grumbled.

"You have achieved some thing though our protest ended like this."

"How can you say so when you know our people feel humiliated? Heads broken and limbs wrecked." Ettanu and Kandan doubted.

"That is exactly what you have achieved from today's experience; you feel humiliated and it has gone deep into your heart hurting you always. This hurt will strengthen your will to resist, and if not today, tomorrow you will overcome."

"Like many before him Meenan too will be forgotten soon."

Kallu realized this eternal truth.

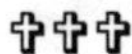

Twenty Nine

"Untouchability is the unique instrument of subjugation the native genius invented to keep the meek in fetters. To legitimise the rule they secured the gods on their side claiming the law was divinely ordained. It's dishonest." Rev Aaron Griffith burst out in righteous anger. He was visiting Jayanthan Namboodiri and wife whom he had saved.

The cruel killing of Meenan had distressed Rev Griffith. He grieved for him, a promising young man simple and guile-less. He did not believe the man was capable of committing a murder. His was a cold blooded murder, with the collusion of the higher ups.

Jayanthan sat listening, sympathising with the aggrieved family. Personally he was grateful to the *Padre,* Meenan and his wife Kallu, whose self-sacrificing service had saved his wife, Uma, from the jaws of death.

"No soul is born untouchable; it's the mind that creates the dichotomy," he rationalised. He and his wife had been living under the scanner for their condemnable association with the untouchables.

Eachara Warrier announced the arrival of Vamadevan Namboodiri and his associates; they had come to haul Jayanthan and his wife over the coals, again. Jayanthan was in the eye of a storm vis-à-vis his unorthodox interaction with the untouchables. Uma's sojourn with the outcastes and her midwifing the *Pulaya* woman had outraged the orthodox community.

"Yes, bring them in." He instructed the steward and asked Rev Griffith to stay on. Eachara Warrier ushered in the interlocutors.

"This is my friend, Rev. Aaron Griffith, a missionary who works among the untouchables." Jayanthan introduced the Priest, emphasising what he did. Vamadevan was scandalized; he stood staring into the eyes of the missionary, rather suspiciously.

"I am sure you have heard of him."Jayanthan added.

"Not much; I am not much impressed with what he does." Vamadevan brushed him aside.

"But he is doing a lot to uplift those miserable souls." Jayanthan again tried to provoke him.

"Who cares? Let the untouchables be their burden."

"You find only beef eaters for company!" It was an indictment of Jayanthan but the sting was directed more at the missionary.

Vamadevan believed both the men lacked the right perspective; he quoted:

"It's sin, o! God it's sin, never atoned
in this life or the next.
To drink the milk of a cow that ate the green
which tufted the earth,
where gushed blood from the veins of a lamb
slit, nourished the soil."

"Not what goes into the mouth but what comes out defiles one." Rev. Griffith observed casually. Vamadevan didn't pay any attention; he trooped out with his companions."A society that doesn't generate internal forces to bring about change is static and doomed." Rev. Griffith observed, adding:"Men like you should act."

"Knowledge is power which is denied to the oppressed. They live as know-nots and therefore, powerless to defy the law; they are taught to believe its violation invites divine wrath; the system ensures that the toilers remained suppressed."

"You have the power to us her in a silent social change." Jayanthan told the Priest.

He said the orthodox societies resisted change by closing the door against the agents of change; Christian society was open, outward looking with the walls of exclusion broken.

"The question of the untouchables admits one practical solution." Jayanthan paused.

"Yes, what could it be?"

"You are not bound by taboos; you admit untouchables into your society. Once integrated with you they will certainly inherit all the privileges the Christians enjoy today. That will save them."

Rev Griffith pondered over the advice; he found the reasoning sound. For, the Christian community enjoyed a social status at par.

"Yes, I understand what you mean. I thank you but I need your support."

"Which you will have in plenty." Jayanthan assured him.

Rev Griffith walked down the steps; he was determined.

A few weeks later, on a summer evening, a company of *Pulayas* led by Ettanu entered the precincts of the Marine Shrine at Kudamaloor; they entered by the unguarded western flank of the church ground, stopping at the foot of a heavy built granite Cross that stood at the entrance.

A flock of women and children from the neighbourhood had assembled at the foot of the Cross, a few with lighted candles and others holding small oil filled earthen bowls with cotton wicks *(diyas);* they placed the lights on the rock, and stood solemnly looking up to the Cross with hope.

They stood gaping at the stream of *Pulayas* who had silently walked into the compound. It was an unusual spectacle with so many of them entering a church together.

It was odd too; for, the men wore white *mundu* that reached down their knees with a light cotton shawl flowing down their shoulders. The women too had worn a *mundu* with its end crimped into a chunky fan hanging behind; a jacket with a close cut neckline inching down to the waist line overlapped the top of the *mundu* covering their torso. The women's garb concealed all the curves hither to shown in the buff, except the face. The strange sight of the *Pulayas* walking in ceremonial attire shocked a few, who thought it defiance.

"What is it? Will we have a new God?" Ettanu's youngest son Koran, asked his brother Chennon pointing at the Cross.

"You keep your mouth shut; it's not any God. It's only a Cross."

"But what is a Cross?"

"I don't know; but someone died on it long, long ago."

"I suppose *Veluthachan* will tell us. Or we will ask our Maria *Ammachi*, she knows." Chennon jostled ahead to stand close by the Cross, wanting to climb atop.

"Chennon, don't do it; keep down." Mathai warned him and Chennon promptly drew back.

Rev. Griffith came with a broad smile on his face with the Sacristan following him. Emmanuel and Rosma too joined them to assist in the ceremony with a bundle of white veils with golden borders. Rosma placed a piece over the head of each female; she showed them how to cover their heads leaving the face uncovered by holding the seams of the veil collected together over their chest. Pylee, the Sacristan instructed the crowd to stand in two lines, men in the front followed by women. Rev. Griffith led them immediately behind Pylee who walked in front holding a crucifix aloft in his hand, solemnly.

Koran who walked at the tail end of the line along with a few other boys filched an oil lamp from the Cross; he walked down slowly, carring it in his cupped palms. The procession stopped at the aisle of the church with Rev. Griffith entering. Jayanthan and Uma, who had arrived to witness the ceremony, stood by the left side of the aisle, watching the rituals that the Priest had commenced. Kuriacko handed over to each of the catechumenates a candle, instructing:"You light it only when asked to."

Pylee escorted Kallu along with her baby to the font where she stood facing the Priest, holding the child in her left arm. Manka rushed in to help her and the Priest signalled Emmanuel and Rosma to move closer to stand by the side of Kallu and her baby as godparents. Rev. Griffith looked at her, solemnly, asking:

"What name do you want to give your son?" Kallu stood puzzled, staring into the faces of the Priest and Pylee.

"Micah." Rosma whispered into her ears.

"Micah." Kallu repeated.

The celebrant asked a series of questions most of which Kallu answered, occasionally helped by the godmother. Pylee lighted the candle and Rosma helped the child to hold it in his tiny black hand.

"In the name of the Father and of the Son and of the Holy Ghost I baptize you Pathrose Micah." Rev Griffith pronounced solemnly.

He blessed Kallu, called her Sarah and baptized her, prophesying that she would see many generations and enjoy the peace of the Lord in her life. He blessed Manka, called her Liza and baptized her.

"Ettanu, you are the eighth among the children of your parents and so they had called you Ettanu, meaning the eighth, and today I baptize you Octavius."

Rev Aaron Griffith baptized and admitted him too into the church. On that day he had baptised ninety souls from twenty seven families; ever since, they were collectively called ninetiers denoting their original number.

"Beloved children in Our Lord Jesus Christ."

Rev Aaron Griffith addressed the congregation of the neophytes, whom he had assembled in the nave of the church soon after the ceremony; they sat on the floor on both sides of a carpeted central passage, turned towards the altar, agape with excitement; the women occupied the rear timidly. The Priest stood in the sanctuary facing them. He looked at their faces and found them exuding a rare joy.

They earnestly believed that they had a great man in the person of their *Veluthachan* to fall back upon, when they groped in doubt or landed in trouble. They believed that they, being Christians, were no longer untouchables. Finally, they thought they had discovered a God who had promised to love them as his own children.

Happier was Rev Aaron Griffith who believed that God had sent him to emancipate a tortured and exploited community destined to live a brute life. He taught them to dream big and he shared with them a vision.

"Today I have baptized you, and you have become Christians; and I want to remind you that to live a Christian life is very simple if you observe only, and I say only, one commandment of our Saviour Jesus Christ." Rev Griffith paused for a moment looking into the eyes of those who sat before him, and also Jayanthan and Uma who stood attentively in the aisle.

Jayanthan looked puzzled, as he had always heard of Ten Commandments, not one. As the elders waited straining their ears the youngsters cast their roving over the carved ceiling and the altar wall feasting on the icons and intricate inlays.

"Yes, one commandment, Love. You love God and love one another; the rest follows. For, God is Love and He is our Father and we are His children, and remember love bonds us together."

"When you love your God you love one another, and when you love one another you love your God." Rev. Griffith explained to them.

"This is the church where you are free to come and worship when ever you like but certainly on Sundays." He looked into the face of each, whom he recognised by name; their faces, he thought, though meek mutely articulated a new hope for a better life. Rev. Griffith realised it was his words that strengthened their will to tread a new path daring the powerful. He was confident that they had God on their side taking care of them. He guessed that being neophytes they needed one person to lead and guide them.

"I suggest that Octavius be your *Moopan,* the elder person to guide you. Besides, the Reverent Fathers of this Parish would be your spiritual leaders and teachers. Obey them."

"In the name of the Father and the Son and the Holy Ghost I bless you. The Peace of the Lord is with you."

The ceremony over, they trooped out of the church, bowing before Rev Griffith in whom they thought they had found a saviour, and folding their hands before Jayanthan who had been standing beside the Priest. Sarah came out of the church holding her baby in her arms; she stood before Uma with a smile that soon faded away as a surge of emotions overwhelmed her.

"Rev Griffith, you have taken upon your shoulders a great responsibility. I found them very enthusiastic had with great expectations." Jayanthan told him, adding "A mere change of religion or bearing new names doesn't help them; what they need is a change in their life."

The treatment meted out to the untouchables in his community had troubled him for years. He believed the intervention of the church would show them a way out.

"The theory that birth determines one's destiny is rather irrational." He opined

Rev Griffith had a vision to bring about changes in the society; his intention was not simply to multiply the number of Christians by converting the *Pulayas*. He was moved by the miserable life they had been damned to live.

"Organization and education usher in changes." The Priest explained.

"The church provides a viable organization and by getting integrated with it, this community will find social mobility, denied to them presently, possible. Being part of the church gives them a new identity."

"The stone that collects the pollen shed by the jasmine blossom too retains its fragrance." Uma remembered the old axiom.

"Yes, very true. I think the Christian presence is slowly but certainly inducing changes in our social milieu; it's a welcome influence, really catalytic." Jayanthan recognized the potential of the Gospel of Love.

"If what I preach makes you a good person what more should I expect?" Rev Griffith asked as he sauntered with Jayanthan and Uma.

Emmanuel's big boat had sailed down, punted by Ittathan baptized Isidore and Kandan renamed Christopher. Octavius, the *Moopan* sat on the mid-thwart; he sat looking into the distance rather thoughtful.

"Pakkothamma, what is the name *Veluthachan* has given you?" Manka, who had her name changed to Liza asked Octavia's' wife. It was difficult for them to remember their new names.

"*Ediyey*, what is your new name?" Octavius asked his wife; he failed to grasp what Rev Griffith had pronounced. Too many people and too many names that refused to yield to their tongue confused them. Octavius' wife too remained uncertain.

"Ammachee's name is Philoma." Maria, the daughter-in-law of the family came to their rescue. Philoma found the new jacket of raw cotton irritating and uncomfortably itchy. Quietly, she pulled the jacket over her head; it caught but with the narrow slit of the neckline refusing to allow the head to pass through.

"Philoma's head is too big for the slit." Liza said as she helped her to pull the jacket off.

"Too much clothing sweats you heavily." Philoma tried to explain away her action; she threw the chatta over her shoulder carelessly and sat on the edge of the boat. What she did prompted a few other women to follow.

"Octovicha, please tell us, what do we stand to gain by becoming Christians?" Isidore's son David asked him the first question that he faced on becoming their *Moopan*. Octavius himself was unsure as to what they gained yet he ventured to answer the question. He remembered what *Veluthachan* had told them earlier.

"*Veluthachan* told us that we have discovered our God, the Saviour."

"Will the God help us get three measures of paddy as our daily wage instead of the two that we receive now? Will Konna *Thampran* listen to our God?" David raised a relevant question. He guessed that Konna *Thampran's* God was not the one that they had discovered presently; he wondered why he should accept one that was not his own.

"Our God will give us the wisdom to do things intelligently; that will give us strength. It's not the volume of grain that determines our future; of course, we need food too," Mathai's wife Maria, who had heard David's questions, saved her father-in-law.

"Yes, what Maria said is true; we will become strong." Isidore believed that Maria, whose family had joined the church earlier, knew better.

"Will we become strong enough to kill the murderers of our Meenacha?" Chacko, son of Octavius asked; he wanted to take revenge on the mahout; he added: "That *Aanakkaran* should be punished."

"No. You need not punish him. I have already forgiven him." Sarah, who sat listening to the discussion, intervened.

"Why? Why should he not be killed? He has killed our Meenacha." Chacko was annoyed at Sarah's breaking in but what she said further confused him; he wondered what the new idea of forgiveness was.

"I have already forgiven them; we pray to God to forgive us as we forgive our enemies," Sarah explained. Chacko was not convinced though he sat back, grumbling.

"So far we have been forgetting their wrongs, now we are forgiving them too. Still, we have no strength to oppose them." He thought the new teaching was ineffective, still leaving them at the mercy of their tormentors.

"One thing I wanted to tell you definitely. We are Christians and we are no longer untouchables." Octavius declared with pride, as the crowd appeared lapsing into silence, quite unconvinced of Sarah's act of forgiveness.

"How do you know for certain? Will the *Thamprans and Thampratis* accept us as equals?" It was again Chacko's turn.

"They have to. Emmachan and Rosma are Christians, and they are not untouchables. There cannot be two rules for one people." Octavius asserted with reason.

"Let us test and see." Chacko relented. But he was not willing to leave it at that; he decided to visit the *Tharawad* one day to enter the house to see how the high caste would respond.

"Remember, *Veluthachan* wanted us to attend the *Kurbana,* the Holy Mass, on Sunday. No excuses; all must come, wearing clean clothes." Octavius reminded them as the boat shored.

"On Sunday morning we will meet you at the church." They assured each other, as they got off the boat en route home; they appeared happy.

Back home, Octavius was thoughtful.

"*Veluthachan* is all for us but what about the other Fathers?" He noticed that none of them came to witness the ceremony. He neither asked this question nor shared his doubts with his brethren but it was a fact that really bothered him. He wondered whether the great expectations that had driven his men into the church were real. He guessed that though Ittathan, [baptized Isidore], lacked formal schooling, he was wise and was right when he observed precisely:

"We're people with no gods of our own; their gods don't open their eyes on us, they keep the doors shut against us. For, our sight defiles the gods who run away from their pedestals seeing us, leaving their temples desolate. If gods do not want us why should gods' men care for us? So we are defilers as well." Isidore explained to him and what he said was clear to Octavius.

"As far as I know, *Veluthachan* doesn't despise us, he certainly loves us and he declares that his God loves everybody, high or low." Isidore continued.

Octavius and his people believed as Isidore explained. "We trust in *Veluthachan*'s God; at least His abode is not barred to us and He doesn't run away at our sight."

"And we ceased to be untouchables, hopefully."

Now, Octavius had more questions seeking answers.

"How will Konna *Thampran* react once he learns that we have become Christians?" He shuddered at the thought of facing Konna Kaimal whom they had already crossed. Though they had dared him, egged on by Simeon, whose Christian courage had blinded them. He feared that the axe would fall on them any day. In the night as he slept, instead of the new God it was Konna Kaimal who stood before him, with his face contorted with rage and eyes red, summoning him out.

"Ninety of our *Pulayas* have joined the Christian church; perhaps they will become more demanding." Kocharayan brought the news to Konna Kaimal.

"By joining the church they do not cease to be *Pulayas* and *Pulayas* they will remain receiving the same two measures of paddy." He declared.

"Let them be the Christian's burden. The land is ours; to eat their daily gruel they have to earn the two measures which we hold; they have to come to us. Will the *Padre* feed them? We feed them." He asserted.

But the *Pulayas* had great expectations which Rev Griffith had shared with them in Christian abundance.

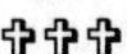

Thirty

It was Sunday morning, the first Christian Sunday they had been excitedly awaiting. Getting up early morning posed no problem; they readied themselves for church.

"Konna *Thampran* has arrived." Philoma announced, disturbing Octavius' peace. He was lazing on the mat dreaming of the first Mass in the church. Octavius lay proudly watching his wife and children busying themselves, getting dressed. Maria stood by the rear door helping Agnes, who was formerly Chakki, doing her hair, and instructing her in the Lord's Prayer; the girl stood struggling with its mystery and its strange phrasing, prompting her to ask:

"Will the Lord give us bread too?"

Before she could answer a shout echoed,

"Ettanoo…" An impatient Konna Kaimal screamed. Octavius was slow to appear before the lord and Konna concluded that the man did this in protest against his refusal to meet him when he came along with his horde.

"Maybe his new found Christian arrogance. How could he be so impudent and conceited? I'll teach him a lesson." He looked back; he had a retinue of half-a-dozen men with him.

But Octavius saved the situation; he rushed out and stood before Konna Kaimal, with his arms crossed across his chest, head bent and shoulders slouched in abject submission as he did in the past. He was careful to remove the white *mundu* he had worn around his waist for the church; he guessed his dress would enrage his lord. The deep sense of subjugation that remained ingrained in his psyche hadn't been erased overnight by the new Faith. Konna Kaimal concluded he was still the old *Pulaya.* Yet he decided he shouldn't be shown any leniency.

"You, rascal; don't you know that I am here waiting for you."

"No *Thampra*, I learnt when my wife told me."

"O! Do you expect me to send you advance notice?"

"No *Thampra.*" Octavius said slouching his shoulders further. The precept of Christian equality Rev Griffith had sunk into his psyche seemed to have evaporated.

"Don't you know these men have come to pluck the nuts? Am I to wait at your convenience?"

Octavius had rightly guessed the purpose of Konna Kaimal's visit with his retinue. A weekly off was never a bondsman's right.

Octavius lived in a sprawling coconut grove owned by the *Tharawad*; he was bound to work for the landlord on a nominal wage besides the *oozhium*. On every forty-fifth day, a team of tree climbers reached the grove to cut the nuts. The harvesting was supervised by the big boss personally; he came by boat punted by two men, carrying an easy chair for him to relax and watch the operations. Paramu Nair was to keep a detailed account of the trees climbed, nuts yielded, nuts dropped by the trees and pilfered. Octavius had to account for the nuts found lost, the charges automatically slapped on him.

Four climbers clambered up the trees; they cut down the ripe bunches that crashed on the ground scattering the nuts. Greater the number each tree yielded, the sight of its free fall and the sound of its crash brightened Konna's face; he sat counting the bunches and estimating the nuts as they came down.

Octavius stood silently behind Konna Kaimal, gazing at the climbers and watching the nuts filling the ground; Konna Kaimal's face suddenly turned cloudy for, he found Ettanu's wife and children absent and even Ettanu remaining indifferent. It was their duty to collect the nuts and the fronds.

"Ettanu?" Konna Kaimal jumped up from the chair and stomped towards him; Ettanu drew back alarmed at the menacing expression on his face.

"Where are your woman and children? Don't you know you have to collect the nuts?" Octavius stood still, daring not to look into the eyes of his boss.

"Aren't you listening?" Konna Kaimal bawled out.

"Yes *Thampra*, but they have gone to church; *Veluthachan* told us not to work on Sundays." Octavius told him rather nervously.

"church? *Veluthachan*? No work on Sundays? Whose Lord's days? Who determines? I am the Lord here and I say you don't eat on Sundays either." He shouted as Octavius stood shivering.

Ettanus becoming Christians was no news but the temerity of his servant in casually making it known and declaring that they didn't work on Sundays angered Konna Kaimal. For him, it was sheer defiance.

"You are my servant, your woman and children as well. You have to do my work first; your church and *Padre* are not my concern. Go and collect the nuts immediately. I'll decide what to do with you later." Konna Kaimal withdrew shaking his head ominously; Octavius knew that the frown on his face implied that a disaster awaited him.

He conjured up the vision of the entire newly baptized community attending the morning Mass, socializing and exchanging pleasantries with the congregation, including the ancient Christians. Ettanu had great expectations about the first day's worship in the church.

He had prided himself at *Veluthachan* nominating him the *Moopan* of the ninetiers; it was his privilege to lead them into the church. He expected the old, aristocratic Christians waiting at the entrance to receive them into the church; many of them were personally known to him as rich farmers. He believed it was great to sit in the church along with them worshipping the same God.

Collecting the nuts that ran into a few thousands single-handed was an enormous task; soon he found himself weak and exhausted. Kocharayan was following the climbers but returned to Octavius when he found the man lagging behind.

"Ettanu, hurry up; we have to return by noon," the mahout shouted. He felt peeved at the mahout's intervention. His addressing him by his old name was unacceptable to him and he decided to correct him. He also believed that he need not address him as *Thampran* as he was no longer an untouchable, slave.

"Kocharayan, I am no longer Ettanu, I am Octavius." The erstwhile timid, servile man stood up and declared with pride.

The untouchable's audacity to address him by his first name stunned Kocharayan, who stood staring at him. Octavius continued picking up the nuts; the mahout's icy stare went unnoticed; but a chance glance chilled Octavius' heart. The mahout charged at him; Octavius unobtrusively moved to another corner to avoid him but the mahout followed him, itching for a row so that he could haul him up before the boss. He yelled derisively.

"Ettanu.... you Ettanu *Pulaya*? How dare you address me by my name?"

Octavius refused to respond and his snub angered the mahout.

"Your new name...what is it? It's for your woman and children to address you; maybe for that *Padre* too. For us, you are still Ettanu, the *Pulaya*."

"No, I am no more a *Pulaya*; I am a Christian, and understand that we are no longer untouchables." Ettanu proudly asserted.

"*Pfooo*...Christian? This is it." Kocharayan caught the man and struck him on his cheek. As Octavius struggled with the mahout Kadutha, the tree climber interrupted, yelling:

"*Thampra*...no...don't do it."

The mahout meekly drew back, eying Kadutha sheepishly. Kocharayan knew that the chopping knife wielded by a toddy tapper and the chopper held by a coconut tree climber were formidable, and Kadutha had one held in his hand.

By mid morning the members of his family returned from the church. Octavius had busied himself with picking up the nuts; he lacked the will to face them for his cheek was swollen and left eye still remained red. Philoma promptly removed her upper jacket and rushed into the ground along with the older boys to collect the scattered nuts. Mathai too was bare breasted but the other boys did not care to bare themselves more for the fun of wearing a shirt than to irritate their lords. Mathai had warned them but the youngsters declined to oblige him. Little Agnes stood by the courtyard of the hut holding on to the fingers of Maria whose white dress and Agnes' colourful frock made them conspicuous.

"Who are those *apsaras*?" Konna Kaimal asked Kocharayan derisively as he saw the girls standing well dressed in his presence. This frightened Maria who quietly withdrew into the hut dragging Agnes along.

By mid afternoon the work was over and Octavius and his family piled up the nuts in a heap. The stalks of nuts for Konna Kaimal to determine the nuts dropped by the trees and nuts pinched by pilferers were presented.

"One hundred and eight nuts dropped." Paramu Nair announced looking into the eyes of Konna Kaimal and peeping at Octavius. It was for Octavius to account for the nuts dropped.

"How many pinched?" Konna Kaimal was impatient. Paramu Nair carefully examined the stalks again to detect telltale marks left on the stalk when the nuts were pinched.

"Forty-seven." Prompt came the reply.

"Ettanu?" He stood before Konna Kaimal who turned towards him; the storm of anger that blew over the loss of nuts turned Konna Kaimal's face into an ugly gnarl. Mathai had brought from their hut eighty-one nuts they had collected as dropped by the trees.

"Where did the twenty-seven go? Who pinched them?"

"*Thampra*… we haven't pinched any; it was mostly from trees that stood on the rim of the compound, easily accessible to late night prowlers." Octavius tried to explain. Every night they had been diligently watching the grove until mid night but the sneaky thieves had always outwitted them "It's not for me to come and catch them; that is why you are here." Konna Kaimal stood staring at him; he said:"You have failed in your duty."

"*Thampra*, the dropped nuts are those fallen in the water and carried away by the river; we haven't taken a single nut." Octavius pleaded.

"No excuses; to compensate the *Tharawad* you and your family will work for us ten days with no wage. If you fail, you will receive twelve lashes. You know what happened to Chathan." Konna Kaimal dismissed them tersely and walked away.

"We are leaving two thousand, eight hundred and fifty eight nuts." Paramu Nair told him. It was obviously Octavius' duty to hand over the exact number to the contractor. Octavius sat back grieving over the fate fallen upon him, twelve lashes or ten days *oozhium*.

"He could have ordered us to the gallows instead of starving us to death."

"Why don't you eat your gruel?" Philoma came searching for him; she guessed he was hungry. He had had no food since his supper the previous evening.

"It's mid afternoon, no harm in skipping the mid day meal; who knows what we will have for tomorrow." He sat immobilized, his left cheek covered his hand to hide it from his children. Philoma too decided to forgo her lunch; she sat by his side. He didn't know how long he sat watching the heap of nuts awaiting the contractor to arrive.

In the evening some of his fellow Christians came, and found him sleeping leaning against the coconut mound; they woke him up.

"This morning we missed you in the church." Christopher said casually.

"Our life is not in our hands." His reply was clear to his friends; they could guess why he couldn't attend church.

"In a way it was good that you didn't come; there was no place inside the church. We stood outside" Isidore explained.

Being new and strangers to the Sunday Mass they reached the

church late, thinking the ritual required one just to show one's face any time. A few, who had in fact arrived on time, tarried outside timidly looking for Octavius to lead them in. Mathai arrived along with his wife and other women; he too was uncertain.

"Why do you wait outside? You are free to enter the church as you arrive; nobody will come to invite you. Let us go in; it's already full." Maria urged them moving ahead, and waving to them to follow.

They waited in the open peeping in for a glimpse of the colourful ceremony.

The neophytes felt disappointed; they found the ancient Christians unfriendly. No one came to welcome them. They looked at them as if they were unwelcome intruders. The younger generation felt hurt and doubted whether their decision to join the church was right; they argued and began to question the wisdom of their elders.

Isidore's son David and Octavius' son Chacko expected no change to occur in their life by joining the church. They reasoned:

"We were mere *Pulayas* earlier; now everybody calls us Christian *Pulayas*. Does it mean any change?

"We are just tolerated, that too for the sake of *Veluthachan*."

But the women among them, though equally hurt, were not in favour of breaking off.

"We never had a God of our own to worship; our lords never allowed us to enter their temples as they said we defiled them. Now we have our own God and we will abide with Him. I am sure these people will change their attitude slowly." Sarah argued. Maria and Liza supported her.

"Does *Veluthachan* know what happened in the church last Sunday?"

He knows; he had a report from Pylee, the sacristan.

For almost three months, the neophites had been arriving for the Sunday Mass individually, rather unpunctually. Those who reached ahead of time nervously stood outside expecting the arrival of their group. They stood wavering and totally overawed at the sight of the powerful personalities striding into the church. By the time the number of Neo-Christians swelled, the church got filled to capacity. Their feeble attempt to enter the church disturbed the worshippers already inside who demurred forcing the *Pulayas* to withdraw shamefacedly. They prevailed upon the Vicar to chastise them from the pulpit, and he obliged them.

"Next Sunday, let us come ahead of the time," Christopher suggested.

"The church is not large enough to accommodate all those who come for the Mass; those who come first naturally find a place inside. You come early and nobody can stop you from occupying the nave." Rev Griffith assured them as he heard their problem; they felt reassured though a few youngsters looked sceptical.

On Sunday morning they arrived at the ferry in strength. Christopher and Joseph had gone around in a boat to collect all the members from their homes. They stood in a single line and walked slowly, but the chimes of the bell warned them; it was the second bell for the Mass.

"The second bell is ringing; you have to quicken your steps." Octavius announced, his warning spurred them and they reached the church before the third bell. They stopped bewildered.

The church was almost empty. Pylee was inside lighting the twelve candles on the steps of the altar on either side of the tabernacle.

Octavius stood immobilized; he was unsure how the high-born would react. With the people behind him surging forward he could no longer resist the temptation to lead his people into the church.

He stepped forward cautiously and entered the church with his people following. They squatted wherever they found space.

Gradually, the regular worshippers began to arrive; the sight of too many *Pulayas* in the church surprised them though they had heard the news that the Missionary Priest had converted a few. Those who came early sat comfortably, wherever they found place but when more people arrived it posed problems; many found themselves barred to stand outside. They were annoyed. Some who thought that the *Pulayas* had encroached upon their privilege were unwilling to let the *Pulayas* sit in the nave. They forced their way into the church pushing aside the intruders; the *Pulayas* resisted. Kurian Edathon who had arrived late felt outraged at the impudence of the *Pulayas*; for him, sharing the floor with the *Pulayas* was anathema. He stood in the aisle, snapping his fingers; many from among the worshippers looked back and he selectively summoned the *Pulayas*. A couple of them meekly stood before him.

"You sit outside." He showed them the door. A few ignored his summons and stayed inside the hall. Their refusal wounded his pride. He walked up to a man who had refused to respond to his summons. He lifted the man up, dragged him and pushed him out. Some of his companions were miffed. The men who had been shown the door tarried outside, talking among themselves. Those who remained inside felt restive.

As the congregation rose up for the readings from the Gospel the remaining *Pulayas* found it easy to sneak out. Isidore squeezed himself out bumping a man who had blocked the door; offended, the man retaliated by pushing Isidore down. Rattled, the *Pulayas* collectively resorted to a raucous protest, the only weapon they had.

In the melee that followed several of them were hurt and thrown out forcibly. Their women came out screaming, Sarah carrying her baby in her arms and Christopher's wife dragging her four-year-old grand-daughter to safety. Isidore's nose was bleeding as the man who stood blocking the door had punched him but he was scared to name him. Philoma removed her jacket promptly, and wiped the blood from his nose and lips.

"I will put this jacket to a better use, he said."

The *Pulayas* quickly dispersed without waiting for the Mass to conclude. Philoma left behind her blood stained *chatta on* the granite steps of the church as she walked away.

She blamed her husband for all their woes, the genesis of which she attributed to his decision to let his son marry a Christian girl.

"We are neither here nor there." Philoma concluded as Octavius walked behind her still unwilling to be disillusioned. He believed that *Veluthachan* would solve the problem for them; he waited on him, hopefully.

Rev Aaron Griffith had his hands full.

✞✞✞

Thirty One

The missionaries emphasised the fundamental truth.
"Education liberates man; universal education is a right." But a conservative royalty shot down the idea.

"It's not the policy of the Government of His Highness to spend funds from the Treasury of the Deity to promote universal education. Besides, learning is forbidden for the untouchables."

Undeterred, the missionaries decided to go ahead with opening of schools; the mounting pressure from the missionaries persuaded the royalty to relent.

Edavapathi, meaning mid *Edavam,* coincided with the first of June; the monsoon seldom failed to keep its date with the land. The arrival of the monsoon was eventful; the rains revived life on the earth which became green.

Arrangements had already been completed for the opening of a new primary school. Recognition for the school was finally granted by the government. The building was large enough to eventually accommodate four classes, though the intake for the first year was limited to class one. Rev Griffith had funded the construction.

A day before he visited the premises along with Jayanthan to make sure that every thing was in place for the class to begin on the date. The sky was cloudy and a midnight outbreak of monsoon was almost certain

"Monsoon is welcome but not tomorrow morning." He prayed watching the dark clouds that marched eastward.

The day arrived. For the first-time pupils the experience was exciting though a few felt nervous. Many pupils arrived well ahead of time, walking briskly into the premises but many appeared confused and unwilling to walk in; their guardians escorted them. Inside, a class room was set up with three benches put on three sides; on the fourth side a small table was placed facing the pupils with a wooden chair behind. Rev Griffith had ordered for a few more benches which, however, failed to arrive.

"How many can be seated on these benches?" Rev Griffith asked.

"Maybe twenty-five or maximum thirty," the Headmaster replied.

During the past four weeks the three men, Jayanthan, Rev Griffith and the Headmaster Raman Pillai had been visiting parents with children aged five or above. Treading the countryside, talking to parents irrespective of castes, at times arguing but frequently drawing flak was an arduous task. They received a mixed reception; a few enthusiastically offered to send their children but many appeared sceptical and reluctant.

The upper castes feared that a school sponsored by the Missionary would certainly have a good many untouchables. His obvious pro-untouchable stand was unacceptable to them. They feared free mingling of the children would lead to the breakdown of the social system. But ironically the lower castes too remained sceptical; they feared their children might be accused of defiling the upper caste children inviting reprisals.

"If you admit only upper caste children, I will send both my nieces." Govinda Marrar, who played percussion instruments in the temple assured his visitors, and added cautiously.

"My elder niece is nine, she may turn pubescent any day. I cannot take the risk, so I don't want to send her to school."

"It's a natural occurrence, why are you vexed?" Rev Griffith tried to assuage his fears but the response from the man was anger: "You don't know what our culture is; we have Namboodiris giving *Pudava* to our girls. Do you know what it demands?"

"Govinda, don't get agitated; there is nothing unusual about it. If you don't want to send the girls to school forget what we have told you; the matter ends." Jayanthan spoke firmly as they walked away.

"*Ammava*, why don't you allow us to join the school? It's very interesting as they teach many useful things; singing, dancing, sewing and writing." The youngest girl urged her uncle the elder Ratnamma who stood behind the sacred basil mound had nudged her sister forward to plead with their uncle.

"Namboodiris don't look for learned girls." Govinda Marar told them plainly. The opposite was true; the educated girls never fell for the Namboodiris.

Their next encounter was with Pulpara Narain Pillai,a landlord and textile dealer. His sister had two sons, twins and two daughters aged seven and five. He agreed to send the boys but the girls he found no reason to be educated.

"The girls need no schooling; they should learn how to raise a family from their elders," His glib answer stunned Rev Griffith, but the other men with him found nothing new in his argument.

"But what about your own sons? you have two." Jayanthan asked him.

"That is for their uncle to decide. I don't question his right." He had no regret in disowning his responsibility to educate his own children.

The next port of call was at the house of Thomman Mappillai, a flourishing Christian trader and agriculturist; he raised paddy, coconut and sugarcane on land he owned and leased from a local landlord. He processed the yields in his backyard and sold rice, coconut oil and jaggery. His residence was a veritable beehive of activities.

When the school promoters entered Thomman Mappillai's premises, he was busy in measuring out coconut oil that he had contracted to supply to the local temple; a few more customers waited to buy rice and jaggery. The householder appeared vexed as he faced varied customers demanding different items. His eldest son Yacob told him of the arrival of the Priest and a Namboodiri; the news irritated him, still he rushed out entrusting his son with the unfinished task. As he approached the exalted visitors, he removed his head gear as a mark of respect, ordering his son to place a bench for the guests.

"Praise is to Jesus." He wished the Priest, simultaneously folding his hands as he turned towards Jayanthan with a smile.

"Mappilai is terribly busy, I suppose." Jayanthan complimented him in appreciation of the scale of his activities.

"Oh... not much." He tried to be unassuming.

"How many children do you have, Thomman?" Rev Griffith asked as he saw a swarm of children frolicking around with a toddler, perhaps the youngest, attempting to climb up his shoulder. Thomman lifted the child up and held her in his arms.

"I have fourteen children; she is the youngest, not yet two. My eldest son is twenty eight; he helps me in the business; he has three kids."

"Very good; yours is a blessed family. But do they go to school?" Rev Griffith enquired.

"No. They don't read much; in fact, they don't need much reading; everyone is good at calculating." Thomman added, after a little thought. "That is enough for our business."

Jayanthan knew that no amount of canvassing would convince Mappillai to change his mind. Rev Griffith thought of tackling him from another angle.

"Thomman, don't you want to read the Bible at home?"

He was not concerned with the Bible, he told the Priest candidly.

"Father, we recite all the thirty-three prayers and a full rosary every day."

They understood that Thomman was a hard nut to crack but they decided to try their luck anyhow; they put the question straight.

"Why don't you send at least the younger children to school; we have now a school near your house," Rev Griffith suggested.

"That is very difficult, Father. Every child does some useful work in this house. The girl, just above this one, is taking care of this girl. How can I spare her? The one above her looks after the chicks, the boy above him is looking after the goats and cattle. I need more children to keep this household going." Thomman was very proud to inform them how gainfully his family members were engaged.

"At least send one among the fourteen to school, and see the difference." Taking advantage of his spiritual affinity with a fellow Christian, Rev Griffith pleaded with him adding, "Education ushers changes in our life."

"Father, do you think that schooling will bring about changes in a person?" Suddenly, Thommam Mappillai sounded serious.

"Yes, certainly." Rev Griffith and Jayanthan together assured him. Thomman stood pondering for a while, and then he selected one the who, he thought, needed change the most in his household.

"I will send my wife to school; she needs change."

The school promoters sat stunned at what Thomman had decided. Rev Griffith had a difficult time convincing Thomman this was unacceptable.

"Thomman, this is a school meant for little children. We expect you to send at least one of your youngsters." Thomman pondered, and reluctantly then agreed.

"Okay Father I will send one to oblige you."

"I thank you. What is his name?"

"Gheevarghese."

"At least one." Jayanthan heaved a sigh of relief as they walked down the pathway.

They met a good number of the local population; many were enthusiastic, many lukewarm and many just not interested. The dominant groups that resisted schooling were from the upper caste who feared that by sitting along with the untouchable children, their wards would be defiled.

"Remaining undefiled is more honourable than getting educated," the mahout of the temple elephant told Jayanthan to his face. The team missed Parvathi's house but she searched them out to tell that she would send her children to school.

The resistance they came across in getting the children enrolled was an experience for Rev Griffith. He discovered that socio-cultural inhibitions had become sanctified and inviolable on the hallowed matrix of religion. A convenient practice had become a rule.

At the end of the day, Rev Griffith felt disappointed; he found his protégés, the *Pulayas*, rather lukewarm. Most of the children, timid as they were, shied away at the very suggestion of schooling; the hang-over of the past seemed to have frightened them away. The parents too appeared less enthusiastic, their fear being the cost involved and the loss of earnings. However, a few came forward seeking admission. Rev Griffith's offer to provide each child with two sets of dress failed to lure many. He thought he would recommend to the Parish committee to grant two measures of rice to each family which sent their wards to school. This was mainly aimed at the *Pulayas*; he expected it to be a community supported programme.

Kunjan, the tavern keeper visited Rev Griffith along with Octavius to seek admission for his daughter. Kunjan was not sure whether his daughter would be admitted. Rev Griffith was glad that Kunjan took the initiative.

The first day of school arrived. Kunjan was the first parent to get to the school; he reached along with his daughter, both looking nervous. They stood at the door undecided, wondering whether they should enter. Those who came later, of the high caste community, walked past them into the office where the Headmaster was seated. Several parents who had come escorting their children waited on the premises with apprehension. The air was thick with rumours about the caste men's threat to physically resist the entry of the untouchables and the untouchables' determination to frustrate any attempt to stop them.

"I heard that the caste people have brought a few men under wrestler Manian Pillai to chase away the untouchable children." The disclosure alarmed Kunjan but he stood undaunted for he knew Jayanthan Namboodiri and Rev Griffith supported the weaker communities. They affirmed: "You are the children of this land; you have equal rights."

"The grown up *Pulayas* will accompany the children, with their sickles."

"The *Pulayas* can turn fierce if they are piqued."

"Why are you standing there? Get away, you defile us." Govinda Marar who had finally decided to get his nieces admitted, shouted at Kunjan; he drew back holding his daughter's hand to a corner sufficiently away from the door.

"Kunjan, have you got your daughter enrolled?" Rev Griffith who had just arrived walked up to him and asked.

"Ugh… I am just waiting."

"Smart girl… what's your name?" The Priest asked her with a chuck under her chin; the child shyly drew back hiding behind her father, but announced:

"Ammukutty."

"Good girl… Ammukutty."

He took her by her arm and entered the room signalling Kunjan to follow.

"Raman Pillai, please help them; left to themselves, they will never reach you." He advised Kunjan to wait at the desk.

The Headmaster was not pleased with the unsolicited patronage the Priest had extended to the outcastes but he was forced to oblige.

"What is her name?"

"Ammukutty."

"You may go; leave the child in the class." He noted her name in the register. The dismissal, was peremptory. Ammukutty was afraid to enter the classroom but her father pushed her in. She stood in a corner petrified with fear, silently watching the youngsters of the upper castes rollicking about with gusto.

Suddenly, the crowd lapsed into silence. The few parents who had waited for the class to commence appeared bewildered at the unexpected sight of a long file of children entering the school gate trailing behind Rev Griffith, with Sarah, Octavius and Christopher guarding the rear. Rev Griffith decided to lead them personally into the classroom, as he had feared the rumoured threat to stop the *Pulaya* children at the entrance, might result in a fracas.

Ammukutty was happy that she saw at least one person who would keep company with her in the class. It was Octavius' daughter Agnes.

"Chakki…we will sit together," she rushed towards her excitedly.

"We will sit together, but remember I am now Agnes, not Chakki."

The first bell went beckoning the children to a new world of knowledge.

The sound of the gong echoed across the skyline and sent a message of promise to everyone. The crowd that waited to watch the brawl missed it but not altogether.

Rev Griffith's protégés, numbering nineteen, eleven boys and eight girls, made an impressive entry. As they entered the class they stood covering the first two benches that they occupied. The other children also rushed into the class but found the remaining one bench not enough to seat twenty-two of them.

"You urchins get off the benches; squat on the floor as you do at home." Govinda Marar rushed to the classroom along with the wrestler Manian Pillai, yelling at the children; they stood up instantly, dazed and frightened.

The class teacher, Devaki Amma, rose to the occasion demanding the aggressive Govinda Marar and the wrestler move out of the classroom; she recognized it was her duty to keep order in the class for it was the first school in the village.

"None should violate the sanctity of the classroom by forcibly entering when the teacher is in the class. Please go out."

Devaki Amma's order silenced the aggressors, who turned back and saw the School Inspectress Elizabeth Philip standing close-by. The men drew back hiding their sheepish faces; a shawl that hung down his shoulders helped Govinda Marar cover his face as he walked out of the class.

"Devaki Amma, please continue the class." The Inspectress gave her freedom to manage the affairs.

"We don't allow any distinction nor do we discriminate on the basis of caste or religion; here all are equals. Do you understand children?

"Yes teacher." The children answered earnestly in unison. It was for the first time that some one in authority had pronounced that all were equals, though its significance had gone largely unregistered.

"Very good; now please sit down." The children on the right sat on the two benches while the children on the left stood uncertain as they had only one bench available. A few children had to sit on the floor which was clean and plastered with cow dung.

"Now I shall take the roll call. I'll call out your names and each should stand up to say '*Hajjar* teacher.' Do you understand?"

"Yes teacher."

Devaki Amma opened the attendance register. The names were entered in alphabetical order; but she found the very first name weird and unfamiliar.

"*Aamakutty.*" She watched the face of every child present in her class.

"*Aamakutty.*"She called out the first name found written in the attendance register. She once again watched the face of every child who sat in front of her but saw none responding. She found them giggling. She repeated for the third time "*Aamakutty.*"

The pupils could no longer restrain themselves; they broke into a guffaw, inviting a stern look from the teacher.

"Be silent." She ordered, waving her hand that held a cane. The class lapsed into silence. Devaki Amma concluded that the pupil *Aamakutty* was absent; she proceeded with the roll call.

"Aanandavalli."

"Hajar teacher."

"Agnes."

"Appukuttan."

"Not present teacher." Some one informed the teacher

"Aravindan, Avaraham, Gheevarghese, Ratnamma, Vasudevan, Velu." And the roll call continued. The teacher was happy that she found only two absentees, Appukuttan and *Aamakutty*. She asked.

"Have I left out any one?"

"This pupil's name was not called out." Agnes who sat next to Ammukutty pointed out as Kunjan who had remained outside came forward to enquire why his daughter's name was omitted.

"Are you *Aamakutty*?" The teacher asked the child; instantly the entire class burst out into another peal of laughter.

"No… I am not, teacher." Ammukutty protested as she started crying.

"She is not…she is not." Both Agnes and Kunjan too testified. Devaki Amma appeared puzzled; she guessed there was something sinister in the odd name.

"You better talk to the Headmaster; take the child also."

"Sir, what's an *Aamakutty*?" The strange question surprised everybody except the Headmaster.

"Literally, *Aamakutty* means a baby tortoise," Raman Pillai's said.

"Sirs, does my daughter look like a baby tortoise? You look at her and tell me whether she is one." Kunjan asked everyone present, earnestly.

"Ammukutty, please come." Rev Griffith extended his hand, and the child slowly walked towards him; he wiped the tears on her cheeks and asked, bending over her.

"Why do you cry?"

"Everybody calls me *Aamakutty*."

"What is there to be ashamed of in the name *Aamakutty*?" Raman Pillai turned towards Kunjan:

"Who is a tortoise? It's the divine incarnation of Hari, the God." He explained and asserted in the same breath. "*Aamakutty* means daughter of Hari, the God. Don't you know that much? And aren't you proud to be called the daughter of Hari?"

This surprised everybody. Jayanthan sat amused at the cunningness of the man. The silence that followed emboldened the Headmaster to repeat to Kunjan. "Do you feel ashamed to be called the child of Hari, the God?"

Kunjan seemed to have been subdued but when he asked his last question Raman Pillai had to literally swallow his words.

"Children of Hari we are, perhaps, yet we are untouchables to our gods."

Mullakatt Raman Pillai, the unknown village schoolmaster, created history of sorts when he propounded an obscure theory that the untouchables were the children of Hari, the God incarnate as tortoise.

History didn't record it though that long before Mohandas Karamchand Gandhi rediscovered the untouchables and rechristened them Harijans, meaning the children of God, there was a man in God's Own Country whose ingenuity had bestowed upon them a divine hallow.

Kunjan's daughter returned to the class and her name in the school records stood corrected to read Ammukutty, which the class teacher Devaki Amma cautiously pronounced, correctly.

"Ammukutty."

Nevertheless, the pupils in the class addressed her tauntingly as, *Aamakutty*.

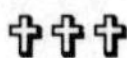

Thirty Two

The children of the untouchables were irregular in their attendance; the sowing and the harvesting season kept them busy, helping their parents earn an extra measure of grain; foregoing the additional income was painful. For them, learning was low on priority. Besides, the children found schooling a tortuous experience except the occasional periods of games. The games too had become embarrassing, for the upper castes boycotted the games if the untouchables entered the field.

Most appeared frightened and timid in the presence of the bossy upper castes. They remained withdrawn, overwhelmed by cultural inhibition. The upper castes found immense sadistic pleasure in inflicting mental torture on them, they jeered at and avoided them, rendering them subdued.

Their parents lacked the means to provide them with the texts and dress. The pupils attended classes unwashed, wearing soiled clothes. The upper caste children naturally shunned them; a good many slowly dropped out.

The unrelenting efforts of Rev Griffith and Jayanthan persuaded many to return but the number of drop-outs continued to be high. Rev Griffith visited the homes of the neophytes regularly to ensure their children attended the school; he patiently listened to their woes and positively encouraged them.

"A mere change of religion doesn't end your suffering; education alone will lift you up. Make a little sacrifice and send your children to school."

"I baptised you not to add numbers but to educate you; if you remain unlettered the mission of the church remains incomplete."

He tried to convince them. They listened to him silently, knowing that schooling was not affordable.

"*Veluthacho*, we don't earn enough for our gruels; what the children earn goes to fill an extra bowl. Where do we find money to educate them?"

Isidore spoke the truth; his companions nodded their heads in approval. The missionary was not unaware of their plight; he concluded that mere opening of schools would not fulfill his mission but the problem defied a solution. He guessed what they needed was positive support but raising funds was a gigantic task.

The enormity of the problem daunted him not. The first planned step was a discussion with Father Edathon, the Vicar. His attitude was however a forgone conclusion. One evening, after the vespers, Rev Griffith visited the Vicar in his office.

"Father Griffith, I hear that your *Pulaya* wards are dropping out." Rev Griffith ignored the sneer in his words, and said:

"Yes, Father. They have a very hard time; with two measures of paddy a day how do they manage?"

"Half of which they barter for palm toddy." The Vicar interjected.

"Not all but a few; but their work is hard; they are poorly paid too. This has to be remedied."

"How? Do you advocate a wage raise too?" Rev Edathon warned the missionary.

"Don't put wrong ideas into their heads." Father Edathon had reasons to be worried; his fraternity owned extensive land employing farm hands. Any suggestion to increase their wage would hurt them a lot.

"Such ideas coming from a Priest of the church would foment unrest," he warned him.

"If not today, it will certainly have to be done tomorrow." Rev Griffith thought it was inevitable.

"That need not be a missionary's concern." Father Edathon retorted.

"Father, do you think the church will be able to spare some funds to support them?" Rev Griffith cautiously placed his request before him. An instant return of the just vanished simper was his taciturn reply, though he wilfully broke the silence when he said:

"I don't intend to sell the church property to educate the *Pulayas.*"

"They are no longer *Pulayas*; they are baptised Christians." Rev Griffith asserted. It hurt him to realise that the Vicar was unwilling to admit them into the fold as Christians.

Father Edathon thought the missionary's dabbling in local politics was uncalled for. Educating the *Pulaya* children or advocating a wage increase were not part of the Christian mission; and he told him bluntly.

"Father Griffith, I think you are unfamiliar with our custom; our mission is to look after the spiritual welfare of the Faithful. You are expected to say the Mass, hear their confessions, teach the children the catechism, solemnise the marriages, baptise the babies, and, of course, bury the dead." Father Edathon concluded.

"Father, you have left out an important function." Father Edathon looked at the missionary wondering what more was there.

"Preaching the Gospel to the meek and the humble, the maimed and the condemned..."

"Oh! Those you had in plenty in the former Roman world joining the fold; here long ago we had the Brahmins joining the church. We are the descendants of those four whom Thomas, the apostle had baptised."

Rev Griffith felt it was futile to discuss the matter with the Vicar.

"The Congregation should contribute for the schools." Rev Griffith urged the believers from the pulpit. They listened to him patiently.

"*Oru Pidi Ari* a day will solve the problem to some extent." He explained to them, calling the women folk together.

"When you cook one measure of rice a day, spare a handful from it; put it in a pot and save it for the school. At the end of the month or when the pot is full you bring it to the church as your contribution for the school fund. Can you do that much sacrifice for a good cause?" He looked into the eyes of the women who stood before him.

"We can…we can." They assured him whole-heartedly. Rev Griffith called that scheme '*Pidiari.*

Every hungry child who attended the class received a mid-day meal, a bribe to get the poor children to school. The Priest then confronted the men who stood a little apart watching the Pastor talking to their women. They expected the Priest to stop with the women agreeing to save for the school.

"Now it's your turn." Rev Griffith confronted the men; some appeared wary, were really rich.

"Why do you look glum? There is a way out for you too and a only little sacrifice is needed on your part. Are you willing, like your women?"

"Yes, Father." The Priest noticed that only a few joined the chorus. One man who stood in front but quietly disappeared behind the crowd to evade a direct request from the Priest, for he was immensely rich, and feared that he might be called upon to give more.

"Haven't you read what Jesus said…"

"He doesn't read Father…he's unlettered." A man who stood behind the rich man interrupted the Priest. The interruption triggered a mild giggle but the Priest ignored it.

"There is more reason for you to listen to the words of Jesus. He said:

"Whoever has two shirts let him give one to his brother who has none. I am repeating to you what he had commanded us; not to give one out of the two but one out of the ten."

He explained:

"It's simple; listen, if you have ten coconut palms in your garden spare one for the school; every time you pluck the nuts, keep the yield of this tree separate and send it to the church. Do you agree?"

Again, the ayes were not many but nos were also few, and he felt the response was not bad. The rich man siad, "Father you said if I have ten in my compound spare one but if I have a hundred in my compound how many should I spare, and if I have several compounds what will happen?"

He appeared troubled for he was rich; he didn't want to displease the Priest who, he thought, decided the destiny of his soul but to give more than the legitimate minimum was really hurting; it was the genuine concern of a rich man, and he was really rich. His question provoked laughter. The Priest too joined in. When the laughter subsided he answered him.

"It's a tricky question that admits a broad or narrow interpretation. What you give I leave to your generosity. You can give one for every ten or one for all the tens as it pleases you."

Though unlettered the man was good at figures. He found one for every ten leading to a big number that, perhaps, he could afford but was not willing to give. After much thought he said,

"Father…I will give you two trees; one for the ten and one for the rest fo the tens."

"As you please; thank you. May God bless you."

He was Thomman Mappillai who had offered to send his wife to school instead of one of his fourteen children. The Priest called the scheme '*Kettu thengu.*'

As Rev Griffith turned back to return to his room the rich man followed him wanting to speak.

"Those who offered many palms may not turn over the yields to you but I will send you the nuts the two trees yield."

"Good. May God bless you."

It turned out to be a successful beginning to raise funds.

The government lacked social orientation. It had never occured to the royals that educating the children was the duty of the State. Traditionally, teaching remained a private affair between the teacher and the student. The aspirant lived with the *Guru* rendering him services in return for the knowledge imparted. Untouchability being divinely ordained the outcastes stood barred from the precincts of knowledge; so they lived unlettered.

Men like Rev Griffith championed the cause of universal education. It attracted flak from the aristocracy. Quietly, the missionaries ventured into education; the schools they opened became popular even among the caste aristocracy. Of course, those schools had its doors open to the untouchables as well. The revolutionary experiment silently proved that the high and the low could sit together with no curse of the gods on either; though an alien idea it thrived. The State could no longer resist the just aspirations yet many hurdles remained.

The State administration remained in a shambles, entangled in religious bigotry. The treasury was considered the fief of the State's presiding deity; spending money to educate the untouchables was declared repugnant to the deity and the rulers abided by the diktat. Lack of social vision and prejudiced impressions blurred the focus of governance.

One evening Rev Griffith visited Jayanthan to discuss the future of the school with him; finding resources had become a major problem. He wanted to explore the chances of securing a grant from the State; he sought Jayanthan's support. He had access to the palace and was a consultant to the Prince on State business.

"The administration is in the hands of obscurants; it's not easy to get new ideas across their closed minds. Still we should try." Jayanthan agreed.

They proceeded to the capital. Jayanthan managed to get an audience with the Prince. They reached the palace gate and were promptly ushered in before the Maharaja of Travancore.

"You should not emphasise the need to educate the untouchables; your case should be limited to general education." Jayanthan warned the missionary. He guessed that teaching the untouchables was not a royal priority.

"But I don't want to conceal the truth." Rev Griffith stressed.

"No denial. The school is by the church for the Christians and the rest; the untouchables are logically in." Jayanthan explained. Rev Griffith understood the difference.

"We have been doing well without schools for years and years.

Why do we need schools now?" The Maharaja threw his first question.

"Your Highness, I understand that a government's goal is to promote the welfare of the subjects; development ensures public welfare and growth is knowledge driven. Generating and disseminating this precious knowledge is the function of education. Societies are competing. In this race the government's role is crucial, and the Administration needs competent man power at all levels." Rev Griffith paused for a moment.

"I humbly submit this is why we require schools to produce growth promoters."

The Maharaja sat quietly as Rev Griffith presented his case. The concept of growth, change and welfare impressed him and its linkage with knowledge was undeniable. Without consulting the Diwan or the Queen Mother, the real power behind the throne of Travancore, the Prince quietly favoured an experimental partnership with the Missionaries in promoting education. He feared the orthodox lobby might create impediments to release funds from the Treasury to educate the untouchables. For, in Travancore the treasury belonged to the deity.

Rev Griffith waited confidently for a verdict; but the Maharaja withdrew into his private chamber, the Diwan following.

"His Highness will receive you tomorrow," the Diwan announced; the meeting abruptly stood terminated.

"The Maharaja agrees to the Missionaries promoting schools with a grant-in- aid." The Diwan announced the following day in the presence of the Prince.

"But on one condition," the Diwan added. Rev Griffith stood wondering what the Diwan had in mind.

"You shall not admit *Pulaya* pupils in the schools," the Diwan clarified.

"They are not *Pulayas* or untouchables; they are Christians as we are." Rev Griffith insisted.

"They are Hindu outcastes whom you have converted; they continue to be *Pulayas.*" The Diwan countered, emphasising: "a change of name or religion never renders an untouchable a touchable."

"A person is rated high or low not on the basis of his name or religion but on the basis of knowledge he commands; here we impart them knowledge that makes them high. You have the truth in your own scriptures, only if you care to discover it; the story of a *Chandala* becoming a learned man and a revered guru, the great Valmikhi." Rev Griffith pointed out. And he added:

"That is how we abolish social iniquity and uplift the disadvantaged."

"When you deny them their right to gain knowledge you keep them suppressed; it's unjust. This goal prompted our foray into the field of education." The Missionary explained.

"If we abandon our mission we cease to be Missionaries."

The King subsequently concluded that modern education was necessary to bring about changes in the society. He recognised the potential of the Missionaries in spreading education.

"We should encourage the Missionaries to open schools all over the State." The Prince gave a positive signal to the Diwan.

The *Sircar* Missionary partnership eventually became a model for the spread of education in the State.

✞✞✞

Thirty Three

"Sarah immichee, wait." Mathai's eight-year-old daughter Catherine yelled from the riverside as she climbed up the riverbank and rushed forward; she knew that Sarah was going out. Sarah stood and waited in the courtyard of the hut with a basket in her hand, for the girl to arrive; she had a few mussels in her basket that she had collected the previous day.

"Kathri what makes you cry?"

"Sarah *immichee*, *Vallicha* doesn't talk, his eyes look wild, never closing; mamma says he has stopped breathing." She tried to describe with difficulty, a death, as she perceived it. Sarah stood stunned at the news, dropping the basket onto the ground. Octavius was dead!

"Liza, our Octavicha is gone…he has left us." Sarah screamed; she felt her legs failing as she slouched to the ground, supporting her head with hands.

"What did you say, Sarah?" Liza rushed out of the hut where she was minding the gruel that was on the boil.

"I said Liza our Octavicha is gone."

"Octavicha is dead?" Liza repeated blankly. Chitha, too was shocked. Sarah saw the mussels in the basket slowly crawling away but made no attempt to collect them.

Octavius was a great source of strength both for Liza and Sarah and for that matter for every one in the community. *Veluthachan* had named him the *Moopan* of the community, a responsibility he had been discharging with great care; he had worked hard to keep the folks together, against all odds.

Sarah and Liza were the first to reach Octavius' hut. The body was laid on a mat with an old pillow supporting his head. Maria had closed his eyes; she had also straightened the limbs and placed a small crucifix on his chest; it was an Avelian cross that Rev Griffith had presented to Octavius, when the Priest returned from Rome. Octavius had always held the cross close to his chest, kissing it every night before he retired to sleep and every morning prior to his departure for work.

Rev Aaron Griffith arrived with Kuriacko. He gave the dead person a final absolution, and sat by the dead man's side consoling his widow and children, though he himself looked sad and distraught. The dead man was a Christian. The Priest's concern was how to give him a Christian burial, now that he was dead. He could imagine many hurdles in the man's last journey to the cemetery.

Whoever heard the news took upon himself the responsibility of informing his neighbour and in no time the news of Octavius death spread everywhere. Whoever heard the news visited his hut. His kith and kin, friends and fellow workers, including those whom he had befriended in the last *oozhium* camp came to pay their last respects; each had a good word about the man.

Jayanthan and Uma came along with their son Sidharthan. Those who stood in the courtyard made way for them. Jayanthan placed a red hibiscus on the chest of the dead body below the cross. They bowed and slowly drew back.

Mathai felt embarrassed for he had nothing to offer them for a seat except a few old mats. Sarah and Maria came forward to speak to Uma.

"Where is Micah?" Sidharthan asked turning to Sarah; he was one year junior to Micah in the primary school but was a member of the Kabaddi team that Micah had captained and together they had won several trophies.

"Micah has gone to inform some of our relations who live quite far."

The Namboodiris had a few words with Rev Griffith as well.

"Rev Griffith, do you think I can be of any help to them?"

Rev Griffith never refused charity either in giving or in receiving.

"Mathai, come here." Jayanthan beckoned Mathai who stood in attendance a little away from the group. Mathai moved forward, and Jayanthan dropped into his cupped palms a few silver coins. He quietly accepted with a glance at the Priest who gave him a positive nod.

Octavius was the first member of their community to breathe his last since they had become Christians. They were unfamiliar with the burial procedure the church had prescribed, but they expected a decent burial in the cemetery instead of the abominable fate of throwing the dead into the depth of the river with stones tied.

"When do you plan the burial? Where do you bury him?" They asked Mathai, he being the eldest male member of the family. He looked uncertain though he guessed it would be in the church cemetery.

"He will certainly be buried in the church cemetery." Simeon asserted; he added: "We are baptized Christians and our dead cannot be thrown into the river. The dead body of a Christian is sacred; he shall rise again from the dead when the Lord comes in glory to judge the living and the dead." What he explained was more for the non-Christian mourners.

"Have you sent some one to the church?" He turned towards Mathai.

"Not yet." Mathai had no idea how to proceed. Together they consulted Rev Griffith who advised them to send someone to the church to inform the Pastor. Isidore and Christopher were sent to the church to make arrangements. Micah accompanied them, as the Vicar personally knew him.

"What brings you here at this odd hour?" Micah, claiming familiarity moved closer to the Priest.

"Praise is to Jesus."

"Oh! Praise is to Jesus; but tell me what is this all about." The

Vicar responded with indifference; the *Pulaya* face always had been abhorrent for him.

"Octavicha is dead; we have come for permission to bury him." Micah looked into his eyes earnestly.

"Who is he? I am yet to see him." The Vicar was curt and brief.

"*Veluthchan* knows him and we come to the church regularly." Christopher who had been regularly attending Sunday Mass submitted humbly.

"It's not enough that *Veluthachan* knows you. I am the Vicar I should know you." Rev Edathon asserted his claim to be the boss.

"Father, don't you remember me? I have been rowing you in the canoe whenever you visited some of the parishioners." Micah guessed that the Priest needed a reference to refresh his memory. Yet the Vicar refused to recognize the young man, and brushing him aside told them:

"The key to the cemetery is with the caretaker Edathon Vakkachan; you better meet him." He dismissed them peremptorily.

They rushed to the caretaker's house to find him not at home; a servant they met at the boatyard told them that the man had gone to his threshing yard. Isidore knew where his farm was and they proceeded to the site. They skirted around the huge paddy heaps and finally spotted him bargaining with traders who had come to buy the paddy. They hesitated to go nearer lest they annoy. Their attempts to catch his attention failed, for though he had seen them he preferred to ignore them, they being menials.

Micah finally walked straight to him with the other two men trailing behind; seeing them come closer Edathon Vakkachan looked at them enquiringly,

"Why have you come? Can't you wait for some time?" He was unhappy at this intrusion.

"No, It's urgent. *Veluthachan* has sent us."

"Why? What happened to him?" He knew that the *Pulayas* were men under the Missionary Priest's special care.

"*Veluthachan* is fine but Octavicha is dead."

"Oh! Ettanu.... Octavius; is he dead? What do you want me to do? Vakkachan knew that death entailed unforeseen expenses that the *Pulayas* would not have anticipated; they were not in the habit of saving either. He concluded the men had come seeking assistance.

"You collect five measures of paddy and go. I have other business to attend." He dismissed them.

"No Sir, we haven't come for any collection."

"What else? Be quick; I have other important matters."

"Sir, we need your permission to bury him in the church cemetery."

"In the church cemetery? See Ittatha…oh! What's your new name?"

"*Veluthachan* calls me Isidore."

"Yes. Isidore. There is not enough space in the cemetery even for us; our number is increasing. My father had seven children and I have now eleven children, and they have three or four each so far; it's bound to go up fast. Where will we go if we fill the cemetery with the *Pulayas*? Vakkachan paused for a moment.

"It's enough that you dump the dead in the river as was done in the past. Does it make much difference? I don't think so. But we cannot do it. I'll explain to Rev Griffith."

He turned back to go but as an after thought he added:

"Isidore, you may collect ten measures of paddy; I know you have expenses."

They didn't stay back to collect the ten measures; they too had other matters to attend to. Edathon Vakkachan continued with his urgent business, undisturbed by the need of the dead man for six feet of earth to lie in peace until the Lord called him up for His second coming.

Micah reported to Rev Griffith the failure of his mission and Rev Griffith looked a failed man. The mourners had become restive and they came out with several suggestions. A few of them looked agitated and many reticent.

"Aren't we Christians as the others?"

"Are we untouchables in our own church?"

"Why don't we throw him into the river; let him follow his fore-fathers who had gone before him." Kunjan, the tavern keeper opined but some resented his comments.

"A Christian needs a Christian burial; you don't understand its significance." Simeon countered the toddy tapper. Miffed at Simeon's remarks, Kunjan walked off with his daughter Ammukutty and her son, Chankaran.

Rev Griffith sat under the canopy of an Aanjili tree that had been mercifully shading the courtyard. Everybody looked up to him for guidance and consolation.

"*Veluthacho* what do we do now?" Mathai stood before Rev Griffith for an answer. For once, Rev Griffith felt he had no solution.

"We don't mind dumping him into the depth of the river." Some one opined from behind but this was overwhelmingly rejected by the rest, and the Priest joined them.

"No, this shall never be." Rev Aaron Griffith avowed, but he still stayed unsure where to bury the dead man.

Peter came to inform that the coffin had arrived.

"Emmachan has sent a beautiful coffin with a black cross inlaid."

"You make arrangements to commence the journey." Rev Griffith's face confirmed that he had made up his mind though he had not disclosed to anyone what the destination was.

The coffin with Octavius' body laid inside was carried to a cargo boat; it rested on the mid-thwart. The mourners boarded the boats; they had men, women and children filling four more large boats. The leading boat had, besides the coffin, a black herald with a white passion cross-inlaid, and a wooden cross with a black hood. The corteges sailed down the river passing Kudamaloor ferry and turned right to enter Konakari canal, off river Meenachill. Rev Griffith had indicated the destination to the punters and they promptly berthed the cortege at the boatyard of the Monastery.

A few old timers recognized the old boathouse, where they had sheltered almost two decades ago, when a flood devastated the land; they remembered it was Rev Griffith who had rescued them.

Rev Griffith, though quite aged and greyed, went up the steps to the monastery to meet the Prior General; he was on time to meet the abbot, who welcomed him.

"What brings you here unannounced?" The old abbot, Rev Cyril, knew by experience that the Missionary was in the habit of visiting only with prior appointment; he wondered what had prompted his visit.

"I have urgent business. Could you please come with me to your boathouse?" The visiting Priest pleaded.

"Of course with pleasure but it's the canonical hour." Rev Cyril hesitated.

"At canonical hours you talk to God but when you come with me you come to do God's work."

The abbot skipped his canonicals and accompanied the Priest to the boatyard, where he stood astounded at the sight of a large crowd of mourners with a coffin in their midst. Rev Cyril made a sign of the cross and stood by the side of the coffin silently for a few seconds.

"What does this mean?" He turned towards his fellow friar; since the abbot was familiar with his friend's evangelical efforts among the untouchables he needed no elaborate clarification.

"I need a little ground to bury a dead of the Lord," he placed his request before the abbot.

The abbot too had problems; what they had was a small private cemetery exclusively for the vestured fraternity; it was unthinkable to admit an outsider into it, and he knew that once open he could not close the door against future demands. He stood debating. He went into consultation with his counsellors and advisors, whom he found evenly divided.

"It creates a bad precedent, and the *Pulayas* are after all *Pulayas*. After their conversion they have become very demanding too." The Procurator who was more conversant with mundane affairs of life argued, and on such matters in practice the counsellors considered his opinion the best. Rev Cyril was in a dilemma; for him the question was not merely a worldly affair.

"It also concerns the spiritual life of a community of God's children.

Whatever be the immediate circumstances that led to the situation it needs urgent correction; we cannot sweep it under the carpet."

"I don't expect you to bury the dead man in your private cemetery; what I suggest is that you grant them a burial ground in a corner of your compound so that the dead man is given a Christian burial." Rev Griffith's suggestion helped to allay their fears. The Abbot's words sealed the agreement.

"On board the chariot of time,
I do sail into the heaven, where
I sight the kingdom that's mine,
the kingdom that's mine for ever."

The immortal lines of the German missionary Wohl Breet Nagel echoed across the paddy fields; the dead body of the *Mooppan* of the ninetiers was lowered into the wet earth. He was the first in memory among the *Pulayas* to escape a watery burial.

"Our story of the *Thonnurans* ends with the exit of Octavius." Sivanandan told his associate Suresh Kuttan.

"The rest is present."

"Now let the Monsignor read it so that we can release it on the occasion of his consecration."

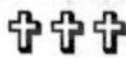

Thirty Four

"A man's tale ends with his demise but the history of a people never ceases; it's an endless stream. Pathrose Micah silently reflected as they summed up the story of Octavius. For the *Thonnurans* he was a mentor, *guru* and pathfinder next only to Rev Griffith; his death was a severe loss as the subsequent events testified. They lost the man who held them together and tended them forward. He instilled them with a sense of fraternity.

"With Ettanucha gone, the bond that kept us together was weakened." Pathrose told Sivanandan as they finalised the story of his end.

"Now, it's on your shoulders to lead them together, though many have reneged,"

Sivanandan reminded him.

"I believe you have been doing a fine job in keeping them together," Suresh Kuttan testified, adding "the present generation avidly recalls your visits to their homes advising the parents to send their children to school, buying them books and even dress."

"Even an occasional threat or an alluring bribe spurred many a skulker back to the class room." They always recognised his services.

And that was how Pathrose Micah had been; for him, every day was a journey of discovery as he trudged the waterlogged hamlets and abandoned village roads searching for his fellow men.

He remembered he was the first to be admitted into the fraternity, precisely eighty years ago. The charisma of their Veluthachan was captivating and the message of the gospel was promising. The support of the Missionary strengthened their will; it gave them the impetus slowly to break their shackles; but still their march was tardy.

Of course, their children had access to the schools and their females dared to cover their breasts, unthinkable a generation earlier. But their transformation from a docile populace to a self conscious community remained incomplete; the millennia long suppression still weighed them down. The ancient Christians under a phoney claim of Brahminical descent looked down upon them. The gradual exit of the Missionaries left the neophytes abandoned with the local church remaining unconcerned. Finally Rome had to find a solution; they per force erected separate churches and clergy to serve the underprivileged.

Many felt the Mission had failed them.

"It was Veluthachan who had discovered us, proclaiming the truth that we are the children of the same Father, God." Pathrose Micah reminded his brethren. He argued that this revelation had inspired great social changes in the country.

"When Mahatma Gandhi called us Harijans, the children of Hari, the God, it echoed what the Veluthachan had proclaimed 'God is the Father and we are His children.' But we remain in our own church, the children of a lesser God."

"The experience of those who had stayed put with all its travails, despair and occasional joy hadn't daunted them. Many left seeing the grass greener over the fence. Kochu Mathai and Joseph alias Krishna Kumar were the living examples highlighting the success or failure of the mission.

Pathrose Micah remembered once walking into the house of Kochu Mathai, a third generation Christian and grandson of Octavius. Among his sons, Mathai's progeny had stayed firm in the church. The credit went to Maria, his wife who saw to it that her children didn't stray from the course.

"May her soul rest in peace." Pathrose prayed silently.

Kochu Mathai came out of the house with a broad grin on his face to receive the grand sire, an honorific the community had bestowed upon him in recognition of his age and élan. He extended his hand to help him climb the steps but the old man gracefully declined. Micah briskly climbed the three steps and took a chair by the side of a half wall. He was not surprised to find a chair in a *Pulaya* house; he knew the times had certainly changed; a *Pulaya* could aspire to sit on a chair.

Kochu Mathai was a school dropout; he had faced hard times with no regular job or steady income. An occasional call to do an odd job was his only source of earning; his wife worked as a domestic help in the town.

As they sat talking, Kochu Mathai's two children entered the veranda and waited behind him trying to catch his eyes.

"Where do you go to school?" Seeing the children in uniform Micah asked them; but they shied away leaving their father to answer.

"They haven't paid the tuition fee so far; they went to the school but the teacher ordered them out. Defaulters are not allowed to attend the class."

Kochu Mathai's children attended a church school even though the fee was unaffordable; he found the children intelligent and the school reputed.

"Do they give any concession, you being a Christian, and a *Pulaya* too?"

"No concession. Asking for concession disqualifies one from getting admitted." They had plenty of applicants from rich backgrounds. Even when he agreed to pay the fee, the Principal tried to dissuade him; giving excuses to deny admission.

"The syllabus is rather tough and I don't think your children will be able to cope with the studies." Kochu Mathai had learnt that the church school was more concerned with maintaining a higher academic record than uplifting the children from lower social classes; still he pleaded:

"Father, please give them a chance; if they don't do well I will pull them out." His suggestion found no favour with the Principal; for he feared that in the event of the children being withdrawn mid term, the seats would remain vacant, thereby the school suffering a loss of income.

His frequent appearances at the Principal's door and pleadings forced the Principal to reluctantly relent; he believed that children hailing from poor families were a liability; they might drop out or fail, adversely affecting the 'par excellence' grading the school had maintained. Finally, he said:

"All right, as you wish. You may pay the fees."

To his dismay, Kochu Mathai found the admission process not as simple as he had expected. At the paying counter, the bill clerk insisted on him producing a special slip from the manager.

"He asked me to pay the fee." Kochu Mathai insisted, looking at the man behind the counter.

"That is true, for admitting the children but you have to pay a donation towards the school building fund. Can't you see the huge buildings coming up in the compound? Those are for your children and you have to share the cost." The cashier explained to him. Kochu Mathai stood at the counter astounded, oblivious of the restless crowd that stood behind him in the queue.

"How much would the donation be?" Kochu Mathai enquired, as he moved out of the queue disconcerted.

"That the Principal will let you know. It can be any thing, five, ten…" The clerk tried to put him off.

"Just five or ten? That, of course, I have." He offered, regaining his composure.

"Please go away. I have other business to do." The clerk waved him off.

"It's five or ten thousand." A man who stood behind him in the queue with a thick purse told him, expecting him to move out of the queue.

"Five thousand!" Kochu Mathai exclaimed as he walked towards a window for a whiff of fresh air.

Pathrose sat silently listening to the woes of a poor parent trying to educate his children. He remembered that he had not faced any such problem when he took his son for admission to St Columbus, one of the best Christian schools in Delhi. Pathrose declined to venture an opinion not for want of sympathy. He thought discretion was more advisable, since he was the parent of a Bishop designate.

"You could have sent them to a Government school."

"In Government schools, education is free of course, but there is no teaching. Too much politics and too little teaching; those schools are really in a shambles."

Pathrose knew why the Government school teachers themselves refused to send their children to the schools they taught in; even political leaders privately admired the private schools.

Kochu Mathai's house was a shade better than what a *Pulaya* hut used to be, say eighty years ago. It was built on a better foundation of laterite stones; one room was secured with walls, and there was an enclosure for the hearth. A veranda bound by half walls and sheltered by sun beaten palm-frond curtains completed the structure.

"Why is your house still incomplete? Sunil Dass is also a Pulaya and a daily wage earner; his house has a tiled roofed with mosaic floorings." Pathrose asked him.

"Don't you know the difference between us, though we both are *Pulayas*, grandchildren of same grandfather; he is a Hindu Pulaya and I am a Christian Pulaya; that makes a big difference." Pathrose sat quietly looking into the distant sky.

"Valliappacha, don't you know Krishna Kumar?" Kochu Mathai asked when he saw another cousin of his passing by. Pathrose intently looked at the passer-by, trying to locate him somewhere in his memory. Krishna Kumar stopped; his face was as dark as the face of the other four in the house. Their eyes crossed, tarrying for a while.

"He's certainly one among us…but?" Pathrose tried hard to place him; behind his stripped shirt and denims, beneath his well combed, wavy hair he appeared oddly familiar. Pathrose hesitated to identify him, though he was sure that the man was one among them, perhaps the scion of the Thonnurans.

"Valliappacha, he is a grandson of Christopher uncle." Kochu

Mathai solved the problem for him.

"Is he Yohannan's son? When you said Krishna Kumar I thought he was the son of some Krishnan."

"No…no; he is not, but his name is Krishnan." Kochu Mathai tried to explain the matter and turning to Krishna Kumar.

"Don't you remember, this is Valliappachan? Pathrose Micah, our grand old lady Sarah aunt's son, the one who went to the war with Japan at a very young age, and returned alive?" he asked.

Krishna Kumar stood cool, feigning unfamiliarity; apparently he abhorred any one from among the *Pulayas* getting too familiar with him.

"Don't you remember the one who escorted us to the school when all of us together started going to school? He bought us the text books and slates"

Pathrose instantly remembered Yohannan's son, baptised Joseph almost thirty five years ago, Pathrose and his wife being the godparents. Again it was at his persuasion that Yohannan finally agreed to put the boy into the school. Yohannan's pigheaded opposition melted away one night when Pathrose invited him home, served him with two large drinks of army rum and on the strength of the drinks he ordered Yohannan to send the boy to school, also promising him that he would get his son recruited into the army; the promise, though a blank cheque on a non-existent bank, helped to water down his opposition.

"That year when I was on leave I got three boys and two girls admitted in the primary school; you both were among them."

"Joseph!" Pathrose hailed the young man wanting to embrace him; he rushed towards the well groomed youth.

"No… I am not Joseph… I am Krishna Kumar." The young man in the denims protested.

"No. To me, my son, you are still Joseph."

Krishna Kumar stood exasperated at the impudence of the old man, unconsciously raising his hands to shield himself from his embrace. Pathrose abruptly stopped short of embracing him. Krishna Kumar averted his eyes,

"I am getting late. I have to reach my office." He excused himself, stepping forward.

"Alright, my son. I will see you later." Micah remained stunned at the manners of the young man. He felt pained. Slowly, he returned to Kochu Mathai's veranda.

"Valliappacha, he shuns us though he is one among us."

Pathrose knew it was difficult for successful men to treat with camaraderie a less privileged compatriot.

Krishna Kumar's two sons, Ravi Dass and Ram Dass also walked past along with their mother Sree Devi, unmindful of Kochu Mathai's children who were still hanging around; more children came, passing by in small droves; Strangely none cared to seek out the company of Kochu Mathai's children; these kids were invariably absent from school; They were habitual defaulters.

"Valliappacha, do you know that woman who just passed by?"

"No. I don't."

"She is Krishna Kumar's second wife. She is the granddaughter of our Mankott Ravunni Achan, who they said your father had murdered." The insinuation in the allegation startled Pathrose, who instantly stood up protesting; staring into the eyes of both Anna and her husband.

"My father never committed such a heinous crime as vouchsafed by Jayanthan Thirumeni and Sidharthan Kunju." Pathrose asserted.

"Valliappacha, she never meant that your father committed the gruesome murder; we are sure he was implicated." Kochu Mathai intervened to pacify the old man; a mollified Pathrose resumed his seat accepting a glass of coffee that Mathai handed over to him.

What Anna said was absolutely unintentional. It was only to let him know how the society had changed over the years; a *Pulaya* youth taking his wife from an erstwhile aristocratic and high caste family.

"I am glad that the society no longer sneers at a caste woman finding her husband from among our clan, once untouchables…it's good."

✞✞✞

Thirty Five

Pathrose was hurt; he sat brooding about how yesterday's transgressions had become today's norms and the customs for tomorrow. He thought Krishna Kumar's ascent was too fast and too steep. He wondered how the young man's change from Joseph to Krishna Kumar had alienated him from his roots.

The Missionaries came, preached the message of equality, established schools; the Pulayas hopefully accepted the gospel. But where did they stand now?

It was the primary school founded by Veluthachan, the first school that admitted the children of the untouchables, a historical event. Pathrose Micah himself was a pupil in the first batch. No newspapers had reported that a *Pulaya* boy Pathrose Micah sat with a Brahmin boy Siddharthan though it caused raised eyebrows. Pathrose Micah passed out of the school after four years.

But later years saw the children of the untouchables quietly abandoning schooling. Pathrose Micah kept the date with the academic calendar to ensure the *Pulaya* kids joined the school by persuasion, threat or bribery, the last in his armoury being two pegs of Three X rum for the parent.

One year he found, in a class of thirty five, four boys and three girls came from high caste families. The next were the Christians who constituted the majority, numbering fifteen; nine boys and six girls. The *Pulayas*, all baptised, numbered seven, five boys and two girls; others, made up of blacksmiths, carpenters and goldsmiths numbering six, four boys and two girls.

The school atmosphere was rather tense with the children overwhelmingly caste conscious. To begin with, it was a gender-based division, the girls stayed together, shunning the boys. The high caste pupils, being vegetarians, avoided pupils from other social groups dubbing them, *champu theenikal,* meaning flesh eaters.

The class on the opening day was remarkable; the *Pulaya* pupils whom Pathrose had escorted to the school, wore *mundu* and jacket, carrying a slate and a language reader. The sight of the well dressed *Pulayas* caused heartburns; other children had come wearing a mundu around their waist, leaving their torso bare with a mere slate in their hands. The sartorial elegance of the *Pulayas* invited censure from a group of high caste parents who protested to the Headmaster.

Problems began to confront the *Pulaya* children. The language reader was the cause. The language teacher found most of the children without the text book, except Pathrose's protégés. The teacher asked them to share their texts with others; when this was repeated the *Pulaya* boys found themselves invariably deprived of their own books.

"Why should we give our texts to those kids? the boys protested silently. One day the teacher asked Joseph to give his book to Shivan, and Joseph readily obliged; the second day the teacher asked him to give it to Damu, and Joseph again obliged. The third day when the teacher asked again, Joseph said:

"Mam, I didn't bring the textbook as it fell into the water."

In the evening when they returned home Joseph told his friends:

"Telling a lie is profitable sometimes." And they laughed together.

At the end of the third year the *Pulaya* pupils' number had dwindled to four; Kochu Mathai, Joseph, Martin and Markose. It began with the girls; whenever there was a birth in the family the eldest girl had to stay back to look after the baby and the arrivals were quite frequent too. During the harvest season they had to stay back invariably to help their parents in their work. Besides, the harvest field was an important source of extra income which the parents could not afford to forgo. The girls frequently stayed back and eventually dropped out.

The end of the fourth year saw another casualty. Markose had a very poor record, forcing the teacher to detain him. He could have repeated but he opted out. Kochu Mathai, Martin and Joseph scraped through as the teacher subsequently explained to Pathrose, who as a self-appointed guardian folllowed their progress whenever he came home on furlough.

Markose happily joined the ranks of the farm hands.

Primary education was free but the payment of a fee was mandatory in the higher classes; the fee frightened the *Pulayas* who lacked the means. They were frequently ordered out as defaulters. Next, it was Kochu Mathai's turn to be relieved of the humiliation when perforce stopped schooling.

One evening when he reached home he noticed an unusual crowd in the courtyard, the usual quietness of the home disturbed by loud whimpering and hushed up conversation. A neighbour quietly took him aside and told him. "Kochu Mathai, your father is no more."

The books that he had tucked under his arm dropped down unaware onto the slushy ground; the young boy slumped down; Kochu Mathai's fate was thus sealed.

A few days later Joseph stopped at Kochu Mathai's house;

"Kochu Mathai, will you be rejoining the school?" Joseph asked looking into his friend's eyes.

"No…. I want to but I can't. I have to support my mother and siblings."

If he were not continuing, the teacher wanted to know whether he would spare his text book for another pupil. Kochu Mathai agreed; they parted silently hoping they would meet, if not in the school then back home. But as luck favoured him, Joseph climbed the ladder to become Krishna Kumar; slowly he distanced himself from his former friend.

"The untimely death of my father wrecked my dream. I wanted

to finish Matriculation and join the army where nobody would care for my caste." Kochu Mathai breached the silence they had been sitting in.

Joseph and Martin were the only surviving students from the batch which had started schooling nine years ago; finally Joseph too stood facing with the stark realities of life.

"If I complete tenth standard, perhaps, I will get a primary teacher's job in a Mission school," he believed. Being a *Pulaya*, though a Christian, he could not dream of a job in the government.

Nine years of schooling had brought about a lot of changes in his life; he had been observing personal hygiene religiously. He was black but handsome, with his curly hair oiled and combed back close to the scalp, making sure it remained that way until he returned home; his teeth remained sparkling white against his dusky lips.

"Kaar Varnan." One morning when he entered the class, his caricature was drawn on the blackboard with the byline in bold.

"Who is Kaar Varnan?" The children were laughing at him.

"Joseph, are you the one?" Another loud howling greeted the teacher as Joseph sat with no spirit of disavowal; the epithet stuck on him.

"Kaar Varnan is the name of Lord Krishna; you need not be ashamed of it." The teacher tried to assuage his hurt feelings.

At home, more troubles awaited him; his mother had suddenly fallen sick and she was advised bed rest and medication; the physician said that she might not live long. Yohannan appeared sad and bewildered. Of his three sons and two daughters, the youngest girl being two years old, Joseph alone went to school, the others stayed back to share the drudgery of life.

One night Joseph retired early though he had his English lessons to revise, for the lamp slowly went off with no kerosene to sustain the flame. As he lay on the mat struggling with Lord Tennyson's poem, the Lotus Eaters that he had to recite in the class, he heard a subdued conversation between his parents from the other side of the wall.

"There is a proposal for our daughter; you know the boy, our Chacko's son Esthapan, a good young man."

Yohannan's report satisfied her as she too had known him; but an important question nagged her, the big dowry they might demand.

"We don't want any dowry; you give whatever you can afford." Chacko assured. Yohannan was happy; his wife wondered how could there be such good people.

"Why don't you follow up before he changes his mind?"

"He may not change but there is one condition, seems rather difficult."

"Chacko is looking for two, a girl for his son and a boy for his daughter."

"Let him search for a suitable boy; we will wait until he finds one."

"He has already found one; he expects the consent of the boy's parents."

"Then both the marriages could be celebrated together."

"Perhaps"

"Who is the boy and who are his parents?"

Yohannan paused for a few seconds, silently debating on how to answer her; finally he told the truth. "We are the parents and our son Joseph is the boy."

The disclosure killed her enthusiasm; she thought the girl was a mismatch for Joseph and it would be unfair to ask him to marry a mere country bum. Their son was educated and he spoke English. She sought to foil Chacko's attempt to foist his daughter on Joseph.

"What is this girl before him? He deserves a superior alliance." They discussed and argued. Yohannan believed his son was fast asleep so they continued to debate. They slowly slipped into sleep but their son stayed awake for the rest of the night.

"Where is Kaar Varnan?" One morning the class teacher asked casually after she marked the attendance; she noticed that he had been absent for a week. Her question was greeted with giggles that baffled the teacher.

"Teacher, he got married last week." The news stunned her; she felt sad as another promising *Pulaya* boy was on his way out.

"You are too young to get married. You could have waited for a few more years." When Joseph returned after his marriage the teacher chided him. He knew the teacher was unaware of his compulsions. He was helpless before the pleadings of his parents. His father explained to him as his mother looked at him silently imploring.

"My son, you know Margarita is well past the age of marriage; if we don't get her married soon our community will ask why. We can't ignore them. And, of course, she too needs home of her own. Your mamma is bedridden and she needs constant care. Once Margarita is sent away who will take care of the household? If I stay back who will earn the gruel for the family?"

The father's passionate plea troubled the son's conscience; he guessed it was his duty to lighten his father's burden. He succumbed to their pressure and agreed to marry Chacko's daughter in exchange for her brother marrying Margarita; he had only one condition, that the marriage would in no way interfere with his schooling. Both the parties agreed.

"Chacko neither demands nor offers any dowry." Yohannan affirmed but the condition Joseph had put forward was a dampener.

"How is it possible?"

"I will take care of the situation." Rebecca assured him.

She had made up her mind. She would ask the girl to sleep in the kitchen with Joseph continuing in the veranda.

"We'll sleep where we already do, in between them. Won't it be enough?"

"I will place a lamp midway between the veranda and the kitchen." She knew that old mothers had always found a sentinel in the flame of a lamp, to keep away the devil that lurked around to trouble newly married couples.

The marriage didn't help Joseph; he found himself in deeper trouble. Margarita married away, Rebecca eternally invalid and the new bride refusing to join the farm hands, the family income had steeply dwindled. Rosa, the daughter-in-law, stood stubborn in her refusal to work on the farm.

"I am only a servant in your house, not your wife. Am I right?" She asked her husband. Their marriage remained unconsummated; Joseph stood helpless.

Towards the end of the ninth year of Joseph's schooling, his name again appeared among the defaulters; it meant he would be debarred from appearing in the annual examination. He guessed the threat was real and the outcome devastating. The sum needed was beyond the means of his parents. Joseph stopped going to school as he found he stood no chance to raise the money. One day early morning Joseph left home without telling anybody where he was going. He walked quite a distance and exhausted, he appeared before his in-laws. It was his second visit to them since his marriage almost a year ago. Chacko was at home flaying an animal assisted by his sons.

Joseph stood by trying to catch their eyes but the father and the sons ignored him; He decided to wait around ignoring the personal affront to his dignity. He thought the need was his and he should meet it head-on with them. He took Chacko aside.

"I have come to meet you."

"I thought so. What makes you come here?" Chacko sounded remote. "I have my exams."

"Well, that's your business." Chacko shrugged his shoulders.

"You can help me pay the fees.

"No. I don't have any money to waste… you may go." Chacko walked away picking up the cleaver; suddenly he turned back to ask: "Are you studying to become the Peshkar?"

The scorn in his words hurt Joseph; he returned empty handed, on the way back stopping at Neelimangalam, the spot where he had heard in legends of the spilling of the blood of his kin, a woman and later her son who had challenged the established order. He stepped into the river; the fresh water of Meenachil cooled his feet, imbuing him with a fresh zest for life.

"I am not willing to shed my blood here. I want to live." Joseph thought.

✞✞✞

Thirty Six

The night was young yet darkness was thick with the canopies of huge trees converging over the road making visibility rather poor; walking bare foot on the road was most painful. Yet he went on, unmindful of the hurdles.

Farther ahead, he saw groups of people walking briskly. Gradually the small groups streamed into a large rally in an ambience of red festoons and flags. Joseph found himself unintentionally merging with them.

He sat inconspicuously by the corner of the ground, as he feared that taking part openly in a Red rally would invite disapprobation. He listened to the long diatribes delivered from the dais by different speakers. They enumerated the woes of the common people, peasants, workers, landless labourers and the iniquities they were exposed to, injustice meted out to them, rights denied and trampled upon; the last speaker, a young man asked them many questions that touched the nerves of the audience. Everytime he posed a question reacted with anger.

Joseph felt impressed by the young man who criticized the authorities, taunting and challenging them. Joseph admired his guts; he joined the mob in applauding him.

It was Suresh Kuttan. Joseph recognized him; he was a few years senior to Joseph in the school, but he hadn't seen him for a long time. Joseph wanted to meet the speaker; he waited for the crowd to disperse.

He sat by the corner of the dais but soon fell asleep.

The day break saw him on his feet again searching for Suresh Kuttan. Finding his home was rather easy but the trudge was trying. It was quite far and the young boy was soon exhausted. The sight of Kuttan, sitting by a washer man's stone relieved him of his worry. A few bundles of soiled clothes and a couple of water pots lent credence to what he had heard about his occupation. Kuttan had little difficulty in recognizing Joseph.

"You are Yohannan Chettan's son, Joseph, aren't you?"

"Yes, I am."

"I remember you. Have you finished schooling?

"Not yet; but I am almost dropping out." Joseph mumbled.

"Oh No! Why? Don't do it."

Suresh Kuttan took his arm and led him into his house. Kuttan asked him whether he had had his breakfast; the young boy hedged the question. The host guessed his dilemma.

He rushed into the kitchen and brought a bowl with a few portions of boiled tapioca soaked overnight in water; the guest did not say no for he was really hungry. The tapioca fuelled him to recount his long story, traversing the years of his wretched life.

"You now know why I said I am dropping out."

The young revolutionary sat quiet, his eyes gazing at the sky and mind probing the possibilities.

"I thought you are not a Christian becuase of your name." Joseph observed looking at an old picture of Jesus Christ on the wall, side by side with another picture of a person whom he could not recognise.

"Whose picture is the other one, some saint?"

"In a way yes; a saint, Karl Marx."

"Who is he?"

"A saint, as you have discovered."

Joseph thought he had heard the names of several saints but not of this one.

"Joseph, it's true I am not a Christian but a Hindu as you guessed;

but I am an ardent believer in Jesus Christ and a fan of Marx also. And I need to be a Hindu too." Joseph looked confused. Suresh Kuttan had his own reasons.

At a very young age he had become a Christian, converted by a missionary Priest. Suresh Kuttan, whose baptismal name was Emmanuel, heard of Christ from several preachers and unconsciously began to love his personality. He searched for him, discovered him and accepted him as the eternal beacon of his life.

For ages the world had seen great men, sages, preceptors, prophets, *rishis* who had taught mankind; Jesus Christ alone proclaimed a unique message hitherto unheard of:

"God is the Father and men are his children."

"Which means that men being the children of the same father are equals. This proclamation confirmed for the first time the truth that men are equal, thus claiming equal rights on this earth, none claiming more and none receiving any less. This immutable Christian principle provoked Marx to prescribe a remedy for the social iniquity that afflicted mankind."

"I have a different problem; how do I go about it?" Joseph confronted him with his personal problem.

"I too faced the same situation; I solved it by relegating Christ to my heart as I needed him, and changing my name." Joseph understood the meaning of what he had been advised to do; when he left Suresh Kuttan's house he knew how to overcome the obstacles.

"Never give up your schooling." Suresh Kuttan said as the young boy took leave of him.

Soon Joseph returned with a resolve to continue his schooling. He entered the class and sat quietly on the last bench, hoping that the teacher would not haul him up immediately, for non-payment of fees. He looked into his pocket to make sure he had the weapon to defend himself, in case the teacher tried to rake him over the coals.

"Joseph, have you paid the arrears?" After marking the attendance, the teacher turned to the habitual defaulter.

"No Ma'am." Joseph slowly rose up and answered rather casually.

"Who asked you to enter the class? Take your books and go out," the disgusted teacher ordered him; she turned to Martin.

"Martin, have you paid all the dues." He too rose up meekly, averting his eyes from the teacher and his classmates.

"No; my father said he would pay after the harvest."

"Get out, both of you; this is not a store to get things on credit." An irritated teacher bellowed. Joseph walked up coolly and stopped before the teacher. Martin too followed him.

"Yes? Can't you see the door is open?" The teacher's mocking remark was greeted with suppressed laughter from the class. Joseph ignored them; he took out a folded paper from his pocket and extended it to the teacher. He didn't answer when the teacher asked him what it was; he knew the teacher could read it for herself.

"This is to certify that Joseph Y, son of Yohannan has changed his religion and has become a Hindu *Pulaya* after being duly converted by a competent authority. His name is Krishna Kumar. No school fee should be levied on him and he shall be provided with financial assistance to execute his studies."

"Go and take your seat." After carefully reading the document twice, the teacher ordered him. As the class sat silently watching him, Krishna Kumar followed the order making a smart about-turn. Martin who stood observing the high drama followed Krishna Kumar, naively believing that the order applied to him as well, as he was also the son of a *Pulaya;* but he was promptly stopped.

"No… you are not in; you are out."

"Why Mam? I am also the son of a *Pulaya*." Martin pleaded.

"Maybe; but you are a Christian *Pulaya;* he is a Hindu *Pulaya,* he alone is eligible to receive government support. Martin quietly walked out with tears in his eyes.

"Christian *Pulayas,* Hindu *Pulayas!* Does it make any difference? He is a *Pulaya* as much as I am; why the difference? Nobody answered Martin's question; he silently walked down the steps.

"Joseph had determination." Pathrose Micah complimented him.

"But he was cunning too." Kochu Mathai quietly observed.

"Why do you say so?"

He ran away with Sree Devi, a high caste woman whose Tharawad's bondsmen Krishna Kumar's ancestors were. She bore him two sons. When they attained the age of five, the parents got them admitted in a public school.

"What is your caste?" They stumbled upon the caste question. Sree Devi wanted to bring them up in her own caste, Nair, which she claimed was more respectable and legitimate too. For she followed the matrilineal system of descent. But her husband wanted them to be brought up in his own caste, *Pulaya*.

"Kris, look in our family I am the only member with a caste that is my caste, Nair. Our children should inherit my caste and don't forget that the family share that I had inherited is the proof of my caste descent." Her argument sounded cogent and irrefutable but he didn't consider her pragmatic; he tried to enlighten her.

"You are familiar with the Vedic division of men into four castes, and al those who existed beyond perpetually lived as untouchables. Now, the government has legally instituted a fifth caste of all the untouchables together designating them, the Scheduled Castes. Do you understand?"

"Yes, but so what?"

Sree Devi didn't see anything new in what he said:

"To put it simply, if our children are *Pulayas* by caste, which they are certainly, they stand to gain in life. Do you understand?" he patienthy explained.

Ravi Dass and Ram Dass were happily admitted in the school as *Pulayas,* claiming all the privileges that went under the label.

The story of Kochu Mathai and Krishna Kumar exemplifies two phases of the untouchables' quest for justice.

✞✞✞

Thirty Seven

Early in the morning, Pathrose Micah's modest house appeared soulless, quite unusual for the former soldier, well known for his morning callisthenics. No one could believe he was still asleep when the sun had already risen half way up.

Pathrose Micah emerged from his room; he saw his son sitting, lost in thought. He drew back leaving him alone, and busied himself with making breakfast. They ate together, the son never allowing his eyes to meet the father's. Pathrose Micah knew his son had been to the Archbishop's house the previous day and returned late in the night.

Msgr Micah was not hurt but concerned at the outcome of his visit. As he got into the car to return home, Thomas Chandi found his face shorn of the ebullience that carried him up the stairs of the colonial style mansion in the morning. As they drove down, Msgr Micah sat by his side glumly.

"Do you have any date decided?" Chandi asked him without deflecting his eyes from the potholed road; he was keen to know when his friend would be consecrated a bishop. He wished it to happen before his wife Nirmala returned to the States after her holidays.

"It's the phoney piety of a closed mind." Msgr Micah mumbled; he found no change in their attitude since his first visit. It was humiliating too, he remembered.

It had all begun in the early morning of the second day of his arrival at his paternal home. He took the first train to the diocesan town to meet Archbishop to present his credentials; he did not expect any hurdles in his mission. His father was baptised and married in the parish church and he never doubted his claim to be a Faithful. Besides, the Archbishop was personally known to him rather intimately for almost a decade; he had been acting as his unofficial minister-in-waiting whenever he visited Delhi, taking him around the capital and helping him find his way in the city to meet officials and a few Christian elites. The Archbishop had found in him a useful ally.

"Father Micah, are you planning to visit your home in the near future?", The Archbishop asked him as he reached him to the airport at the end of his last visit about six months ago.

"I am not sure Your Grace; my hands are full." He answered briefly.

"Whenever you come, you are most welcome to visit and stay with us." The Archbishop smiled at him as he walked towards the departure hall. Father Micah waited for a while watching the Archbishop reporting at the airline counter; he returned as he saw the passengers moving for security checks.

The Archbishop had not forgotten to keep alive his connection with his Priest friend, and Father Micah continued to be always obliging. Finally, he had an occasion to officially meet with his apparent mentor; he being a bishop designate elevated to the Monsignori and the Archbishop being designated to consecrate him.

Msgr Aaron Micah stood in humility and anticipation, holding a white envelope with golden borders, in front of a heavy rose-wood door seeking an audience with the Archbishop. He was reluctant to knock at the door; he looked around for some one but found no one. Many pastors and Monsignors passed him, none caring to acknowledge his 'good morning'.

"His Grace must be busy." Msgr Aaron Micah guessed and he decided to wait patiently. He was sure the Archbishop would personally come out to escort him in, once he knew who the visitor was.

"Where are you from?" An officious looking young Priest asked him.

"I am from Delhi, Father," "I am Msgr Aaron Micah."

"Oh! Latin?" The Priest sounded disdainful.

"No, Father, I am Indian." He missed Msgr Micah's insinuating smile.

"I am Father Thomas Kattoor, Secretary to His Grace. If you have anything important you may leave the matter with me. I will get in touch with you as soon as possible." Father Kattoor offered.

"Thank you Father but I have urgent business to discuss with him." Msgr Micah displayed his proud possession, the Papal envelope; he justifiably believed it would open before him behind the closed doors of any ecclesiastical abode. Father Kattoor rightly guessed the significance of an envelope bearing the Papal insignia and readily offered to take the letter to his boss. He took the letter and disappeared behind the heavy door as Msgr Micah waited in the lobby.

"His Grace is busy in a discussion on a major project with our Engineers; he will read the letter as soon as he is free. I will contact you in due course." Father Kattoor assured him.

"But, did you tell him my name?" Msgr Micah felt assured that the Archbishop would respond positively once he recognised who the visitor was; he looked into the eyes of the Priest for an answer.

"Of course, I told him and he remembers you." Rev Kattoor reassured him but Msgr Micah felt sad at the obvious rejection.

"Father, when do you think I can expect a call from His Grace?"

"I don't know exactly when but certainly when...."

"All right, Father, I shall wait for your message." Msgr Micah knew he had little choice and he left shaking his counter part's hand warmly.

Msgr Micah's first visit to his much acclaimed mentor ended in a fiasco. He silently walked down the steps.

Back at home, Pathrose Micah waited for his son to return with the exciting news. A good many of his neighbours had assembled in his house to hear the great news. Shouri's son Reji had bought a bundle of crackers which he tied to tree tops to burst into flames the moment the bishop designate announced the date of his elevation to the bishopric.

The night had advanced farther and the crowd had become restive, imagining what might have happened to their dear exalted neighbour. Their wild imagination silently conjured up ghastly visions which they dared not believe. Shouri's mother mutely made a sign of the cross invoking Jesus to protect his chosen servant. The women enthusiastically settled for the recitation of the rosary; but the men, quietly came out of the premises feigning a search for him.

The women carried on, stopping their recitation at any random rattling of an intruding auto-rikshaw or the inane barking of a neighbour's dog; they resumed after every interruption. Finally, they entered the litany with the crescendo of the supplication reaching its pitch; the supplicants with their eyes closed stayed so absorbed in their devotion that they missed the man for whose safety they had been on their knees.

Msgr Micah entered the veranda and stood quietly, joining the prayers. They hoped he had returned with good news, answering their prayers. They mobbed him wanting to kiss his fisherman's ring. The men who had withdrawn from the prayers, rushed to Pathrose Micah's house to hear the great news. Msgr. Micah stood still; his father wondered why his son looked low in the midst of the popular rejoicing. Pathrose Micah had arranged some food for his wellwishers; it was cooked at Shouri's house, and he announced:

"Pathrose Chettan has arranged food for all of us; it's cooked at my house and you are cordially invited to partake of the same."

Shouri slowly moved out followed by his mother and wife. Pathrose Micah persuaded the rest of the crowd to join them; they walked to the venue. Msgr. Micah assured them that he would join them after his vespers for which he was late. The crowd dispersed quietly after the meal without waiting for Msgr. Micah; he ate alone attended on by Shourie who was preoccupied with serving the eminent guest. Msgr. Micah was happy he had escaped the gruelling questions on when he would be elevated.

The next morning Pathrose Micah tarried in his bed unwilling to ask the question. He found the ebullience that had brightened his face the previous morning as he left for the Archbishop's house, totally missing.

"There seems to be something amiss." Pathrose Micah confided to Thomas Chandi who had come visiting them. He found the Monsignor sitting dejected, merely nodding his head to acknowledge when he wished him 'good morning.'

"Do you have the date decided?" Thomas Chandi was keen to know the date of his consecration.

"Well, they seem to be bent on one more test."

It was really a trial, digging up the past of his forebears, calling upon him to account for their sins which had little direct bearing on his present station in life.

"It is rather unchristian," he alleged; yet he submitted himself to the test.

On reaching the Archbishop's Palace for the second time, he was directed to appear before an ecclesiastical commission consisting of three senior Priests, the Chancellor of the Archdiocese and the pastor of the parish which his father belonged to. The third member was Rev Kattoor whom he had met on his first visit. Without wasting much time the Chancellor commenced the proceedings, firing the first salvo.

"Monsignor, please tell us what Catholic you are."

"I am a Roman Catholic," he asserted. "You certainly are; but what Rite do you belong to?"

"My father, who lives in this State, was baptised at a parish in this Archdiocese about eighty years ago. At the time of my birth he had been living in Delhi, and naturally I was baptised in the Archdiocese of Delhi,"

"It's a Latin diocese?" The Chancellor questioned.

"Yes, Latin." Msgr Micah confirmed.

"Please note the admission." The Chancellor instructed Rev Kattoor, who acted as the secretary to the commission.

"Did your father get your name enrolled in the baptismal register of his parish? That would have entitled you to claim a Syrian paternity."

"No. It was not done." The parish Priest affirmed foreclosing Msgr

Micah's option to answer the question.

"Well, I am sorry, the findings go against you; you are not eligible to be consecrated in accordance with our Rite." The Chancellor pronounced the verdict.

"I have more damaging things to report that I have collected from the sources of the parish," the parish Priest intervened. Msgr Micah stood wondering what damaging skeletons he wanted to pull out.

"It's true that Msgr. Micah's father Pathrose Micah, born posthumous, was baptised in our parish as a toddler, along with his mother, a *Pulaya* widow. They were among the ninety neophytes received in the Church by a passionate missionary. But many of them had turned renegades; a few still remain Catholics only in name. Of course, Pathrose Micah stayed committed; he is a practising Catholic." As the Priest paused, Msgr Micah did not suspect it was a left handed compliment.

"But, Pathrose Micah's father, Meenan, was a shady character; he had two women in his life. One he had married and the other he had snatched away from her lawful husband, claiming that she was his first love; he kept both. A criminal, he committed a murder and was apprehended by the police; eventually he was ritually sacrificed to appease an evil spirit. Pathrose Micah is his son, posthumously born to the other woman." The Priest paused.

"Have you finished?" Msgr Micah asked him.

"No wait! more is coming," the Priest raised his head, turning his face towards Msgr. Micah with a scornful stare; he resumed his harangue. "Monsignor, do you know who your mother was."

"Yes, she was a humble untouchable."

"But she was baptised and joined to my father in holy matrimony in the same parish which you preside over now."

"Yes, yes I know!" The Priest perhaps thought it wise not to contest his claim but he had more damaging revelation to make.

"Monsignor, do you know who your great-grandmother was or who your great grandfather was?"

Msgr. Micah knew who his great grandmother was; he was conscious of her relevance in the present context.

"My great grandmother was Neeli Manka, no less than a freedom fighter who had fought to uphold the self respect of the untouchables. I am proud of her." He ran the gauntlet of their censure.

And Msgr Aaron Micah returned home rejected and dejected.

"Christian contribution to usher in an egalitarian society was commendable but it neglected the former untouchables that had flocked to the church." "Reservation was a retributive measure to uplift those who had been denied human rights; why was it denied to them, they still lived *Pulayas* though?" Msgr. Micah asked in indignation.

Nobody answered these questions; they are yet to receive an answer.

"The church too discriminates." Suresh Kuttan pointed out.

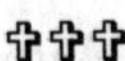

Thirty Eight

Eventless weeks passed into months. The ecclesiastics seemed to have written off the aspiring Msgr. Aaron Micah's claim to the titular bishopric of Arba. He stayed at home keeping a low profile except receiving a few visitors among whom were Thomas Chandi and Suresh Kuttan.

The parochial community largely stayed indifferent to the presence of a bishop designate in their midst; the clerical aristocracy ignored him, for them, he was an outsider and unacceptable.

Pathrose Micah's son though a *Pulaya* was accorded due recognition in his neighbourhood, which perhaps, lacked aristocratic pretensions.

Slowly, his face became familiar; to them, he had become a commoner with no charisma. His helping his father in the kitchen, doing his own laundry and washing the *dishes* lowered his esteem in the eyes of his neighbours, especially the men-folk.

"He may be a fake or a defrocked Priest," a few alleged.

One afternoon the postman came looking for Aaron Micah; he found the house locked. The envelopelooked impressive and official. The postman wanted, in the absence of the addressee, to deliver it to a reliable person. Most of the houses in the colony remained closed except Shourie's; he was sitting in the veranda.

"There is a letter addressed to Rev Aaron Micah but he is not home. Can I leave it with you?"

"Certainly, the last time also you had left with me a letter addressed to him." Shourie examined the envelope and guessed it contained the news they had been expecting. Msgr Micah was late to return. Shourie went to bed, with the letter under his pillow, wanting to deliver it personally.

Early next morning he rushed to Msgr. Micah with the envelope in his hand; he promptly handed it over to him as the Priest stepped out into the veranda. He recognised where it was from, guessing what its content would be. Still standing on the veranda he opened the cover and glanced over the lines. Shourie stood watching his face. The Priest folded the letter, put it back into the envelope and turned back, saying 'thank you Shourie,' leaving the man guessing.

"Father, is the news good?" Shourie was anxious.

"Yes, of course."

"Really…very good…?" Without waiting for any affirmation, Shourie rushed back, rather excited.

Though Msgr. Micah was not explicit, Shourie guessed what the content of the letter could be. It probably contained the message that everybody expected. But he wondered why the Priest hadn't broken the news. He remembered hearing that such news had to be announced first to the congregation on the first Sunday after its arrival. He knew the next Sunday was three days away and they would have to wait to hear the news officially. He was not a regular at Sunday Mass but he decided to attend to hear the news directly. But he thought of rallying the residents of the colony to celebrate the event ahead of the parishioners.

In the evening, Shourie called out the boys who had the crackers and The boys hung the rolls on the trees in front of Micah's house with Reji helping them; they ignited the rolls letting out a chain of explosions lightening the sky and shrouding the ambience in white smoke. The explosions drew the residents of the neighbourhood out in the open; they rushed to Micah's house wondering who had set the sky afire. Msgr Micah came out and stood in the veranda watching the crowd. In the meanwhile, Reji returned with packets of assorted sweets he bought from the local shops.

Msgr Micah was unhappy at the turmoil; it was inappropriate for him to encourage them or participate in the hullabaloo. A few old timers climbed up the veranda and tried to grasp his hand apparently wanting to kiss the fisherman's ring; they felt disappointed to find the ring finger still empty.

"Hallelujah…hallelujanh…" Shourie cried raising the pitch of his voice to higher decibels, and the crowd soon turned into a pious congregation. The women suddenly knelt on the bare floor covering their heads and raising their eyes skyward.

"We praise our Lord and Holy is His name. We thank Thee, O Lord for having raised from amongst us a bishop for us."

An embarrassed Msgr Micah still stood in the veranda.

Pathrose Micah too was confused; his son hadn't so far disclosed to him the contents of the letter; when Shourie went into a full blare, he assumed his son might have shared the news with Shourie and that fired his enthusiasm. Pathrose was happy when he found his neighbours out in the open in a mood of jubilation which the parochial society failed to show.

"Papa, I don't think it proper for us to encourage this show. I don't question their sincerity. You may please ask them to disperse." Msgr. Micah requested his father; the old man stood staring into the eyes of his son.

"Yes, Papa, it's still an open question." He told him. Pathrose Micah understood and told Shourie.

"Shourie, we have to wait a few more days for the final arrangements; until that time there shall not be any public celebration. So I request all of you to return home and continue praying for the cause."

"I thought the letter confirmed the date." Shourie looked sheepish.

"I will let you know in time." Msgr Micah assured him.

The crowd dispersed peacefully.

Later in the week, Msgr Micah called in Shourie briefly.

"Shourie, I will be away for a few weeks. I thank you for all that you have done for me. Please give support to my father as usual. I will meet you when I come back." Msgr. Micah shook his hands.

One afternoon, an Ambassador car stopped in front of Pathrose Micah's house Thomas Chandi was at the wheels. Thomas Chandi quietly kept in the hold of the car a travel bag. Msgr. Aaron Micah occupied the front seat as Suresh Kuttan jumped into the rear. Pathrose Micah, the old man, stood on the veranda watching the car disappear beyond the hedge. The old man looked upset as Kochu Mathai stood by his side trying to console him. The Laksham colony looked empty with the population away and their own bishop departing.

Slowly the people seemed to have forgotten the bishop-designate who had been living as one among them, endearing himself to them. Pathrose Micah had been avoiding the parochial buffs to escape their meddling questions and derisive comments. The local pastor was happy that the burden of a *Pulaya* bishop had been taken away from his shoulders. Pathrose Micah wondered why the church had elevated his son to a bishopric suddenly and dumped him unceremoniously.

He had no news from his son since his departure except a brief note saying that he had reached Rome where he awaited further instructions; what followed was a long silence.

One evening Pathrose was sitting on the floor of his veranda re-fixing a broken chair that he had bought from the scrape market. Unnoticed, a white Maruti car drove up and slowly stopped in front of the veranda; the arrival of the vehicle failed to deflect Micah's attention. Jayanthan Namboodiri's son, Siddharth, who was affectionately Siddharthan Kunju to Micah, slowly emerged out of the car. Indeed, the bang of the door alerted Pathrose. He stirred and rushed into the yard to receive his old buddy, apologetically. The unexpected visit of his old classmate surprised and immensely pleased Pathrose.

"Pathrose, I have come to congratulate you." Siddharth vigorously shook the hand of his friend. Micah stood looking into his friend's eyes, not knowing exactly what the matter was though he could reasonably guess what it could be.

"Have you had any communication from Rev Aaron Micah?" He asked.

"Not much since his departure for Rome, except a brief letter informing that he was waiting for a call from the Papal office." Pathrose sounded low as he took pains to explain the latest position. Siddharth shook his head in approval as he had his eyes resting on the newspaper he had in his hand. Suddenly Pathrose realised it was unfair to make a distinguished visitor stand in the open; he quietly led Siddharth up the steps on to the veranda where he was seated on a chair; he found a perch for himself at the end of a bench.

Siddharth had with him The *Hindu*, the English daily, of the previous day.

"Pathrose, I read a news in yesterday's *Hindu*, date lined Vatican."

"What is it? What does it say?" Pathrose Micah sprang up on his feet, excited. Siddharth read:

"Yesterday, when the church celebrated the feast of the saints Peter and Paul, the Holy Father consecrated three bishops from the three continents of Asia, Africa and Europe. The Asian bishop was Most Rev Dr Aaron Pathrose Micah, as the titular bishop of Arba. He had been serving previously in the Archdiocese of Delhi." Siddharth paused briefly, looking into his friend's eyes. He found him standing frozen, trying to prevent the rush of the tears that had welled up in his eyes, from rolling down his cheeks.

"Micah, why do you cry? Isn't it a happy occasion? I have come to rejoice with you. I congratulate you; be calm." Siddharth embraced him.

"Yes, Siddharthan Kunju I am happy…very happy." Micah emphasised wiping his eyes, his voice quivering;

"There is more to the news."

"It's further learnt that the Pope has appointed the newly consecrated bishop Aaron Micah as the Chancellor of the Sacred Congregation for Oriental Catholics; Vatican's arm that disburses subsidies to the eastern Rite churches, directly under the Pope. He presides over the administration of a huge budget."

The report was concluded with a brief quote from the New Delhi correspondent of the newspaper.

"The bishop is the son of Pathrose Micah, a Second World War veteran of the untouchable Pulaya caste, euphemistically called Thonnurans meaning ninetiers signifying their original number when they were christened by Rev Aaron Griffith, a missionary, almost eight decades ago; the octogenarian Pathrose Micah still lives in his home village Kudamaloor," Siddharth concluded reading the report and placed the paper in Pathrose's hands, perhaps for him to keep as a souvenir.

In the meanwhile, Suresh Kuttan arrived, holding a popular local newspaper, reporting the consecration of Msgr Aaron Micah in Rome. The local paper had a news item which narrated the travails of Msgr. Aaron Micah when he sought to have his enthronement in the State and how he was frustrated in his efforts.

"I thought it was Jesus who had proclaimed for the first time in history that men are equals, the good news that laid the foundation for an equalitarian social order which today every nation endeavours to achieve. Yet it is shocking that what he had taught is repudiated with impunity by his own followers.

A fortnight later, Bishop Micah had a visitor in his office introducing himself, as Rev Thomas Mangalam, an alumnus of the Urban, now living in Italy looking after the socio-spiritual welfare of the community of Catholic Nurses from God's Own Country working in the European Union.

"Your Excellency, my stay in Italy is sponsored by your office; we are your protégé." Rev Mangalam was apologetic that he was late in calling on him; he said he was away in Germany on official business.

"Never mind, please take your seat." The bishop signalled to him.

Before occupying the chair he took out an envelope from his brief which he rather solemnly handed over to Bishop Micah, saying:

"This is from our Archbishop. His Grace wanted me to deliver this letter personally. It's a gift to you from the Archdiocese as a token of our love and affection for you." Rev Mangalam presented him a small red casket, the top inlaid in gold with a miniature of the Mar Thoma Cross.

"I thank you." He said with a broad smile,

"I was, and still am, a great admirer of His Grace. We have known each other for more than a decade. I used to be his personal escort whenever he visited the capital." Rev Mangalam shook hands with him as he stood up to leave, tactfully reminding the new occupant of the office:

"I may have to call on you frequently to follow up on projects the archdiocese presents for your consideration."

"You are most welcome to do so." Bishop Micah assured him.

In the evening, as he returned home the bishop read the letter.

"Your Excellency,

I have immense pleasure in congratulating you on your being elevated to the See of Arba by the Most Holy Father. Please accept our compliments. It's a two-fold recognition that you are appointed the Chancellor of the Sacred Congregation for Eastern Catholic churches, an office of great responsibility which the Most Holy Father rightly thought you were strong enough to shoulder. Wish you all the best.

You might have discovered that the Congregation you are chosen to direct, supports our church. I am glad that finally it has a chief who is from among us. We seek your favour to help nurture this ancient church of ours.

Incidentally, I am sorry I missed the privilege to install you to the see of Arba but I know that my failure became a blessing leading you to the Holy Father, giving him the occasion to install you for greater glory. You need only be mindful of how the hand of the Lord works.

I bless you.

Yours in Our Lord.

Bishop Micah was intrigued that the Archbishop who had declined to consecrate him and even refused to meet him had found time to write to him; it was also the Lord's way of taking care of His servants.

He was curious to see what the well-designed casket contained. He slowly turned the tiny knob; it unlatched a still smaller lever opening the lid; what he discovered was a thick pouch of soft silk. He ran his fingers over the pouch but was clueless about the content.

"Is it a string of seeds?" He wondered whether the senior prelate was trying to pull his legs or it was a ploy to teach him a lesson.

The content turned out to be a string of yellowish-green, well cured cardamom pods carefully crafted into a rosary, each pod strung with the succeeding in solid gold. The tiny Mar Thoma Cross at the end was mounted on a bed of cardamom seeds. The rosary exuded a spicy fragrance as one rolled it between the fingers. Bishop Micah wondered why the Archbishop had taken so much pains to send him a gift that seemed costly and unique too.

"Uniqueness, perhaps, creates a lasting impression." Bishop Micah concluded as he walked down the aisles. His dark shadow lengthened as he walked down the Via Doloroso, silently reciting the rosary. On reaching home he found on his table a tiny Bible bound in red leather with the title printed in gold which read Gods Own Untouchables.

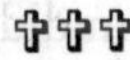

The Epilogue

In God's Own Country, at every ecclesiastical appointment, the Catholic Press went hammer and tongs inventing the candidate's twin hallows of Brahminical descent and apostolic origin. Msgr. Aaron Micah stood deprived of both. But his high profile office, at a young age, with long years before him didn't go unnoticed. Back home at least a few discerning ecclesiasts saw in him a future black Pope.

✞✞✞

Glossary

Achon	A sorcerer, physician and priest to the community of untouchables.
Anna	One- sixteenth of an Indian rupee
Biriyani	An oriental, spiced rice-meat preparation.
Brahmin	The top most caste of the four-fold Indian populace divinely ordained. Brahmins constituted the priestly class; they are the teachers and law givers observing strict form of untouchability. They enjoyed the status of gods on earth, called Bhoosuras. Brahmins in God's Own Country are called Namboodiris.
Bandh	A system of public protest against the government in power by bringing about total closure of activities; though claimed to be voluntary coercion and violence unleashed to bring the society to a standstill, resulting in death and destruction.
Chatta	An upper garment devised by the missionaries with a narrow slit at the neck worn by the Christian women.
Dalit	A common name for all low castes
Edavapathi	Middle of Edavam, a month in the native calendar, corresponding to June first when monsoon arrived in the land.
God's Own Country	The brand name of a strip of the land on the south western corner of India, Kerala.

Kaikaran	A person appointed by the vestry meeting to look after the financial affairs of the Parish.
Kaappi	Coffee
Mooppan	The senior most or head of a group.
Mundu	A plain cloth (dhoti) wrapped around the waist.
Nairs	A constituent of the Shudra caste.
Onam	Originally a harvest festival it assumed a socio-religious garb, the event universally being celebrated with a week long program of eating and feasting in God's Own Country to commemorate the egalitarian rule of Mah bali, considered to be Buddhist but was dethroned by his rivals, the gods employing a dubious stratagem effecting a bloodless coup de maitre. The king was, however, allowed to visit his subjects; they on the occasion celebrated Onam to send the message that his former subjects were as happy as it were during his reign.
Panam	A low denomination silver coin in circulation in the land.
Penkoda	A ceremony of giving a girl in marriage.
Pulapedi	Clandestine Pulaya gangs to avenge atrocities against them.
Pulaya	A community of Untouchables, agricultural labour lived beyond the four fold caste division bound to the earth and bonded to the four fold castes enjoying no rights. Lived forbidden from entering the public thoroughfare and barred from the abodes of gods. Learning was forbidden to them; reciting or listening to the reciting of the scriptures invited the punishment of plucking the tongue or pouring molten led into the ears. Their women were prohibited from covering their breasts or wearing ornaments except pebbles stringed together on thread.

Thalapulayan	The foreman of the farm labour.
Thampran	Milord
Tapasya	Religious austerities performed to please a god.
Toddy	Juice extracted from the spathe of palm, fermented.
Tharawad	A Hindu matrilineal joint family estate with the title resting on the matriarch but administered by her eldest brother on her behalf.
Thonnoorans	(Ninetiers) The ninety Pulayas, whom the missionary priest Rev. Aaron Griffith had admitted into the Church, collectively called.
Untouchables	The Indian populace whose touch or sight defiled the high born.
Vallom	A country craft or a dug out canoe used in water borne traffic.
Veluthachan	St. Andrew, the patron saint of a church on the Arthunkal coast whom the local populace endearingly addressed Veluthachan meaning fair skinned. A Pulaya who met Rev. Aaron Griffith, the missionary for the first time believed he had before him the Veluthachan in flesh. Since that meeting for the Pulayas he was Veluthachan, the living saint.
Vishnu	The second but most popular of the Hindu pantheon of gods Vyshyas. The third division in the caste order assigned to agriculture and trade, in a way the wealth managers. Vydhyan A physician, practicing native medicine.

✞✞✞